THIRD WORLD ATLAS

Second Edition

Alan Thomas

**with Ben Crow
Paul Frenz, Tom Hewitt
Sabrina Kassam and
Steven Treagust**

OPEN UNIVERSITY PRESS
BUCKINGHAM
in association with

 The Open University

Note on authorship

In the case of a graphic publication of this nature, attributing authorship simply to those who originated ideas and selected data is quite inadequate. A large part of any credit must go to the following members of Open University staff:

Carolyn Baxter	Course Manager
Judith Dutton	Editor
Pam Higgins	Designer
Ray Munns	Cartographer

The authors would also like to acknowledge the following members of Open University staff for their valuable suggestions or contributions to the preparation of this atlas:

Jane Clements	Project Control/Rights
Harry Dodd	Print Production Controller
Joe Greenwood	Design Group Coordinator
Garry Hammond	Editor
Caryl Hunter-Brown	Liaison Librarian
David Wilson	Project Control

Members of the Development Studies subject group at the Open University

Published in the United Kingdom by Open University Press, Bingham

in association with

The Open University, Milton Keynes

Open University Press, Celtic Court, 22 Ballmoor, Bingham, MK18 1XW, UK

First published in this second edition 1994

Edited, designed and typeset by The Open University

Printed in Italy by Amilcare Pizzi

A catalogue record of this book is available from the British Library

ISBN 0 335 19077 4
ISBN 0 335 19076 6 (Pbk)

This book is one component of the Open University course 08 Third World Development. If you would like a copy of Studying the Open University, please write to the Central Enquiry Service e Open University, PO Box 200, Milton Keynes MK7 2YZ. If you have already enrolled on the Course and would like to buy any other Op University material, please write to Open University Educational E rises Ltd, 12 Cofferidge Close, Stony Stratford, Milton Keynes MK1 Y, UK.

2.1

CONTENTS

INTRODUCTION

The developing countries, or 'Third World', are home to the majority of the Earth's population, some three billion people. The term Third World is used to describe a range of countries as diverse as Nigeria and Nepal, Peru and Papua New Guinea. The relationship between the First and Third Worlds (or 'North' and 'South', see map opposite) profoundly affects both communities. The North consumes fruit grown on the plantations of the Caribbean, fuel extracted from the oil fields of the Middle East, electronics assembled in the factories of South-east Asia, and clothes spun from cotton on the Indian sub-continent. Likewise, Asian audiences await the latest American 'blockbuster', West Africans emulate the fashions of Paris, and Latin Americans hope to own a foreign car.

The chart on the page opposite shows some of the major inequalities, such as in the distribution of resources, in the world. We hope this Atlas helps explain some of the reasons for these large differences. As we approach the next century it is increasingly apparent that all inhabitants of planet Earth share to some extent a common future. Our destinies are linked not just through trade, telecommunications and so on, but because of the enduring linkages established under colonialism. How limited resources are used today and how we treat our shared environment will determine the world our children inherit.

This Atlas focuses on some of the Third World's *common* experiences, such as its historical linkages with the West, the challenge to provide basic needs, and the effects of competition in the global economy. Even though we have concentrated on unifying themes we hope that this never masks the underlying historical, social and political diversity of developing nations.

Our overall analysis starts from the following questions:

- What is the Third World?
- How was it made?
- What problems does it face and how is it changing?

These questions correspond approximately to the following sections of the Atlas:

1   Definitions of Third World and Development (pp.10–23) explores how various social and economic data are used to define what is meant by the term 'Third World' and how the process of 'development' has been interpreted very differently at different times in the last three decades.

2 The Making of The Third World (pp.24–47) documents the expansion of Europe and its lasting repercussions for the agricultural, industrial and political development of the Third World.

3 Issues and Challenges in Contemporary Development (pp.48–73) looks specifically at the lives of women and children, and the pressing issues of demographic change, environmental degradation, war, hunger and disease, migration and refugees, and international debt. It analyses the changing face of industry and agriculture in developing countries and reviews overall trends as we approach the twenty-first century.

Of course, it has proved impossible to cover everything in just 80 pages. What is included is a summary of the main historical, social and economic processes, using what we hope are clear, innovative mapping and graphical techniques.

On the whole, the Atlas uses data which come from international organizations such as the World Bank's *World Development Report* and the United Nations Development Programme's *Human Development Report*. These organizations rely on figures supplied to them by governments, special surveys, and the research work of planners and academics.

In describing development trends with data there has usually been a choice to do so in absolute or relative terms. Gross national products per head for developing countries have increased in real terms over the last three decades, but relative to developed nations they have declined. Often the same data can be used to present progress or human suffering. Child mortality rates in developing countries were halved from 243 per 1000 in 1960 to 121 per 1000 in 1988, yet this still means that 25 children died every minute. Even the worst of figures may reveal some hope. It is surely a testimony to the resilience of African mothers, often without any formal schooling, that in spite of difficult environments and minimal services 80% of their children see their fifth birthday and most of them are healthy.

Gathering data is time-consuming and costly. Many of the poorest (often war-torn) countries lack personnel, transport and data-processing facilities. Consequently indicators such as access to services and maternal mortality are often broad approximations at best. Others such as literacy involve a degree of subjectivity which makes international comparisons difficult. Data on income distribution and poverty are found only through complex household surveys which may take years to process. Likewise, demographic data are only available by extrapolation from census figures, produced every ten years at best.

Perhaps the most important failing in much of the data available is the lack of differentiation according to gender, class, location, income or ethnic groups. Very rarely, even in developed countries, is there good information on how access to services and general well-being vary for women and men, city and town dwellers, the well-to-do and the poor. Remember that adult literacy rates, gross national

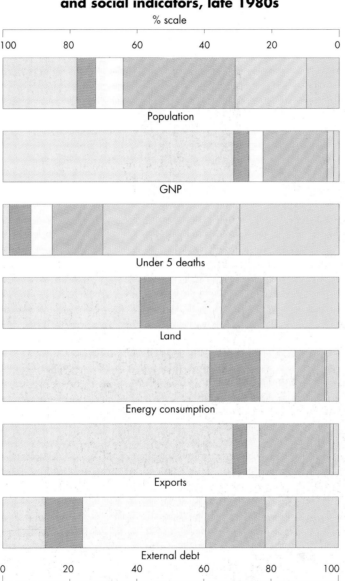

Distribution of world totals between major regions of the world for selected economic and social indicators, late 1980s

% scale

Population

GNP

Under 5 deaths

Land

Energy consumption

Exports

External debt

% scale

Sub-Saharan Africa	East and South-east Asia	Middle East and North Africa
South Asia	Latin America and the Caribbean	Europe, USSR, North America and Australasia

Electronic artwork copyright © 1992 RH Illustration and Design

products and the like are *averages* or totals for the population as a whole and may conceal wide intra-country variations.

In spite of some data being little more than informed guesswork, we believe that they are still sufficiently accurate to show differences between continents and key changes over time. We have tried to make clear when data from different sources or years are used together. A reference section of tables and notes follows Section 3.

This Atlas could not possibly be complete or definitive as a summary of Third World issues. It should, however, be useful in bringing an important spatial and statistical dimension to the study of development. It is hoped that this presentation will add colour to the forces which have shaped the Third World, and highlight some of the issues on which Third World women, children and men have based their hopes and aspirations for a better future.

The map below shows regions of the world on a Peters' projection map and incorporates a North–South dividing line developed for the Brandt report[1]. This particular division of the world into regions derives from World Bank usage and is used on the chart (left) and throughout this Atlas, with the same colour code as here. The Peters' projection is not used for the main base maps of this Atlas; the relative merits of this and other projections are discussed on pp. 6–7.

World regions and Brandt's 'North–South' divide

Electronic artwork copyright © 1992 RH Illustration and Design

This Atlas was compiled over a period when the world's international boundaries were changing faster than at any time since the Second World War. In particular, the futures of the republics of what was Yugoslavia were in doubt. Difficulties are compounded when the latest available 'data' come from a state which no longer exists as such, e.g. the USSR, and/or from the final years of a communist government. What is shown here may soon appear wrong or out of date. You should look carefully at the dates of data given, and at notes and sources, to be sure what is actually shown.

The Earth is an almost perfect sphere. (In fact, it bulges slightly at the equator, which stretches for 40,077 km, whereas the meridian from North Pole to South Pole and back is only 39,942 km.) The way in which a sphere or globe is represented on a flat surface is called a *projection*. All projections distort in one way or another; to visualize this, think of stretching out flat the peel of an orange.

Each projection distorts size, shape, position and distance differently. A cartographer must choose an appropriate projection to suit the purposes of the map. For example, Gerhard Mercator's popular projection (this page) was devised originally in the sixteenth century as an aid to navigation. It is suited for these purposes because true direction is always maintained, so that for example a line drawn diagonally on the map at 45° to the equator always points north-east. Such a map has been commonly used as a reference base on which to put any kind of geographical information, even though other projections might have seemed better. Although shapes are fairly accurately maintained, distances and areas are magnified towards the poles. In fact, Mercator's map is calculated in such a way that distortion continues infinitely as the poles are approached, so they can never actually be shown. Consequently, Greenland, which has a surface area of only 2 million sq. km, appears not merely larger than Brazil, with 8.5 million sq. km, but larger than the whole of South America!

Where a map is centred may be as important as the projection used. Most world maps are centred latitudinally on the equator, which makes it difficult to judge distances across the poles. This problem becomes particularly evident when one wishes to show the close proximity of North America to the northern extremities of the Soviet Union. William-Olsson's projection centred on London (opposite, bottom left) is one which gives a more accurate representation of this relationship. A map ideally is centred geographically according to the features being described, hence the focus on the Pacific rim in the map (opposite, bottom right) intended to show the distribution of natural hazards.

It has been suggested that Mercator's projection is Eurocentric because Europe and North America are disproportionately large and in the top half of the map. Placing the North Pole at the top of a map dates back to the Ancient Greeks, while measuring latitude from the Greenwich meridian, so that London is usually in the middle of a map, derives from the time of British seafaring domination. (An early example of a map which is oriented with the East at the top is shown on p.8, bottom left.)

The way in which a map is constructed is not a neutral process but reflects a cartographer's perception of the world. Dr Arno Peters claimed that his projection 'corrects the Europe centred image of the world as projected by Mercator'[2]. Peters' projection (this page) is equal-area, meaning that regions on the globe which are equal in area are represented by equal areas on the map. It also maintains

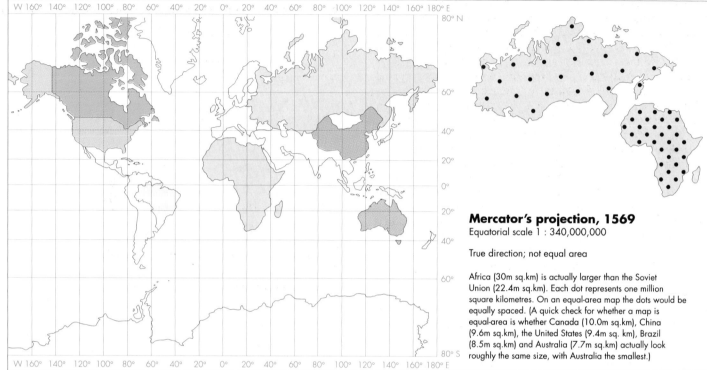

Mercator's projection, 1569
Equatorial scale 1 : 340,000,000

True direction; not equal area

Africa (30m sq.km) is actually larger than the Soviet Union (22.4m sq.km). Each dot represents one million square kilometres. On an equal-area map the dots would be equally spaced. (A quick check for whether a map is equal-area is whether Canada (10.0m sq.km), China (9.6m sq.km), the United States (9.4m sq. km), Brazil (8.5m sq.km) and Australia (7.7m sq.km) actually look roughly the same size, with Australia the smallest.)

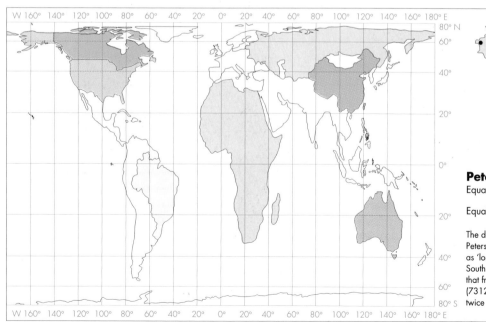

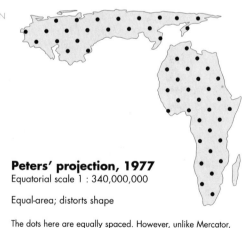

Peters' projection, 1977
Equatorial scale 1 : 340,000,000

Equal-area; distorts shape

The dots here are equally spaced. However, unlike Mercator, Peters does not represent shapes well. Africa is actually roughly as 'long' as it is 'wide'; the distance from Cairo to the tip of South Africa (7050 km) is in fact approximately the same as that from Dakar to the easternmost point of the Horn of Africa (7312 km). On Peters' projection the first appears to be about twice the second.

north–south and east–west directions, but does so at the expense of the shape of land masses, so that continents at or near the equator appear to be squeezed vertically while towards the poles they are stretched horizontally. Ironically, although it is claimed to be a 'third worldist' projection, it is developing countries that suffer most distortion on the Peters map. The Peters projection has been adopted by few cartographers in developed or developing nations.

There are numerous other equal-area projections, mostly based on an oval outline and curved lines of longitude and/or latitude. Choice of projection depends not only on the purposes of the map, but also on the shape and size of the area to be covered. An atlas of oceanography, for example, might choose a base map centred on the South Pacific or the two poles. Most maps in this Atlas are presented on the Eckert IV projection, which is also used by the *World Bank Atlas*. This projection is equal-area but it does not distort shape as badly as Peters'. It is drawn here with lines of latitude and longitude to show how it is constructed. To show land-masses as large as possible, the main world maps in this Atlas have New Zealand moved from its correct geographical position to one which is closer to Australia, and Antarctica and most of the Pacific Ocean omitted.

The next two pages use different types of maps, graphs and diagrams to show socio-economic information. It is worth thinking about how the method used affects the interpretation of data.

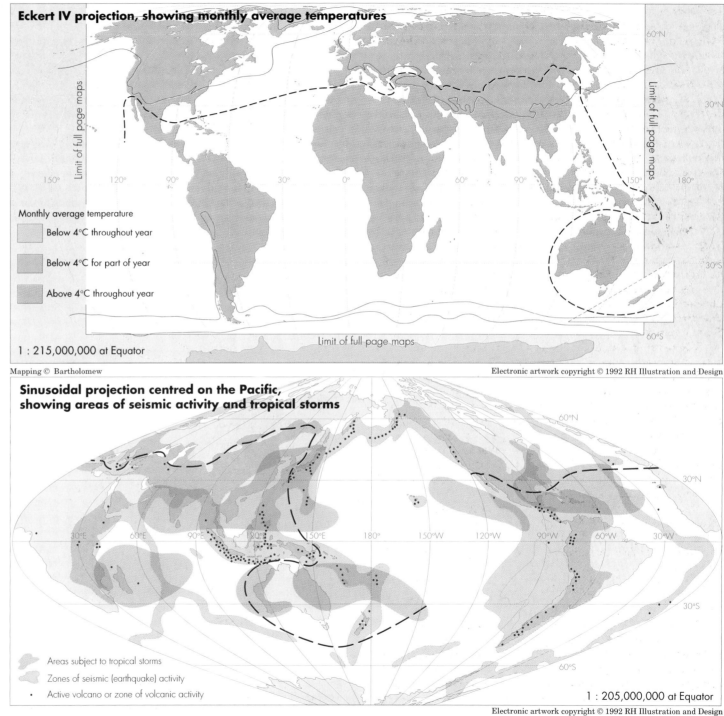

Eckert IV projection, showing monthly average temperatures

Monthly average temperature

Below 4°C throughout year

Below 4°C for part of year

Above 4°C throughout year

1 : 215,000,000 at Equator

Mapping © Bartholomew   Electronic artwork copyright © 1992 RH Illustration and Design

Sinusoidal projection centred on the Pacific, showing areas of seismic activity and tropical storms

Areas subject to tropical storms

Zones of seismic (earthquake) activity

• Active volcano or zone of volcanic activity

1 : 205,000,000 at Equator

Electronic artwork copyright © 1992 RH Illustration and Design

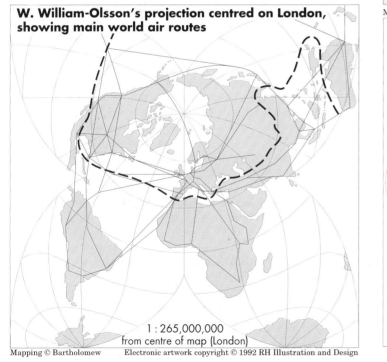

W. William-Olsson's projection centred on London, showing main world air routes

1 : 265,000,000
from centre of map (London)

Mapping © Bartholomew   Electronic artwork copyright © 1992 RH Illustration and Design

Maps are most commonly used simply to display where things are located, with particular conventions for particular purposes, such as navigation or town planning. Alternatively, as with most of the maps (and diagrams) in this Atlas, they can be used as graphic illustrations of how two or more variables are related spatially or have changed over time.

Although no map can be totally unbiased, one can differentiate between a map selected in an attempt to be objective and one used to convey a particular message. The Hereford World Map (below) seems inaccurate because of the incomplete geographical knowledge of the time, whereas the next is a simple but accurate 'equidistant' projection. The third map below is designed to put over a message, although it is no less 'accurate' than the second.

The opposite page shows different ways of relating income, as measured by gross national product (GNP) or gross domestic product (GDP), to population on a world basis. The 'proportional base' maps

may look peculiar at first because the size of a country on the page is determined not by geography but by its population (top left) or GNP (top right). Note that the world is shown divided into the standard six colour-coded regions introduced on p.5. Proportional base maps are also found on pp.15, 53 and 69. The map at the bottom right uses a projection designed by Third World cartographers to give a view of the world 'from the South'[3]; the height of each column represents population density, and the colour shading shows income levels in terms of GNP per capita.

Scatter diagrams are used in this Atlas to show how one variable relates to another. The one opposite relates total GDP and the size of a country's population. A logarithmic scale has been used to accommodate the extremities of the data. Note that GDP is a measure of the size of a country's economy; it is not exactly the same as GNP. The lines indicate the average levels of GDP per capita in each region of the world.

A scatter diagram may show a correlation between two variables, but it is important to remember that even a statistical correlation does not prove that the phenomena are causally linked. For example, countries with more squash courts may have lower levels of infant mortality; it is likely that the number of courts is only a proxy for the wide range of factors associated with more affluent societies and not that squash facilities have a direct impact on the health of young children.

Scatter diagrams relate only two variables at a time. They therefore often give only a part of what may be a multi-causal relationship. For example, child malnutrition levels may correlate with GNP per capita at country level, but they also relate to an almost endless list of other factors such as: agricultural production, access to health facilities, crop prices, and the state of the global economy. It is important to be aware that what a map or graph shows as a simple relationship might only be part of a complex whole.

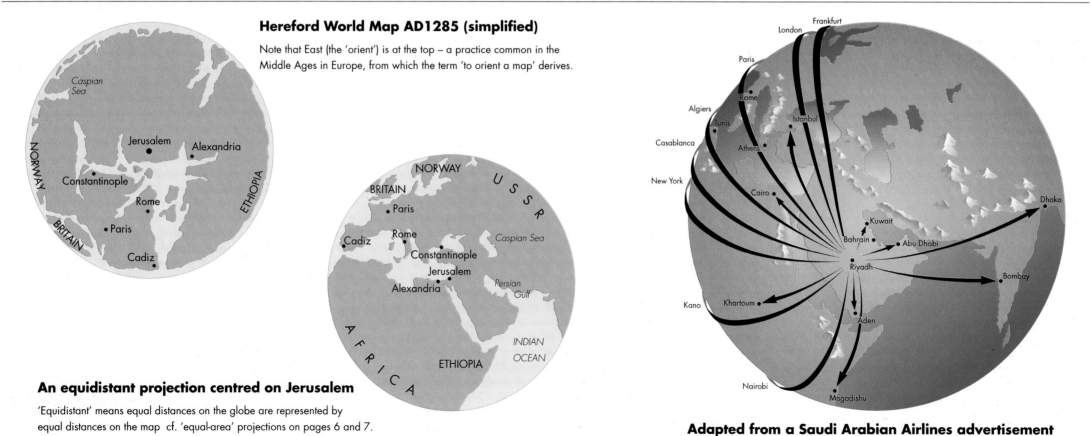

Hereford World Map AD1285 (simplified)

Note that East (the 'orient') is at the top – a practice common in the Middle Ages in Europe, from which the term 'to orient a map' derives.

An equidistant projection centred on Jerusalem

'Equidistant' means equal distances on the globe are represented by equal distances on the map cf. 'equal-area' projections on pages 6 and 7.

Adapted from a Saudi Arabian Airlines advertisement

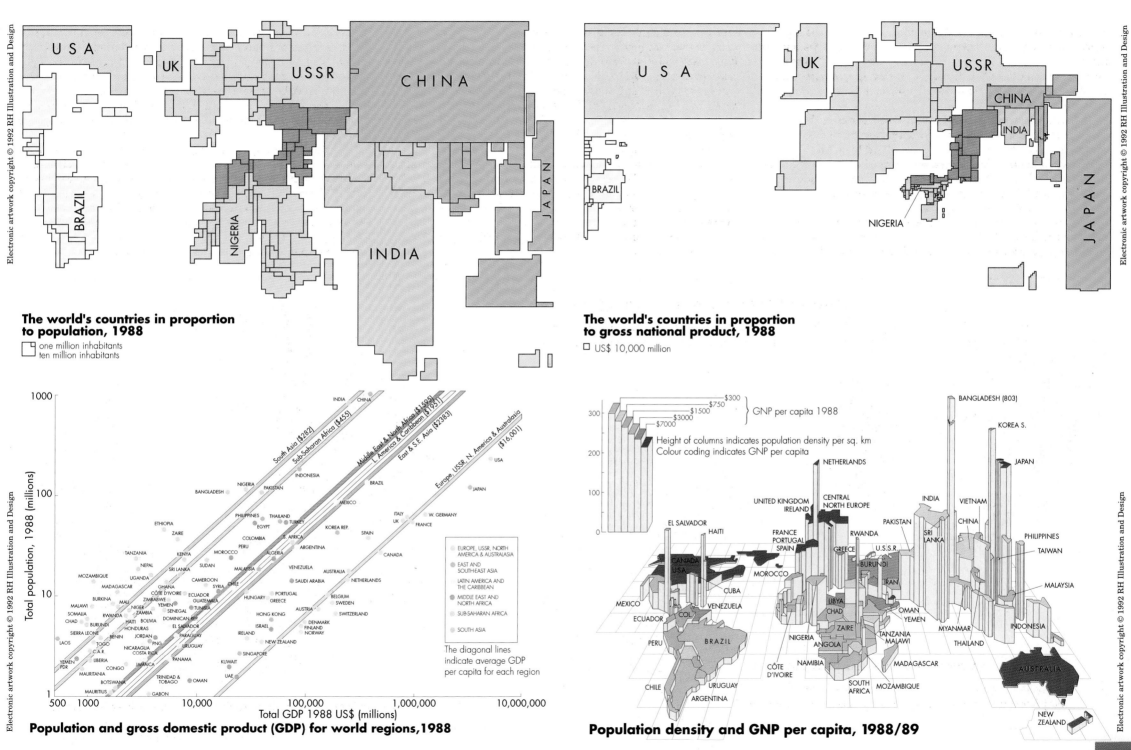

USA
UK
USSR
CHINA
BRAZIL
NIGERIA
JAPAN
INDIA

**The world's countries in proportion
to population, 1988**

☐ one million inhabitants
☐ ten million inhabitants

USA
UK
USSR
CHINA
INDIA
BRAZIL
JAPAN
NIGERIA

**The world's countries in proportion
to gross national product, 1988**

☐ US$ 10,000 million

South Asia ($282)
Sub-Saharan Africa ($455)
Middle East & North Africa ($1592)
L. America & Caribbean ($1951)
East & S.E. Asia ($2383)
Europe, USSR, N. America & Australasia ($16,001)

The diagonal lines
indicate average GDP
per capita for each region

- EUROPE, USSR, NORTH AMERICA & AUSTRALASIA
- EAST AND SOUTH-EAST ASIA
- LATIN AMERICA AND THE CARIBBEAN
- MIDDLE EAST AND NORTH AFRICA
- SUB-SAHARAN AFRICA
- SOUTH ASIA

Total population, 1988 (millions)

Total GDP 1988 US$ (millions)

Population and gross domestic product (GDP) for world regions, 1988

$300
$750
$1500
$3000
$7000

GNP per capita 1988

Height of columns indicates population density per sq. km
Colour coding indicates GNP per capita

BANGLADESH (803)
KOREA S.
JAPAN
NETHERLANDS
UNITED KINGDOM
IRELAND
CENTRAL NORTH EUROPE
INDIA
VIETNAM
CHINA
PHILIPPINES
EL SALVADOR
HAITI
FRANCE PORTUGAL SPAIN
GREECE
RWANDA
PAKISTAN
SRI LANKA
TAIWAN
CANADA
USA
MOROCCO
U.S.S.R.
BURUNDI
IRAN
MALAYSIA
CUBA
LIBYA
OMAN
YEMEN
MEXICO
VENEZUELA
CHAD
MYANMAR
INDONESIA
ECUADOR
COL
NIGERIA
ZAIRE
TANZANIA
MALAWI
THAILAND
PERU
BRAZIL
ANGOLA
MADAGASCAR
CÔTE D'IVOIRE
NAMIBIA
SOUTH AFRICA
MOZAMBIQUE
AUSTRALIA
CHILE
URUGUAY
ARGENTINA
NEW ZEALAND

Population density and GNP per capita, 1988/89

DEFINITIONS OF THIRD WORLD AND DEVELOPMENT

The term *Third World* originated after the Second World War as a political category implying 'positive neutralism' in the context of the Cold War. (For a historical view of the *First World* of Western capitalist nations, the then socialist states of the *Second World*, and the 'non-aligned' *Third World*, see p.47.) However, well before the collapse of Eastern European socialism and the Soviet Union, the main connotation of the term Third World had become 'underdeveloped' or simply 'poor'. The term, in fact, covers a disparate group of countries, including both the newly industrializing countries of South-east Asia and the poorest countries of Africa.

Since the Second World War what has been understood by *development* has also changed, from an emphasis on economic growth to a view of development encompassing the whole of society and implying cultural and political as well as economic and technical change. The chart opposite presents a chronology of some important world events and some ideas which have shaped development thinking. Apart from attempting objectivity in defining war[1], what is included is necessarily arbitrary.

This section focuses in turn on six aspects of development which may be used separately or in combination to attempt to define the 'Third World':

Independence (pp.12–13). The map on p.13 doubles as a basic political reference map, showing states of the world at January 1993 on our equal-area projection. (Data shown on the other maps is generally for 1990 or earlier.)

GNP per Capita and World Bank Categories (pp.14–15) ranks economies on the basis of average income, and shows how the World Bank uses this and other economic factors to classify countries into groups.

Industrialization (pp.16–17) views development as a process of structural economic change from agriculture towards industry.

National and World Integration (pp.18–19) explores development as a process of modernization and internationalization in which Third World countries play a marginalized role.

Social Indicators of Development (pp.20–21) presents some measures of the fulfilment of basic human needs.

Human Development (pp.22–23) introduces the *Human Development Index* and discusses freedom and human rights.

Timeline

EVENTS	WARS	EVENTS	BOOKS	PARADIGMS and CONCEPTS	LEADERS

EVENTS (left column)

- 1991 Independence of Baltic States, break-up of USSR, formation of Commonwealth of Independent States; Soviet Union failed coup d'état
- 1990 Re-unification of Germany
- 1989 Collapse of communism in –90 Eastern Europe
- 1987 US stock market crash; Gorbachev initiates major reforms in USSR
- 1980 Lomé II convention
- 1975 Lomé convention
- 1974 Oil price escalation
- 1971 End of gold standard
- 1969 Non-proliferation treaty
- 1968 Czechoslovakia, Soviet tanks suppress 'Prague Spring'
- 1963 Martin Luther King, leader of civil rights movement, assassinated; Nuclear test ban treaty; 'Hot line' set up
- 1962 Algeria wins fight for independence from France; Cuban missiles crisis
- 1961 Berlin Wall erected; OECD founded
- 1960 U2 incident
- 1959 Kruschev–Eisenhower summit
- 1957 EEC founded
- 1956 Hungarian uprising put down
- 1955 Warsaw Pact formed
- 1953 Stalin dies
- 1952 McCarthyism in USA
- 1949 Yugoslavia/USSR split
- 1947 Marshall Plan
- 1945 UN formed; Eastern Europe becomes Soviet satellite
- 1944 Bretton Woods conference – foundation of IMF and World Bank
- 1942 UN declaration

WARS (vertical bars)

- Yugoslavia Civil War
- Gulf War
- Iran–Iraq War
- Falklands/Malvinas War
- Civil War in Sudan
- Lebanese conflicts
- Angolan Civil War
- Mozambique Civil War
- Uganda
- Afghan Civil War and Soviet intervention
- Eritrean/Ethiopian conflict
- Khmer Rouge massacres in Cambodia
- Indonesian annexation of East Timor
- Wars of liberation against Portuguese
- Vietnam War
- Détente
- Civil War in Sudan
- Massacres in Uganda
- Arab-Israeli conflict
- Six Day War
- Nigerian Civil War
- Conflicts around Bangladeshi independence
- Colombian Civil War
- Cold War
- Vietnamese independence war
- Algerian War of Independence
- Korean War
- Chinese Communist Revolution
- Second World War

EVENTS (middle column)

- 1990 Iraq invades Kuwait; Namibian independence; South Africa, Nelson Mandela released
- 1989 China, Tiananmen Square massacre; US invades Panama
- 1985 Sri Lanka, escalation of Sinhalese–Tamil conflict
- 1983 US invades Grenada
- 1982 Israel invades Lebanon; Mexico's moratorium begins 'debt crisis'
- 1980 Rhodesia becomes independent Zimbabwe
- 1979 Iranian Revolution; Soviets invade Afghanistan; Sandinistas take power in Nicaragua
- 1975 Khmer Rouge atrocities in Cambodia begin; Ethiopian Emperor Haile Selassie deposed; Angola and Mozambique gain independence from Portugal
- 1973 Chilean coup d'état
- 1971 China admitted to UN
- 1969 OPEC set up after Baghdad conference
- 1966 Cultural Revolution starts in China
- 1965 Indonesia, military coup purges 'threat' of communists; Rhodesian whites declare Unilateral Declaration of Independence
- 1964 UNCTAD: Group of 77 declaration; China/USSR split
- 1961 Bay of Pigs
- 1960 Sharpeville massacre
- 1958 Cuban Revolution
- 1957 Ghana independence
- 1956 Nasser confronts UK, France and Israel over 'Suez crisis'
- 1954 French Indo-China independent
- 1950 China occupies Tibet
- 1949 China (excluding Taiwan) becomes a communist state
- 1948 Nationalists win power in South Africa, strengthening apartheid policy; Israeli independence
- 1947 India and Pakistan gain independence

BOOKS

- 1987 *Our Common Future*, World Commission on Environment and Development (Brundtland Report); *Adjustment with a Human Face*, G. Cornia, R. Jolly, F. Stewart
- 1983 *Rural Development: Putting the Last First*, R. Chambers
- 1981 *Poverty and Famines*, A. Sen
- 1980 *North–South: A Programme for Survival*, (Brandt Report) Brandt Commission; *Imperialism and Nationalism*, B. Warren
- 1979 *Capitalist World Economy*, I. Wallerstein
- 1977 *Imperialism and Unequal Development*, S. Amin; *Why Poor People Stay Poor*, M. Lipton
- 1976 *Employment, Growth and Basic Needs*, International Labour Office
- 1974 *Small is Beautiful*, E.F. Schumacher; *Redistribution with Growth*, H. Chenery; *The Challenge of World Poverty*, G. Myrdal
- 1972 *Pedagogy of the Oppressed*, P. Freire; *How Europe Underdeveloped Africa*, W. Rodney
- 1971 *Dependency and Development in Latin America*, F. Cardoso and E. Faletto
- 1970 *Women's Role in Economic Development*, E. Boserup
- 1967 *The Wretched of the Earth*, F. Fanon; *Capitalism and Underdevelopment in Latin America*, G. Frank
- 1964 *Transforming Traditional Agriculture*, T.W. Schultz
- 1963 *The Third World*, P. Worsley
- 1961 *The Stages of Economic Growth*, W.W. Rostow
- 1955 *The Theory of Economic Growth*, A. Lewis

PARADIGMS and CONCEPTS

1990s: Sustainability, environmental sensitivity, human rights, political reform, 'market friendly development', good governance, capacity building

1980s The Lost Decade*:
Neo-liberal counter-revolution (major): free market, reduced role of the state, structural adjustment, export orientation, devaluation of currencies, privatization, 'magic of the market place', efficiency, choice
Neo-populism (minor): vulnerable groups, women and children, marginal areas, holistic development

1970s Debt-led growth*:
Dependency/underdevelopment theory: neo-colonial dependence, First World core–Third World periphery, collaborative elites, unequal terms of trade, dualistic development thesis, First World development achieved by Third World underdevelopment
Community development/basic needs: redistribution with growth, basic, appropriate technology, small scale enterprises, import substitution, renewable materials, equity, community participation, decentralization, rural development approach, New International Economic Order

late 1950s and 1960s The Golden Years*:
Structural change model: advocates structural change from subsistence to industrial economy, facilitated by agricultural 'surplus labour' moving to industry which acts as 'engine of growth' for economy as a whole

1945 to mid-1950s Post war restructuring* after Bretton Woods:
Stages of economic growth: linear stages of development, 'take-off and trickle down', growth, technological transfer, technocratic 'top-down' large scale projects, neglect of agriculture, Harrod–Domar equation advocates mobilization of savings for economic growth

LEADERS (vertical bars)

- Reagan in USA
- Castro in Cuba
- Gandhi in India
- Nyerere in Tanganyika/Tanzania
- Tito in Yugoslavia
- Nehru in India
- Sukarno in Indonesia
- Mao Zedong in China
- Nkrumah in Ghana

*Hans Singer's terms[2]

Most Third World countries have in common their recent political independence and their previous colonial status. However, Latin American countries are often regarded as 'Third World', although they mostly gained political independence in the early nineteenth century, before several European states, including Germany and Italy, existed in their modern form, and while others such as Greece and Bulgaria were still part of the Ottoman Empire.

Independence seems to be a precise term for recent ex-colonies celebrating a particular day on which there was a 'transfer of power'. However, many territories went through a period of 'internal self-government' or as 'dominions' or 'protectorates', and the date on which full independence was gained is a matter of judgement.

An independent state is one which is recognized as such by other states, either directly or through membership of international agencies. The United Nations (UN) was formed at the end of the Second World War and is meant to be a forum for all the nation-states of the world. UN membership has grown from 51 in 1945 to 178 in 1992. Two non-members of the UN are generally recognized as sovereign states: Switzerland never became a member; Taiwan was excluded in 1971 when the People's Republic of China became a member, with the latter claiming the former as an integral part of its territory. (North and South Korea became members only in 1991.)

A few parts of the world still have not attained independence, including some very small islands and military bases. Among others, Hong Kong remains a British colony until 1997; Greenland is a Danish dependency; Guadeloupe, Martinique and French Guiana are French; Puerto Rico is a 'freely associated state' with the USA.

There are also cases of international disagreement over the status of particular territories. East Timor is a potentially independent territory occupied by Indonesia. Some commentators might regard Northern Ireland, or many other areas, as dependent or occupied territories. In Western Sahara, occupying Morocco has supposedly agreed to independent elections, and a new independent state may be formed. This Atlas makes no judgements on unresolved territorial disputes such as these, or that over Kashmir, and bases political boundaries shown on those of *The Times Atlas of the World*.

The 1990s seem likely to give rise to several new states. The diagram below is for 1990; the map opposite shows states of the world in 1993. By this time the republics of the ex-USSR had become independent and the Czech and Slovak Republics had split. For the future, Eritrea is reported to be becoming independent of Ethiopia. Several of the republics of Yugoslavia are separately declaring independence, but are not shown on the maps because of the confused situation. The Palestine Liberation Organization (PLO) is a full member of the Non-aligned Movement, which shows that many recognize Palestine as a sovereign state. In South Africa, because 'independence' was originally ceded to a white minority, the struggle against the white regime can be seen not just as a question of human rights within a sovereign state, but as an independence struggle analogous to anti-colonial national liberation movements elsewhere.

Chart shows periods of independence since 1800 for states that were (a) independent in 1990, and (b) had population over one million in 1990.

The independence date shown is not a beginning: ancient nations (e.g. Poland, Egypt) may appear 'new' because for a long period before or after 1800 they were part of larger empires; or today's boundaries may split countries (e.g. Panama/Colombia) or unite previous political units (e.g. Nigeria).

? Future of state in doubt when this chart was compiled

★ 'Semi-colony' not fully independent for whole period

■ Temporary union (Syria with Egypt; Singapore with Malaysia)

◆ Not members of the UN

● Revolutionary change of form of state

⧅ Period of foreign occupation

Periods of independence (since 1800)

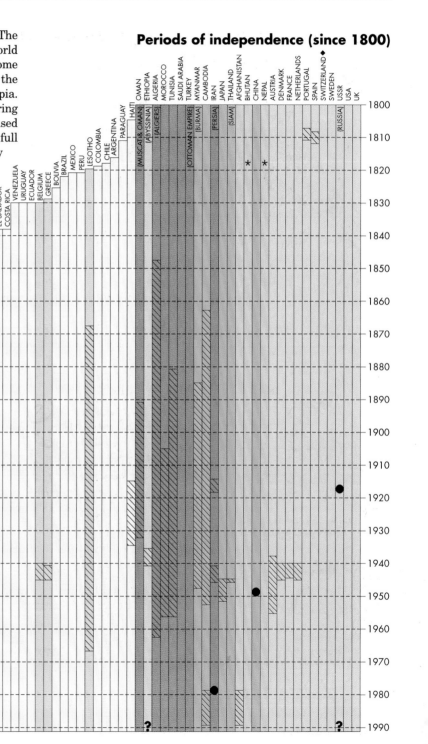

States of the world (1993), with length of time each has been independent

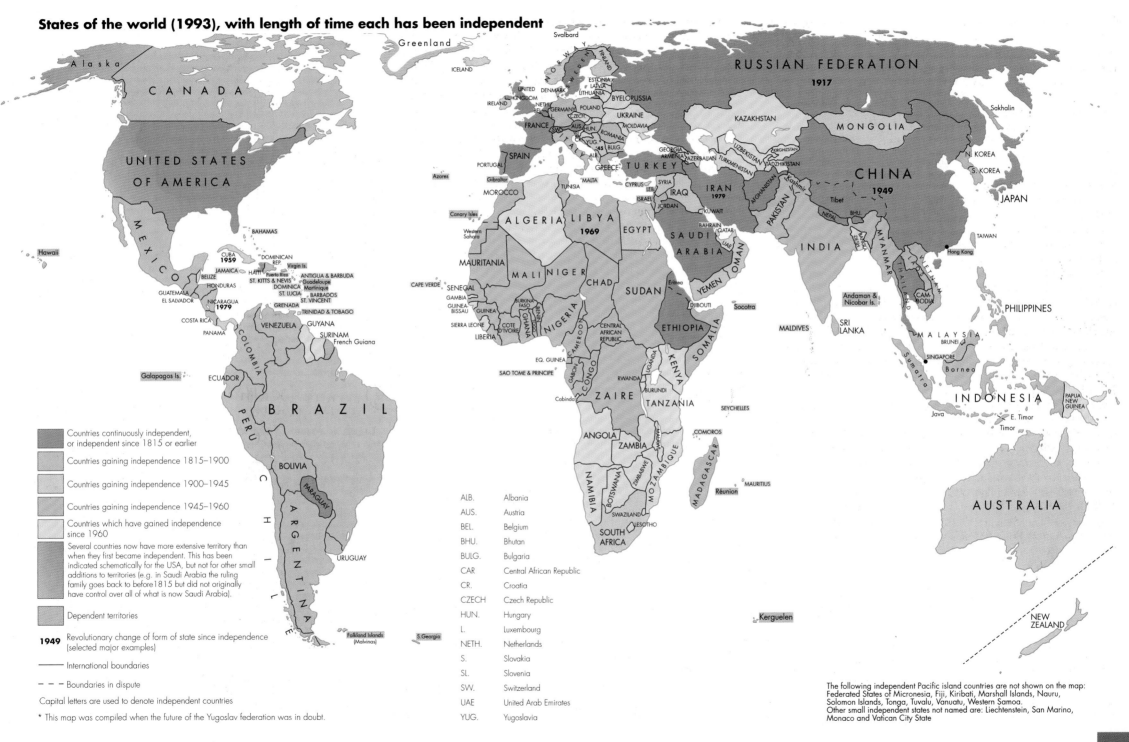

Greenland

Alaska

C A N A D A

UNITED STATES
OF AMERICA

M E X I C O

Hawaii

BAHAMAS
CUBA 1959
DOMINICAN REP.
JAMAICA
HAITI Puerto Rico
Virgin Is.
BELIZE ST. KITTS & NEVIS ANTIGUA & BARBUDA
HONDURAS DOMINICA Guadeloupe
GUATEMALA NICARAGUA ST. LUCIA Martinique
EL SALVADOR 1979 BARBADOS
GRENADA ST. VINCENT
COSTA RICA TRINIDAD & TOBAGO
PANAMA

VENEZUELA GUYANA
SURINAM
COLOMBIA French Guiana

Galapagos Is.

ECUADOR

P E R U

B R A Z I L

BOLIVIA
PARAGUAY

C H I L E

A R G E N T I N A

URUGUAY

Falkland Islands
(Malvinas)
S. Georgia

ICELAND

Svalbard

N O R W A Y
S W E D E N
FINLAND

UNITED DENMARK
IRELAND KINGDOM ESTONIA
NETH. LATVIA
BEL. GERMANY LITHUANIA
POLAND BYELORUSSIA
FRANCE CZECH UKRAINE
AUS. HUN. MOLDAVIA
SW. SL. ROMANIA
CR. YUG.
45 BULG.

SPAIN ITALY
PORTUGAL ALB.
GREECE TURKEY
Azores GEORGIA
ARMENIA AZERBAIJAN
Gibraltar
MALTA CYPRUS SYRIA
MOROCCO TUNISIA LEB. IRAQ
ISRAEL
Canary Isles JORDAN
Western
Sahara

CAPE VERDE
MAURITANIA
SENEGAL
GAMBIA
GUINEA-
BISSAU GUINEA
SIERRA LEONE
LIBERIA COTE
D'IVOIRE GHANA
EQ. GUINEA
SAO TOME & PRINCIPE

A L G E R I A L I B Y A
1969 EGYPT

M A L I N I G E R
CHAD SUDAN
BURKINA
FASO
NIGERIA CENTRAL
CAMEROON AFRICAN
REPUBLIC

GABON CONGO
Cabinda
ZAIRE

ANGOLA

ZAMBIA

NAMIBIA BOTSWANA
ZIMBABWE
MOZAMBIQUE

SOUTH SWAZILAND
AFRICA LESOTHO

SAUDI
ARABIA
BAHRAIN QATAR
KUWAIT UAE
OMAN
YEMEN

Eritrea
DJIBOUTI Socotra

ETHIOPIA SOMALIA

UGANDA KENYA
RWANDA
BURUNDI

TANZANIA
SEYCHELLES

COMOROS

MADAGASCAR Réunion
MAURITIUS

RUSSIAN FEDERATION
1917

Sakhalin

KAZAKHSTAN

UZBEKISTAN KIRGHIZSTAN
TURKMENISTAN TADZHIKISTAN

IRAN
1979 AFGHANISTAN
Kashmir

PAKISTAN NEPAL
BHU.

INDIA

MALDIVES

Andaman &
Nicobar Is.

SRI
LANKA

MONGOLIA

C H I N A
1949

Tibet

Hong Kong

N. KOREA
S. KOREA

JAPAN

TAIWAN

MYANMAR

THAILAND

VIETNAM
CAM-
BODIA

M A L A Y S I A
BRUNEI
SINGAPORE
Sumatra Borneo

I N D O N E S I A

Java E. Timor
Timor

PHILIPPINES

PAPUA
NEW
GUINEA

Kerguelen

A U S T R A L I A

NEW
ZEALAND

Legend:

Countries continuously independent,
or independent since 1815 or earlier

Countries gaining independence 1815–1900

Countries gaining independence 1900–1945

Countries gaining independence 1945–1960

Countries which have gained independence
since 1960

Several countries now have more extensive territory than
when they first became independent. This has been
indicated schematically for the USA, but not for other small
additions to territories (e.g. in Saudi Arabia the ruling
family goes back to before 1815 but did not originally
have control over all of what is now Saudi Arabia).

Dependent territories

1949 Revolutionary change of form of state since independence
(selected major examples)

───── International boundaries

─ ─ ─ Boundaries in dispute

Capital letters are used to denote independent countries

* This map was compiled when the future of the Yugoslav federation was in doubt.

ALB.	Albania
AUS.	Austria
BEL.	Belgium
BHU.	Bhutan
BULG.	Bulgaria
CAR	Central African Republic
CR.	Croatia
CZECH	Czech Republic
HUN.	Hungary
L.	Luxembourg
NETH.	Netherlands
S.	Slovakia
SL.	Slovenia
SW.	Switzerland
UAE	United Arab Emirates
YUG.	Yugoslavia

The following independent Pacific island countries are not shown on the map:
Federated States of Micronesia, Fiji, Kiribati, Marshall Islands, Nauru,
Solomon Islands, Tonga, Tuvalu, Vanuatu, Western Samoa.
Other small independent states not named are: Liechtenstein, San Marino,
Monaco and Vatican City State

13

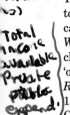

The most common method of attempting to rank countries according to economic well-being is to use gross national product (GNP) per capita as a measure of average income. The World Bank in its annual *World Development Report* and *World Development Indicators* classifies the countries of the world into three main income groups for 'operational and analytical purposes'. In the *World Development Report 1990* the main categories are:

1 *Low-income economies*: GNP per capita US$545 or less in 1988. China and India, with about two-fifths of the world's population between them, fall into this category.

2 *Middle-income economies*: GNP per capita more than $545 but less than $6000 in 1988. Within this group a further division is made to distinguish lower- and upper middle-income economies, fixed for 1988 at $2200.

3 *High-income economies*: GNP per capita $6000 or more in 1988. This group ranges from Saudi Arabia ($6200) at the bottom end of the scale to Switzerland ($27,500) at the top.

4 *Non-reporting non-members*: the USSR, Albania, Bulgaria, Cuba, Czechoslovakia, North Korea, Mongolia and Namibia. Apart from Namibia, this is a subset of the countries previously grouped together as *centrally planned economies*. Taiwan is also a non-member of the World Bank, but is generally not even mentioned in its publications.

Finally, there is a 'non-group' composed of all the members of the World Bank and the UN with fewer than a million inhabitants, which are excluded from the main statistical section of the report.

The categories of low- and middle-income countries together could be considered as providing one definition of the Third World. However, the *World Development Report* specifies that classification by average income does not necessarily reflect development status, thus indirectly acknowledging that GNP per capita by itself is not an adequate indicator. Saudi Arabia, Israel and Singapore, among other countries, are classified as high-income but 'developing' economies.

Even as an indicator of economic well-being, GNP per capita has several flaws. First, since it is an average and does not reveal anything about income inequality, it gives no information about relative numbers of people in poverty: a more egalitarian society with lower GNP per capita may have a smaller proportion of poor inhabitants than a more unequal society with higher GNP per capita. Second, GNP per capita figures use market valuations in internationally convertible currency, usually US dollars. However, the wage represented by a country's GNP per capita in a local currency may buy more (or less) commodities at local prices than could be obtained for an equivalent amount of US dollars in the USA. (An alternative measure of average income which takes this into account is *real gross domestic product (GDP) per capita*, measured in 'purchasing power parity dollars'. This is used in an adjusted form in the *Human Development Index* (see p.22) and included in the tables on pp.74–75. Unfortunately it requires complex statistical estimation, whereas GNP figures come direct from national accounts and currency exchange rates.) Third, market valuations also mean ignoring or under-valuing non-market items, including production for direct use by peasants or others as well as intangible aspects of well-being such as health or an undegraded environment, while assuming any increase in marketed production is a benefit.

As well as groupings based on GNP per capita, the World Bank uses analytical classifications based on two main structural aspects of an economy: exports and external debt. A country can be an *exporter of manufactures*, of *non-food primary products*, of *oil* (and other fuels), or of *services*, or else it is a *diversified exporter*. Low- and middle-income economies are classed as *severely indebted* if certain debt ratios are above critical levels, or else *moderately indebted* or *less indebted*. For example, the *World Development Report 1992* gives the UK as the only high-income exporter of services (most high-income countries are exporters of manufactures or diversified exporters), whereas India is a moderately indebted, low-income exporter of manufactures, Algeria and Venezuela are severely indebted, middle-income oil exporters, and so on. (The tables on pp.76–77 give an up-to-date categorization for all countries.)

Two particular analytical groups are given special emphasis by the World Bank: *oil exporters* and *severely indebted middle-income economies*. In addition, the high-income members of the *Organization for Economic Cooperation and Development (OECD)* are considered as a distinct subgroup of the high-income economies (They are, in fact, by far the majority.) Greece, Portugal and Turkey, all middle-income OECD members, are not part of this group.

The map opposite portrays these groups together with the income-based groups as in the *World Development Report 1990*, on a proportional population base. The diagram below uses the same income data, with estimates for non-members, to give a rough impression of the proportion of the world's population below different income levels.

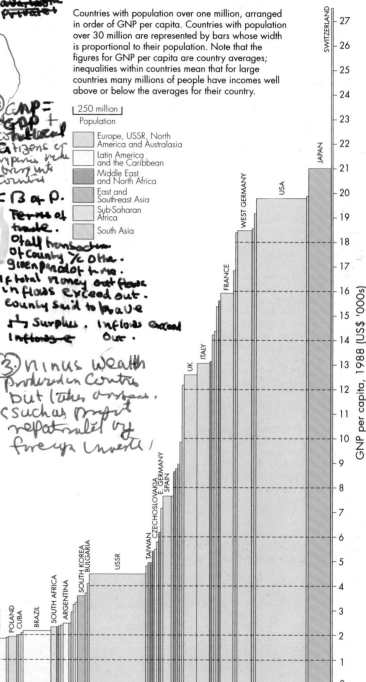

Countries in order of GNP per capita, 1988

Countries with population over one million, arranged in order of GNP per capita. Countries with population over 30 million are represented by bars whose width is proportional to their population. Note that the figures for GNP per capita are country averages; inequalities within countries mean that for large countries many millions of people have incomes well above or below the averages for their country.

250 million
Population

Europe, USSR, North America and Australasia
Latin America and the Caribbean
Middle East and North Africa
East and South-east Asia
Sub-Saharan Africa
South Asia

GNP per capita, 1988 (US$ '000s)

World Bank categories, 1990

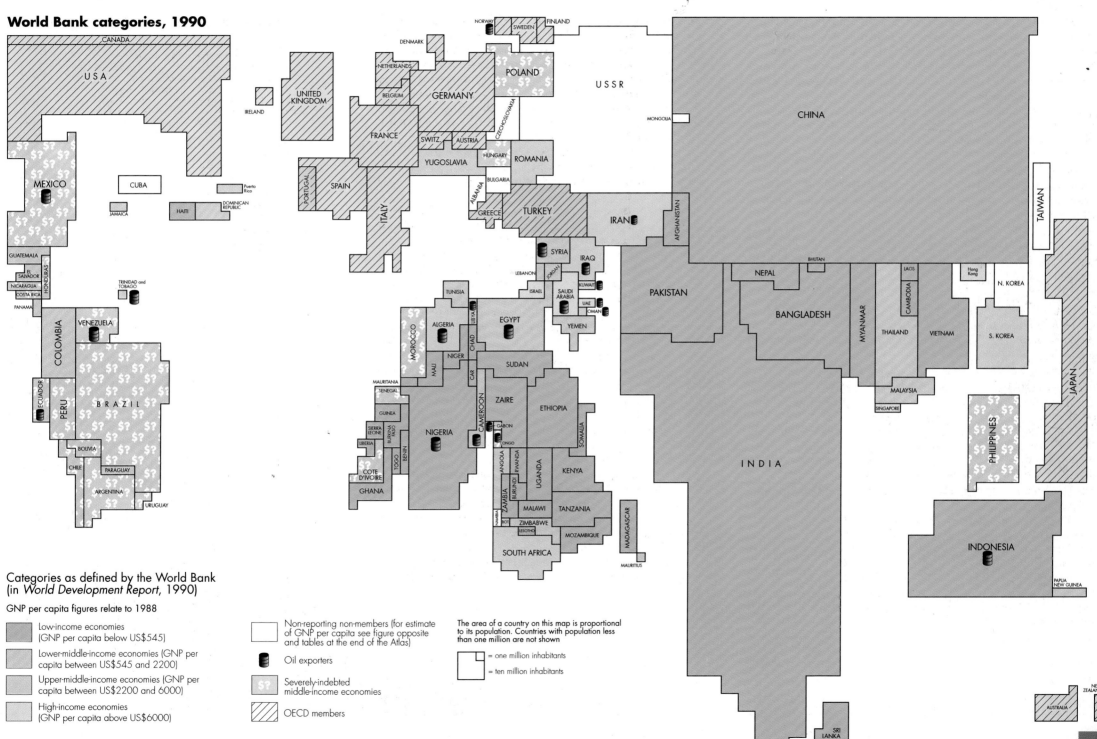

Categories as defined by the World Bank
(in *World Development Report*, 1990)

GNP per capita figures relate to 1988

- Low-income economies
(GNP per capita below US$545)

- Lower-middle-income economies (GNP per
capita between US$545 and 2200)

- Upper-middle-income economies (GNP per
capita between US$2200 and 6000)

- High-income economies
(GNP per capita above US$6000)

- Non-reporting non-members (for estimate
of GNP per capita see figure opposite
and tables at the end of the Atlas)

- Oil exporters

- Severely-indebted
middle-income economies

- OECD members

The area of a country on this map is proportional
to its population. Countries with population less
than one million are not shown

- = one million inhabitants
- = ten million inhabitants

15

Economic activity is customarily divided into three sectors: agriculture, industry and services. 'Industry' includes mining, construction, manufacturing and utilities (electricity, gas and water supply). 'Services' includes wholesale/retail trade, restaurants and hotels, transport and communication, financial services, and social and personal services.

'Industrialization' can simply imply an increase in the proportion of gross domestic product (GDP) that comes from the industrial sector, and within that from manufacturing in particular. The figure on the far right shows how some countries have industrialized in this sense over the period 1965–88.

But industrialization goes deeper than this. It means a transformation in production methods, so that one can speak of industrialized agriculture or the catering industry. Full industrialization implies a cultural change among the whole population.

One influential composite definition is due to Sutcliffe[3], who put forward three 'tests' of industrialization:

Test One: at least 25% of GDP should be in industry.

Test Two: at least 60% of industrial output should be in manufacturing.

Test Three: a minimum percentage of the total population should be employed in industry (at least 10% in Sutcliffe's original; a figure of 7.5% is used here).

The low threshold required in Test Three is because even a small industrial labour force usually has high productivity and generates a substantial service sector. Also, developing countries have a high number of younger dependants, so the proportion engaged in formal industrial employment is often very low.

Sutcliffe then proposed several categories of country:

A Fully industrialized countries passing all tests.

B Countries which pass the first two tests. Manufacturing predominates in a substantial industrial sector but has not spread to affect the whole population.

A/B Borderline cases between A and B.

C Countries which pass the first and third tests. A large industrial sector (perhaps based on mining or oil) affects the population widely, but manufacturing is weak.

D Countries passing only the second test. A small industrial sector is based mainly on manufacturing.

E Countries which pass only the 25% GDP test. There is a substantial non-manufacturing-based industrial sector (again, perhaps oil or mining) which does not affect the population widely.

O Non-industrialized countries which fail on all three tests.

There are two possible paths to industrialization discernible from Sutcliffe's analysis:

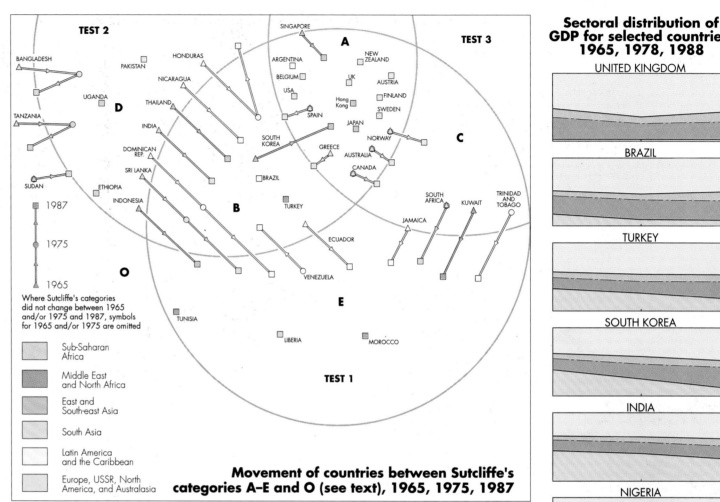

Movement of countries between Sutcliffe's categories A–E and O (see text), 1965, 1975, 1987

Where Sutcliffe's categories did not change between 1965 and/or 1975 and 1987, symbols for 1965 and/or 1975 are omitted

- Sub-Saharan Africa
- Middle East and North Africa
- East and South-east Asia
- South Asia
- Latin America and the Caribbean
- Europe, USSR, North America, and Australasia

D → B → A Manufacturing leads to an increase in industrial output and eventually a shift to a more industrial labour force.

E → C → A A mining enclave spreads to involve the whole population and manufacturing industry develops later.

Sutcliffe's data were for the mid-1960s. His calculations have been reworked for this Atlas for 1975 and 1987. The picture in 1975 more or less confirms the identification of industrialization with the 'developed' West (and East), with some other countries moving along a path towards industrialization.

The map opposite shows Sutcliffe's categories for 1965 and 1975, with information on manufacturing location and output for the mid-1970s. It deliberately does not use recent data, to give a clearer picture. Since the mid-1970s the overall pattern has become more complex. Some countries continue to industrialize; others have moved in the reverse direction by these criteria (diagram above). Even some Western industrial nations no longer pass all three tests. Many have concluded that a process of 'de-industrialization' is now under way. (Pages 49–51 give more recent data on industrial development.)

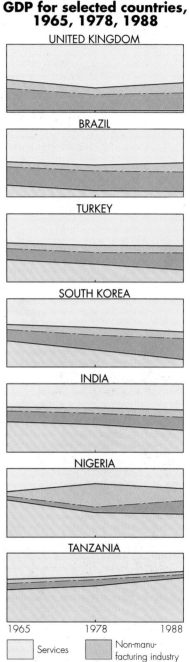

Sectoral distribution of GDP for selected countries, 1965, 1978, 1988

- UNITED KINGDOM
- BRAZIL
- TURKEY
- SOUTH KOREA
- INDIA
- NIGERIA
- TANZANIA

1965   1978   1988

- Services
- Agriculture
- Non-manufacturing industry
- Manufacturing industry

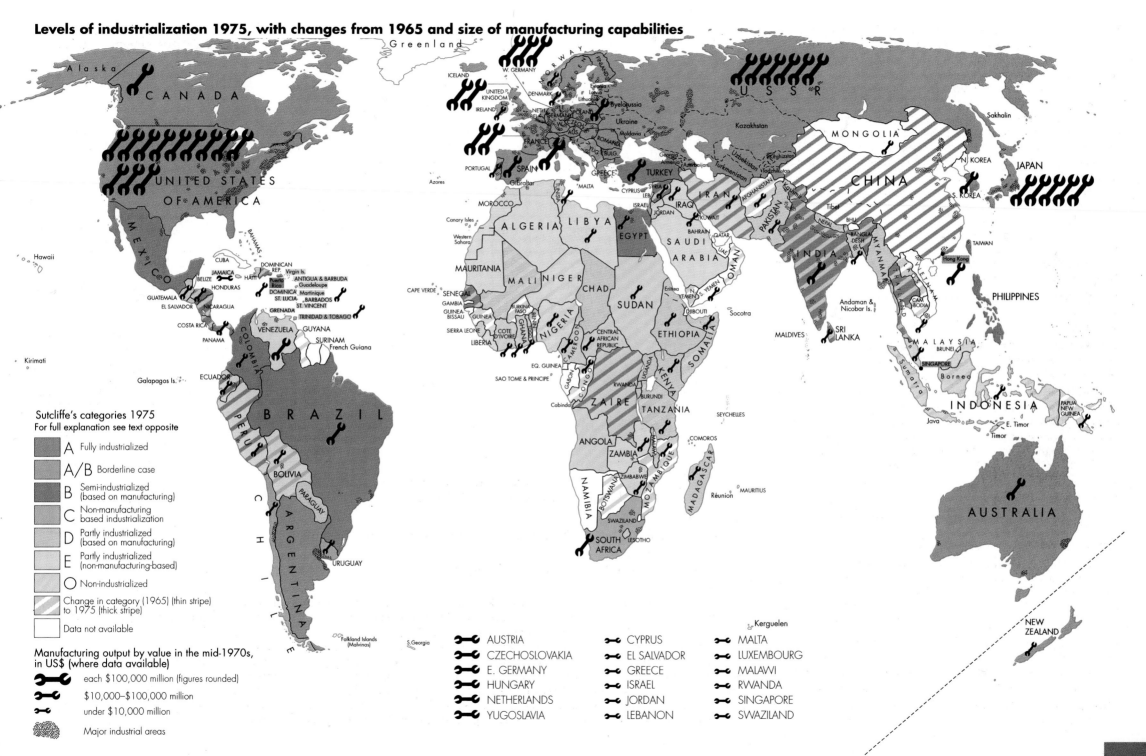

Levels of industrialization 1975, with changes from 1965 and size of manufacturing capabilities

Sutcliffe's categories 1975
For full explanation see text opposite

A Fully industrialized

A/B Borderline case

B Semi-industrialized
(based on manufacturing)

C Non-manufacturing
based industrialization

D Partly industrialized
(based on manufacturing)

E Partly industrialized
(non-manufacturing-based)

○ Non-industrialized

Change in category (1965) (thin stripe)
to 1975 (thick stripe)

Data not available

**Manufacturing output by value in the mid-1970s,
in US$ (where data available)**

each $100,000 million (figures rounded)

$10,000–$100,000 million

under $10,000 million

Major industrial areas

AUSTRIA	CYPRUS	MALTA
CZECHOSLOVAKIA	EL SALVADOR	LUXEMBOURG
E. GERMANY	GREECE	MALAWI
HUNGARY	ISRAEL	RWANDA
NETHERLANDS	JORDAN	SINGAPORE
YUGOSLAVIA	LEBANON	SWAZILAND

These two pages illustrate a number of ideas about how developing countries are linked to the global economy and how they are internally structured. The developed world has been likened to a *metropolis* at the *centre* served by Third World *satellites* on the *periphery*. According to the *dependency* school (prominent in the 1960s) this pattern was the outcome of and the mechanism for a process of *underdevelopment* by which former colonies continued to be drained of wealth and resources.

Thus the *metropolitan* countries of North America and Europe (and, now, Japan) have modern, integrated economies with production, consumption and trade in all types of commodities. The *satellite* countries have 'skewed' trade and communications (mainly to and from the metropolis) and depend on exporting specific commodities to the metropolis.

The map on this page shows how many Latin American, African, Middle Eastern and Asian countries are indeed dependent on producing and exporting one or two commodities, whereas most 'Northern' countries have very diversified exports. The overall flow of world trade (diagram below, right) confirms the idea that the Third World is peripheral. In 1989 exports from the whole of Africa were only slightly more than those of Switzerland alone. World trading power is dominated by developed countries; one-third of all world trade takes place within Western Europe. There was some growth in South–North trade during the 1980s, particularly between Southeast Asia and Australasia. Nevertheless, the diagram shows that in 1988 only 13% of world export trade was between one developing country and another.

Whatever the merits of dependency thinking, the inequality of economic relationships between countries is reflected in the control and utilization of world resources. For example, there are great disparities in energy utilization between regions of the world (diagram, below left), a pattern which could be repeated for most of the world's commodities.

Commodity dependence, late 1980s

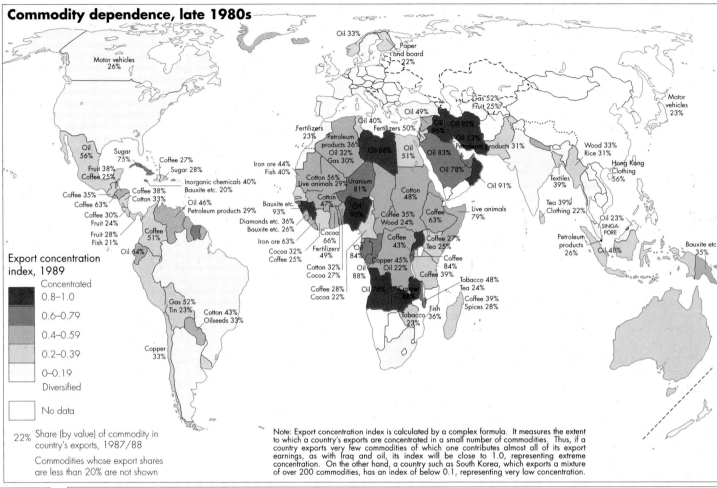

Export concentration index, 1989

Concentrated
- 0.8–1.0
- 0.6–0.79
- 0.4–0.59
- 0.2–0.39
- 0–0.19
Diversified

No data

22% Share (by value) of commodity in country's exports, 1987/88

Commodities whose export shares are less than 20% are not shown

Note: Export concentration index is calculated by a complex formula. It measures the extent to which a country's exports are concentrated in a small number of commodities. Thus, if a country exports very few commodities of which one contributes almost all of its export earnings, as with Iraq and oil, its index will be close to 1.0, representing extreme concentration. On the other hand, a country such as South Korea, which exports a mixture of over 200 commodities, has an index of below 0.1, representing very low concentration.

Energy consumption per capita and population, 1985

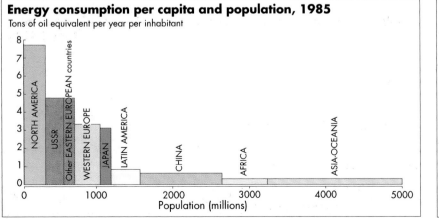

World export trade between regions, 1988 (Total value of all world exports US$ 2,841,000 million)

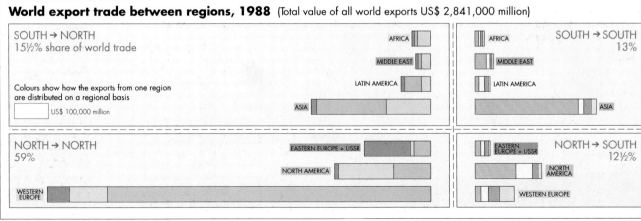

Dependency thinking also saw the metropolis–satellite relationship repeated between Third World cities and rural areas. Third World capitals and other cities were supposedly instrumental in the process of transferring resources from South to North. It was suggested that in developing countries cities comprised two distinct economic tiers: a small elite (often an ex-colonial civil service) with a small modern industrial sector; and a much larger group known as the 'informal sector', involved in activities without regular wages, including street vending, backyard workshops and the 'hidden economy'. This aspect of underdevelopment is by definition hard to measure. The diagrams below show the rapid growth of Third World cities and the size of informal settlements in some of them.

The Third World city also acts as an important entry point for the cultural milieu of fashion, food, soft drinks, TV soaps, films and music, whose total effect is often described as *westernization*. Such influences are difficult to measure objectively, but they are important cultural exports from the First World which can be seen as ensuring continued dependency and a demand for First World products in the future.

Apart from the cities, Third World countries are still relatively isolated in terms of modern communications. In this field, as in others, technological change has tended to consolidate the 'lead' of the modern industrial nations. In the late 1980s, the USA had more than two radios per person, whereas in many African countries there were fewer than one for every ten (see map). With regard to telephones, the situation is even more inequitable: Tokyo has more telephones than the whole of sub-Saharan Africa (excluding South Africa); Canada's 26 million people have 17 million telephones, roughly the same as Asia's two *billion* people.[4] Another indicator of communications is the consumption of newsprint, also shown on the map. There are similar inequities here, with the average North American using more newsprint in a week than the average African consumes in a year.

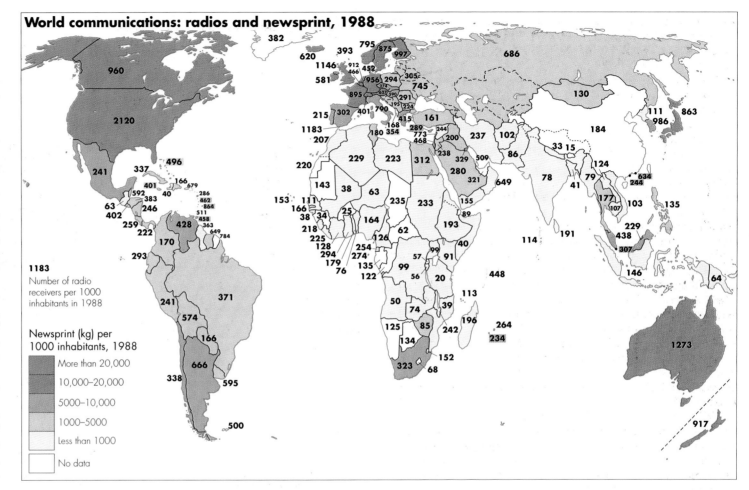

World communications: radios and newsprint, 1988

1183
Number of radio receivers per 1000 inhabitants in 1988

Newsprint (kg) per 1000 inhabitants, 1988
- More than 20,000
- 10,000–20,000
- 5000–10,000
- 1000–5000
- Less than 1000
- No data

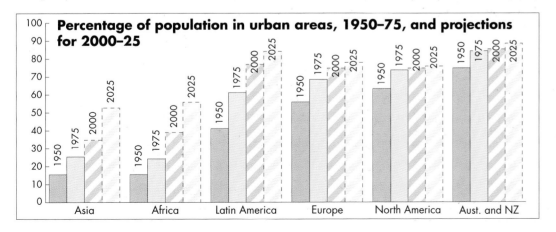

Percentage of population in urban areas, 1950–75, and projections for 2000–25

Asia, Africa, Latin America, Europe, North America, Aust. and NZ
(1950, 1975, 2000, 2025)

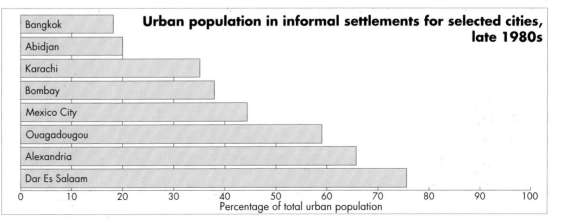

Urban population in informal settlements for selected cities, late 1980s

- Bangkok
- Abidjan
- Karachi
- Bombay
- Mexico City
- Ouagadougou
- Alexandria
- Dar Es Salaam

Percentage of total urban population

Social well-being, and its converse poverty, are multi-faceted: disease, illiteracy and isolation are interrelated and cannot be reduced to a single indicator. The maps opposite show some of the factors that influence social well-being.

1   Rural populations are often the most disadvantaged because they have poor access to economic opportunities and social services. Although the numbers of urban poor are increasing, the relative size of the rural population may still be taken as an indicator of poverty.

2   The status of women is now regarded as an important aspect of development. The ratio of girls to boys at primary school is an effective general indicator for this.

3   Clean water is vital in preventing water-borne disease.

4   The Physical Quality of Life Index (PQLI), developed by Morris[5], is a composite 'welfare' indicator with three components: life expectancy (at age one), infant mortality, and adult literacy. Each component is measured on a scale from 0 to 100. Thus 100 is assigned to the highest life expectancy (78 years in Japan) and 0 to the lowest (42 in Sierra Leone). Infant mortality is calibrated in a similar way, from 0 for the worst (highest) to 100 for the best (lowest) rate. For literacy the direct percentage figures for people over 15 years old are taken. Averaging the three scores gives the physical quality of life index .

Apart from the map, PQLI is also shown on the graph (below left), compared with gross national product (GNP) per capita for selected

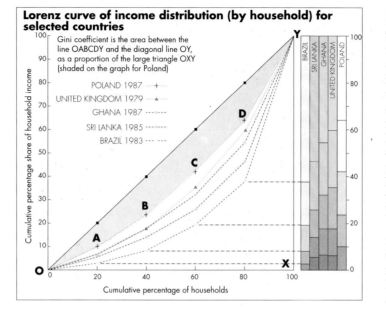

Lorenz curve of income distribution (by household) for selected countries

Gini coefficient is the area between the line OABCDY and the diagonal line OY, as a proportion of the large triangle OXY (shaded on the graph for Poland)

POLAND 1987 —+—
UNITED KINGDOM 1979 —▲—
GHANA 1987 ----
SRI LANKA 1985 ----
BRAZIL 1983 ----

Cumulative percentage share of household income

Cumulative percentage of households

countries. Note particularly the countries with low (or high) PQLI for their level of income. The middle graph (below) shows how two of the components of PQLI, life expectancy and literacy, have improved worldwide since 1960.

Inequality

The equal or unequal distribution of any quantity may be captured in several ways. The bar charts in the figure (above left) are one way of doing this, here for household income; *Lorenz curves*, also in the figure, are another. In a completely equal society 20% of households would earn 20% of the income and so on. In such a case the Lorenz curve would not be a curve at all, but a straight diagonal line. In reality all Lorenz curves are pulled to the right of the perfect-equality line because some households have more income than others. The curves drawn show the cumulative income for each fifth of the population for selected countries: for example, the poorest 40% of households in Brazil had about 8% of the income in 1983, whereas the top 20% had over 60%. (The figures ignore variations in size of households, and distribution within households.)

Gini coefficients are a mathematical way of expressing how much the Lorenz curve deviates from the line of perfect equality: the Gini coefficient varies from 0 for complete equality to 1 for extreme inequality. Countries with polarizations of income, such as many in Latin America, have coefficients around 0.5–0.7; by contrast, formerly socialist Eastern European countries had coefficients of 0.2–0.4.

Another measure of relative equality is the proportion of GNP taken by the poorest 40% of households. The graph (below right) uses this to show that Kuznets'[6] hypothesis, that inequality increases in the initial stages of economic development and then decreases as a society becomes prosperous, is far from conclusive.

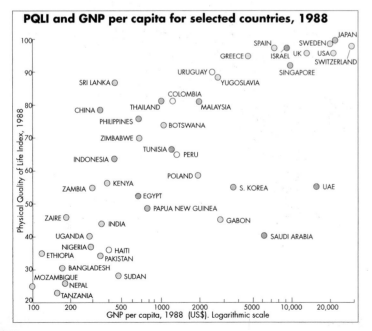

PQLI and GNP per capita for selected countries, 1988

Physical Quality of Life Index, 1988

GNP per capita, 1988 (US$). Logarithmic scale

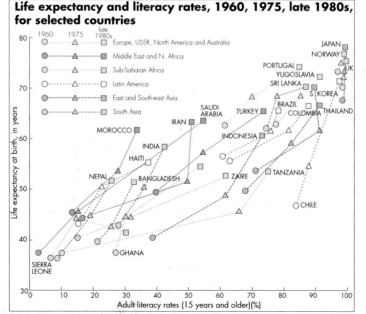

Life expectancy and literacy rates, 1960, 1975, late 1980s, for selected countries

1960   1975   late 1980s

○——△——□ Europe, USSR, North America and Australia
○——△——■ Middle East and N. Africa
○——△——□ Sub-Saharan Africa
○----△----□ Latin America
○——△——■ East and South-east Asia
○----△----■ South Asia

Life expectancy at birth, in years

Adult literacy rates (15 years and older)(%)

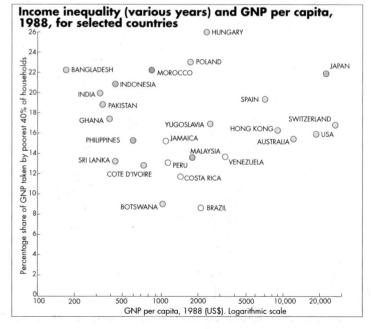

Income inequality (various years) and GNP per capita, 1988, for selected countries

Percentage share of GNP taken by poorest 40% of households

GNP per capita, 1988 (US$). Logarithmic scale

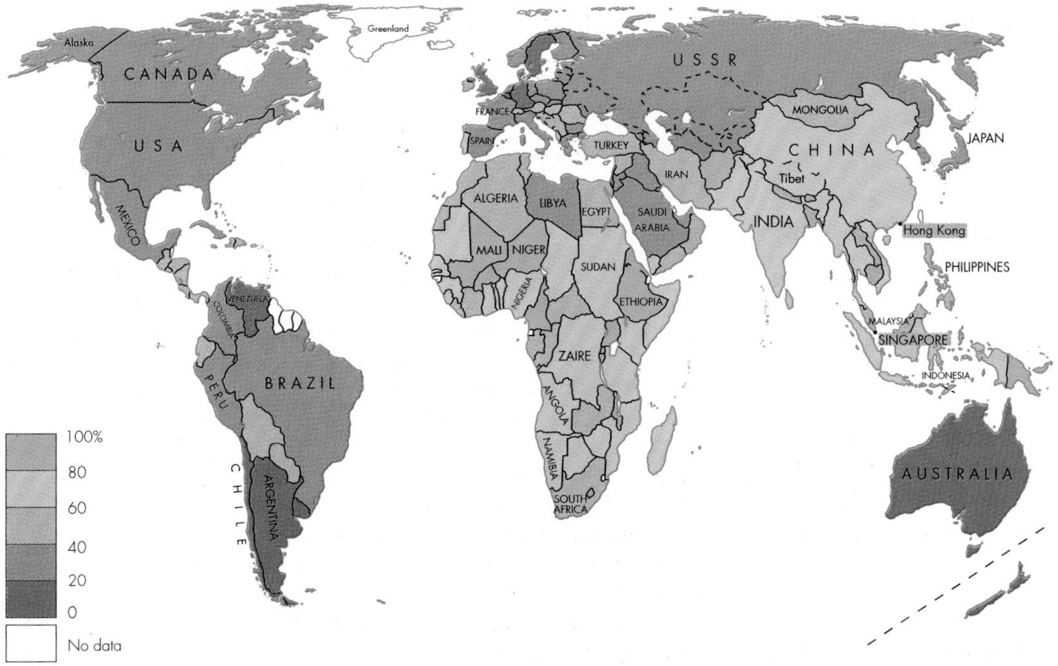

Percentage of population rural, 1988/89

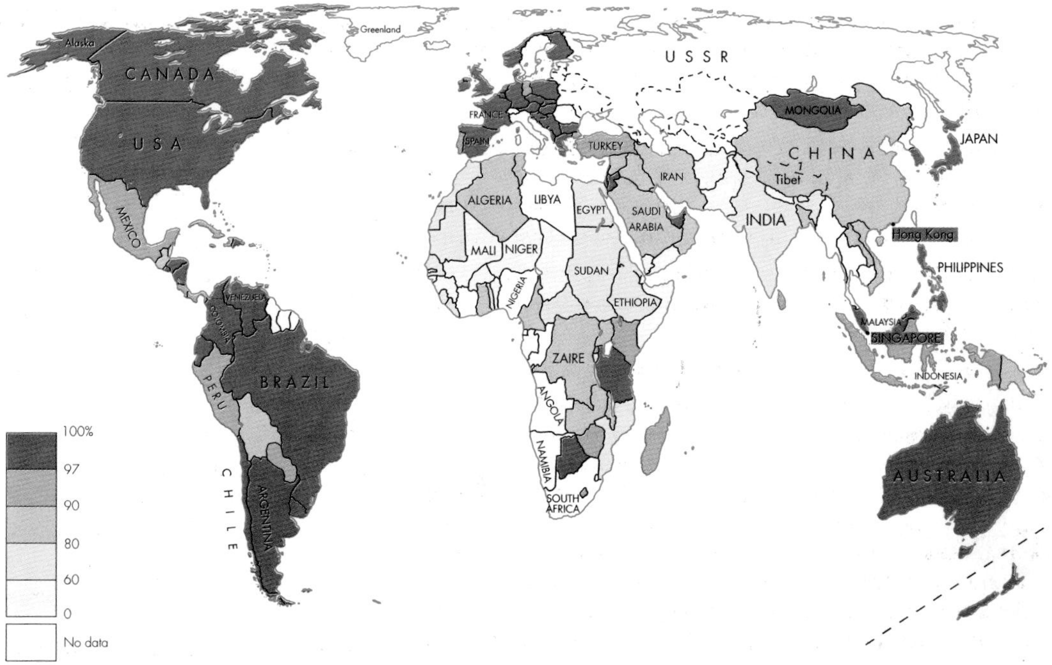

Primary school enrolment of girls as a percentage of boys, 1986–88

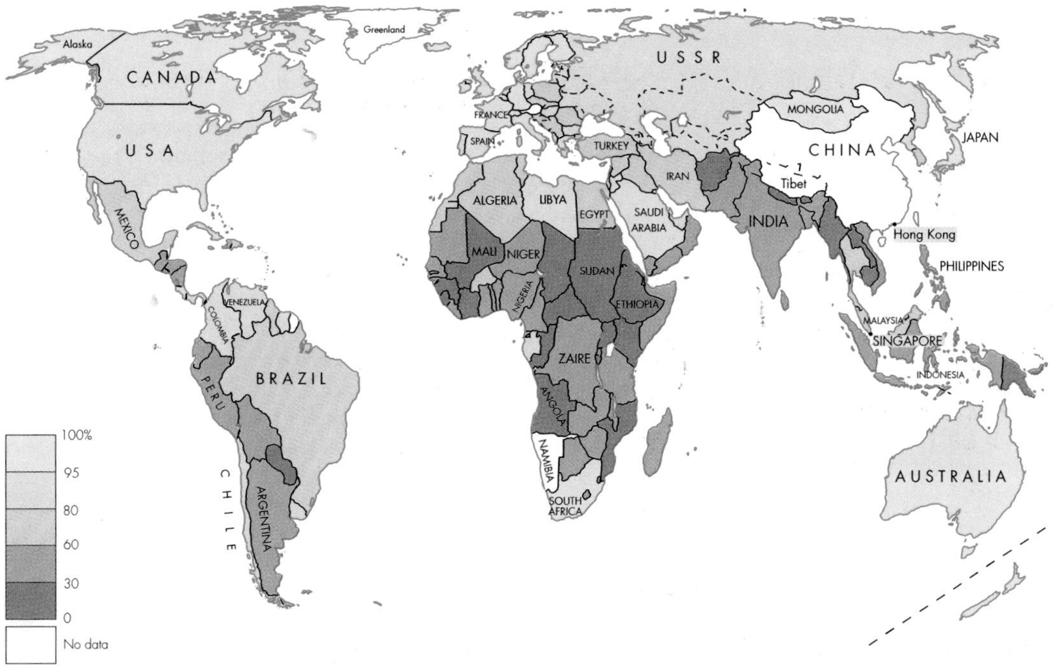

Percentage of population with access to safe water, 1985–88

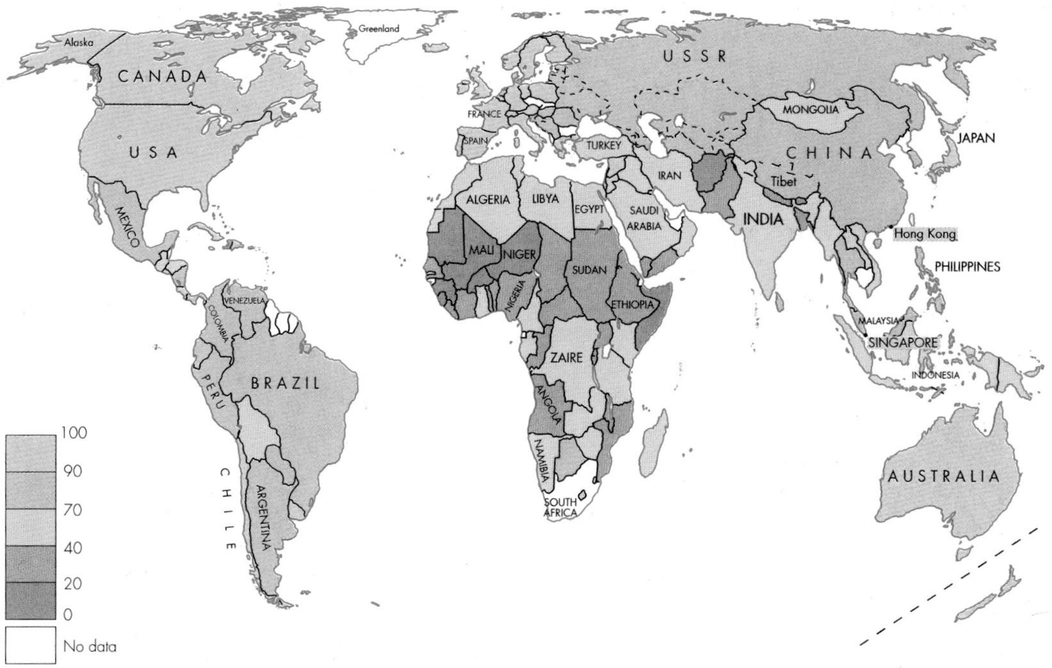

Physical quality of life index, late 1980s

The United Nations Development Programme (UNDP) devised the *Human Development Index* (*HDI*) in 1990 as a composite index combining economic and social welfare.

The HDI gives equal weight to longevity, educational attainment and utility derived from income. A score is derived for each of these, from 0 for the lowest achieved by any country to 1 for the highest. Life expectancy at birth for 1990[7] ranged from 42.0 years for Sierra Leone to 78.6 for Japan, so for this part of the index Sierra Leone scores 0 and Japan 1, with the other countries in between (for example, Singapore, with life expectancy 74.0 years, scores 0.874). For educational attainment, two variables are combined: adult literacy (two-thirds weight) and average years of schooling (one-third weight).

Utility derived from income is measured by a complex formula. It uses *real gross domestic product (GDP) per capita*, or 'purchasing power', rather than gross national product (GNP) per capita, to indicate average income. Then it assumes that as income increases there are diminishing returns for human development. In other words, after a certain point, twice the purchasing power means much less than twice the well-being.

By averaging the three indicators an HDI value from 0 to 1 is calculated. The UNDP's *Human Development Report 1992* gave Canada the highest HDI at 0.982, and Guinea the lowest at 0.052 .

The map below is shaded according to HDI levels. The diagram (right) compares GNP per capita and HDI for 14 countries. Some countries score much better on this index than might be expected if GNP per capita were taken as an indicator of human development.

Countries 'rewarded' by using the HDI include Cuba, China and other socialist and ex-socialist countries. This, coupled with the collapse of Eastern European socialism, has lent weight to an interest in broadening what is meant by 'development' further, to include and even to try to measure democratization, human rights and other aspects of 'freedom'.

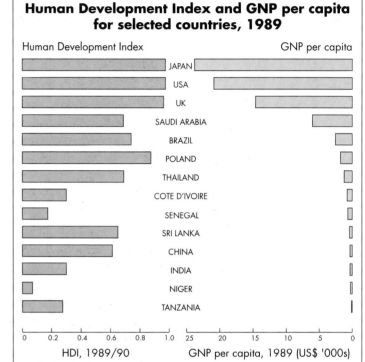

Human Development Index and GNP per capita for selected countries, 1989

Human Development Index / GNP per capita

JAPAN, USA, UK, SAUDI ARABIA, BRAZIL, POLAND, THAILAND, COTE D'IVOIRE, SENEGAL, SRI LANKA, CHINA, INDIA, NIGER, TANZANIA

HDI, 1989/90   GNP per capita, 1989 (US$ '000s)

Freedom and development

The Universal Declaration of Human Rights outlines that: 'Everyone has the right to life, liberty and security of person ... the right to freedom of thought, conscience and religion ... the right to freedom of opinion and expression ... the right to seek, receive and impart information and ideas through any media and regardless of frontiers.'[8] Measuring how well countries abide by these ideals is a difficult, if not impossible, task (the British-based Amnesty International refuses to rank countries according to abuses).

The map opposite is based on information as presented by Freedom House, a US human rights centre. Freedom House designates each country as 'free', 'partly free' or 'not free' on the basis of political and civil liberties. The *most free* have free elections, and all members of the population have freedom of expression, assembly, religion and association. In the *least free* countries political rights are virtually non-existent and citizens live in justified fear of repression for expressing views different from those of the state.

The map also quantifies media freedom, although assessing the extent of state control over information is highly subjective. For example, many would debate the extent to which the media are 'free' in North America.

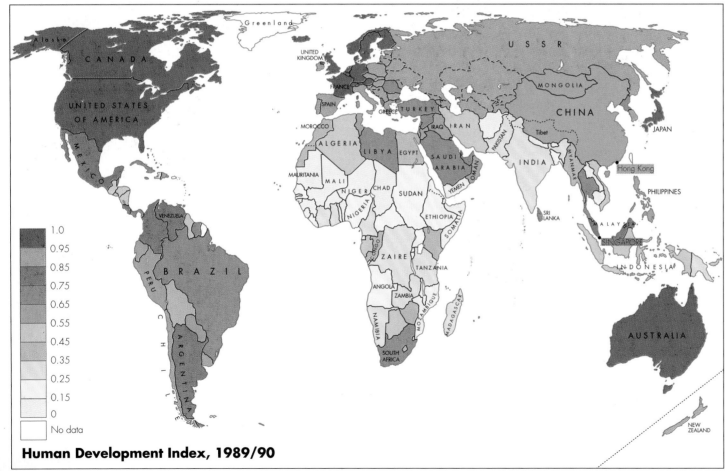

1.0
0.95
0.85
0.75
0.65
0.55
0.45
0.35
0.25
0.15
0
No data

Human Development Index, 1989/90

One view of political and civil liberties and media control
based on 'The Map of Freedom' by the US human rights centre Freedom House, January 1991

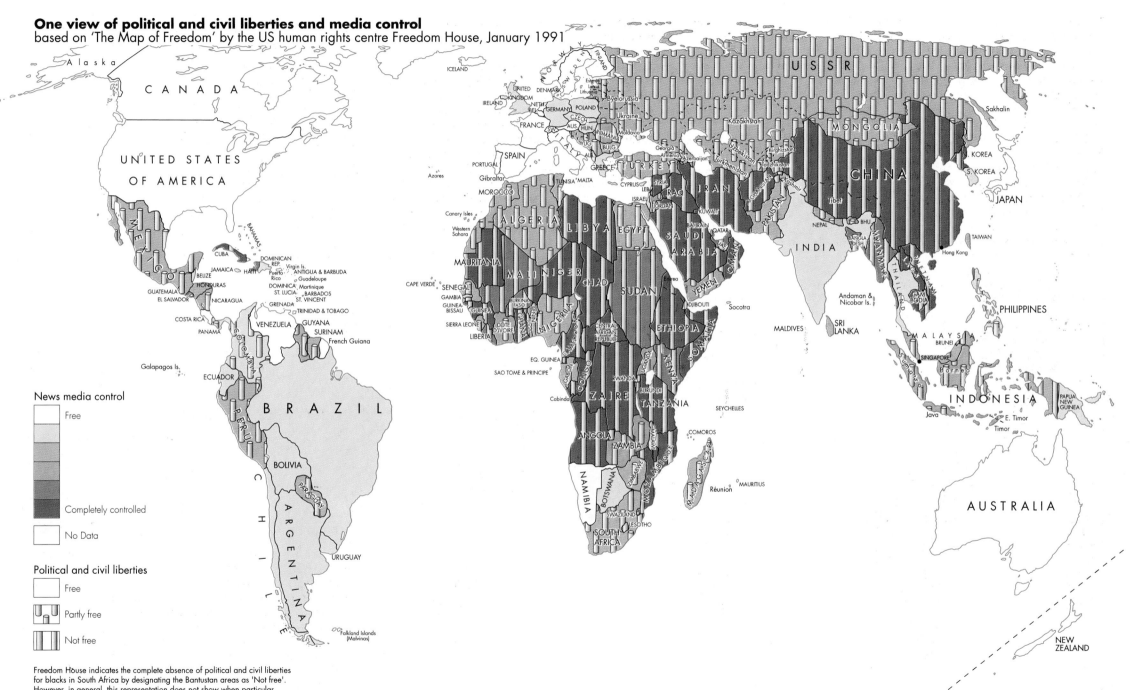

News media control

- Free
- Completely controlled
- No Data

Political and civil liberties

- Free
- Partly free
- Not free

Freedom House indicates the complete absence of political and civil liberties for blacks in South Africa by designating the Bantustan areas as 'Not free'. However, in general, this representation does not show when particular groups or regions have restricted liberties within an otherwise 'free' state, e.g. Northern Ireland or Palestinians in Israel.

THE MAKING OF THE THIRD WORLD

This section, pp.24–47, describes some of the worldwide historical changes which contributed to the emergence of the Third World. Between 1492 and the present, a diverse world was welded into a more homogenous whole chiefly as a result of two forces: the expansion of European political control and the rise of capitalism. These two forces are intimately related but can be studied distinctly; they are described separately in these pages.

Although the expansion of European political control is a discrete and easily identifiable sequence of events in world history, it is not a single, undifferentiated sequence: 'old' and 'new' empires can be distinguished, and colonies where Europeans settled in large numbers were unlike those where a few Europeans maintained control. In the chronology opposite, four main periods are identified: the rise of European commerce, the dominance of merchant capital, the rise of industrial capital, and the development of monopoly capitalism . These four eras correspond to phases in the rise of capitalism but they also distinguish phases in European expansion.

The first wave of European expansion occurred during the first and second eras of the chronology. The 'old' empires of the sixteenth and seventeenth centuries, most notably those of Iberian Europe in Latin America, and England and France in North America, were associated with settlement, plunder and the establishment of control over commerce. The USA and then most of the Latin American countries became independent around the end of the second and the beginning of the third era of the chronology. The third era saw relatively little expansion of European political control, though it did include further British expansion in India and the French conquest of Algeria. It was, however, crucial in the development of industrial capitalism. The final era saw a second wave of imperial expansion, notably in Africa but also worldwide. These 'new' empires arose with the emergence of industrial classes in Northern Europe, and were associated with the creation of a world economy supplying the needs – food, labour, raw materials, markets – of industrial Europe.

During the nineteenth century the prevalent eurocentric view saw the Western world, rooted in ancient Greece and Rome, as the pinnacle of civilization. However, previous civilizations have prospered in all parts of the world to match those of Europe. When Europe began to expand it was not into a vacuum, but it is not possible to describe here all the societies which were partially or completely subdued. The extent of some major civilizations is shown on p.26, and the rise of Islam – a group of societies with a common heritage which frequently stood in the way of European expansion – on p.27. Pages 28–29 show how the world's wealth became concentrated in Europe.

The expansion of European political control

The geographical background to European expansion is shown below. The general pattern of early European expansion worldwide is illustrated on p.30; pp.31–35 provide more detail, with descriptions of the different processes of subordination and expansion in the Americas, Asia and Africa, and the extent of some of the major states overrun by Europe. Maps on pp.32 and 43 show the world in 1714 and 1914.

The rise of capitalism

The initial accumulation of wealth in Europe through plunder and pillage is covered on pp.28–29. Further aspects of the rise of capitalism are described on pp.36–42. These show how agricultural crops were redistributed across the globe to provide for European needs (pp.36–37), how traditional handicraft manufacture was destroyed and supplanted by the beginnings of industrial production (pp.38–39), how trade and overseas investment expanded (pp.40–41), and how the labour force has changed (p.42).

The end of direct European control

The last four pages of this section cover some of the political changes that have led to the modern world of independent nation states. Direct European control has virtually disappeared from the so-called Third World, while world capitalism remains intact as a controlling economic force.

Some of the major struggles fought against European expansion and dominion are shown on pp.44–45.

Page 46 deals briefly with the rise of the USA and Japan up to the Second World War, and the emergence of the USA and USSR as major world powers after it. Most Third World countries have become independent in the context of the 'Cold War' between the USA and the USSR, and have joined the Non-aligned Movement (p.47) to express their desire for the fullest possible independence. However, since the collapse of the Soviet Union and the Eastern bloc, the identity of the Third World has to be seen mainly in relation to the USA as the world's only superpower and centre of world capitalism. Thus, relating the political history of the Third World to the rise of capitalism, as in this section, remains the best way of understanding what has made the Third World what it is today.

The geographical background to European expansion

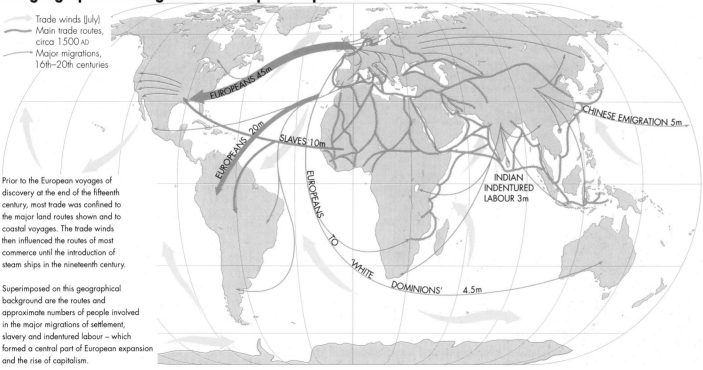

Trade winds (July)
Main trade routes, circa 1500 AD
Major migrations, 16th–20th centuries

Prior to the European voyages of discovery at the end of the fifteenth century, most trade was confined to the major land routes shown and to coastal voyages. The trade winds then influenced the routes of most commerce until the introduction of steam ships in the nineteenth century.

Superimposed on this geographical background are the routes and approximate numbers of people involved in the major migrations of settlement, slavery and indentured labour – which formed a central part of European expansion and the rise of capitalism.

A chronology of European expansion and the rise of capitalism

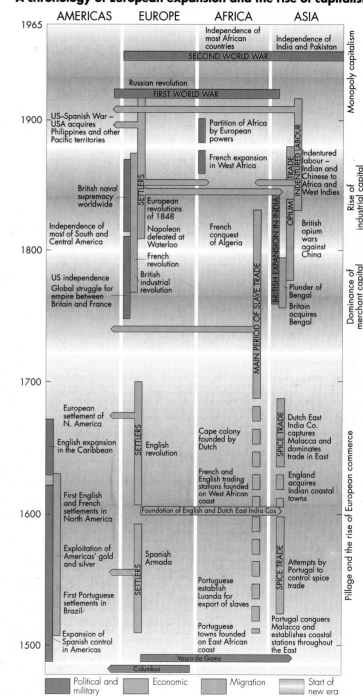

This page shows roughly where and when certain major civilizations and empires extended their political power and cultural influence before the expansion of European dominion.

The term civilization refers to human societies which have attained a high level of cultural and technological achievement together with complex social and political development. It implies the presence of the following basic set of interrelated social institutions: class stratification, differentiated by the degree of ownership or control of the main productive resources; political and religious hierarchies that complement each other in the administration of territorially organized states; and a complex division of labour.

Seventeen civilizations have been selected here, covering a time-span starting with the beginnings of recorded history and continuing after European colonization. Some are 'empires' with a unified political organization encompassing diverse ethnic groups over a wide area. We have chosen to show here only those of particular pre-eminence, longevity or interest. The chronology below indicates when these Third World civilizations prospered. The duration of Mycenaean and Roman civilizations are shown for comparison.

These civilizations and empires are also shown superimposed on the map (right) of the state of agriculture in AD 0. Three methods of self-sufficient food procurement dominate: gathering/hunting, pastoralism and peasant farming. Only in a few relatively small areas, generally where large civilizations emerged, was an agricultural surplus – more than the needs of subsistence – produced. There is a similar map for AD 1500 on p.36.

The earliest civilizations shown are river valley civilizations – Old Egypt, Sumeria and Indus (Harappan) – whose existence depended on irrigation. The technology and social organization required to harness water for agriculture is associated with the emergence of large-scale, centralized states. These three civilizations co-existed for several centuries, and there is evidence of trade

between them, though on a small scale and primarily in luxury goods for the ruling classes. Fundamental differences between them are indicated by the styles of building they left behind: Egypt's pyramid tombs, for example, have no parallel on the Indus, where the civilization left two substantial grid-plan, brick-built cities.

These river valley states organized and taxed peasant agriculture. By contrast, the later African kingdoms depicted on the map co-existed with pastoral agriculture and hunter-gatherers, but gained wealth by taxing trade: in the case of Axum, trade along the Red Sea; and in the cases of Ghana, Mali and Songhai, trade across the Sahara. These states have been described as 'constitutional monarchies', suggesting that power was vested in a single individual, although subject to political controls and not primarily theocratic.

The Mayan Empire emerged in the new world at about AD 0. It reached its greatest extent during the thirteenth century – roughly the same time as Islam reached its first peak in West Asia and North Africa (see p.27). It was a theocratic state exacting tribute from subordinate societies practising rudimentary agriculture (without domesticated animals or irrigation). The somewhat later American civilization of the Inca developed irrigated agriculture.

Production and accumulation of wealth in some of these societies were based on a high degree of labour coercion, frequently slavery. With the Mauryan dynasty in India and the Han dynasty in China, systems of ownership and production had emerged in which the crucial power of the ruling classes was their ownership of land rather than slaves.

Chronology of selected empires and civilizations

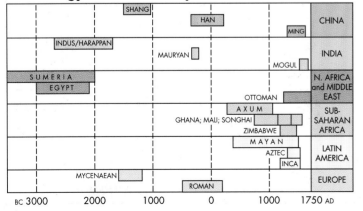

Selected Third World civilizations 3500BC to 1700AD, and agriculture at 0AD

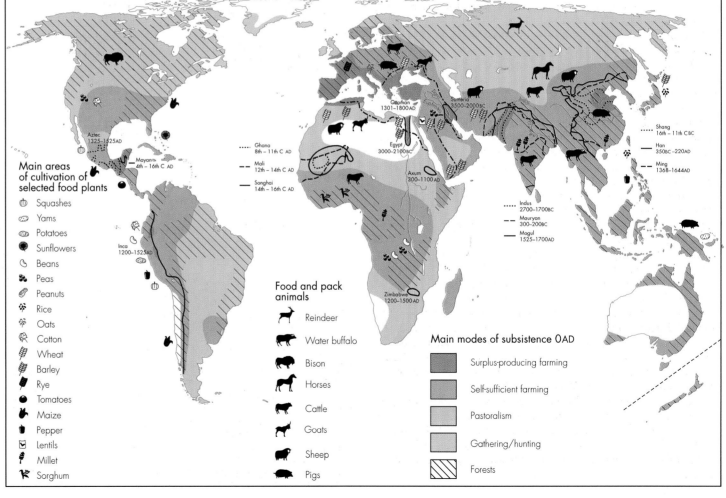

Before, during and after the epoch of European expansion (itself closely linked to the diffusion of Christian ideology), a series of merchant empires adopting and disseminating Islamic ideas controlled large areas of the world. By the end of the thirteenth century, Muslim rulers exercised power over a larger territory than any previous empire, one only subsequently exceeded by the combined territories of the European powers in the nineteenth and twentieth centuries.

The Islamic empires did not rest directly upon a peasant base. The Arab world acted as 'turntable between the main areas of civilization of the Old World'. It provided trading links between Asia and the Mediterranean and obtained its surplus by taxing that trade.

While to Christian Europe the Islamic civilization was (and is) one of 'barbarians', Islam's scholastic heritage carried many ideas through Europe's Dark Ages, ideas which laid the intellectual foundations of Europe's world domination. Egyptian astronomy, Greek philosophy and geometry, Indian mathematical methods, Arab medicine, early maps and perspective painting, all came from or were transmitted by Islamic scholars.

The rise of Islamic empires is marked by two waves of conquest: the first in the seventh and eighth centuries, beginning during the life of ruler and prophet Mohammed (c. 572–632 AD); the second between the tenth and thirteenth centuries. In the first, Mohammed and his successors commanded expansions into the weak and decaying peripheries of the Byzantine and Persian empires (in what are now Syria, Egypt and Iraq), into North Africa and the edges of India and China. The first peak was characterized by the demand for tribute (taxes) from subject societies.

More gradual expansion from the tenth to the thirteenth centuries led to the second peak of Islamic dominion (shown on the map). This enormous trading empire, from which Europe had to wrest trade routes, territory and subjects, included the Eurasian land empires of the Ottoman and Mogul dynasties, which reached their zenith in the sixteenth century. A ruling class of literate and educated merchants extended across the world from Indonesia to Spain and from Central Asia to Mali, having in common the codified practice of the Muslim faith and interests tied to the maintenance of Islamic dominion. The empire did not require centralized control – for the most part the bonds of trade and religion held it together. One serious exception was the protracted clash between the Ottoman followers of Sunni Islam and Safavid Persia, which followed Shi'ism – a divide which 'drove a wedge through the Muslim world'.

During the expansion of Europe, Islam provided a potent unifying force against which colonial rule had to compete. That force was never subdued, as the resurgence of Islam in the twentieth century has shown. The small inset map shows Islam alongside Christianity as one of the two major global – as opposed to regional or local – religions.

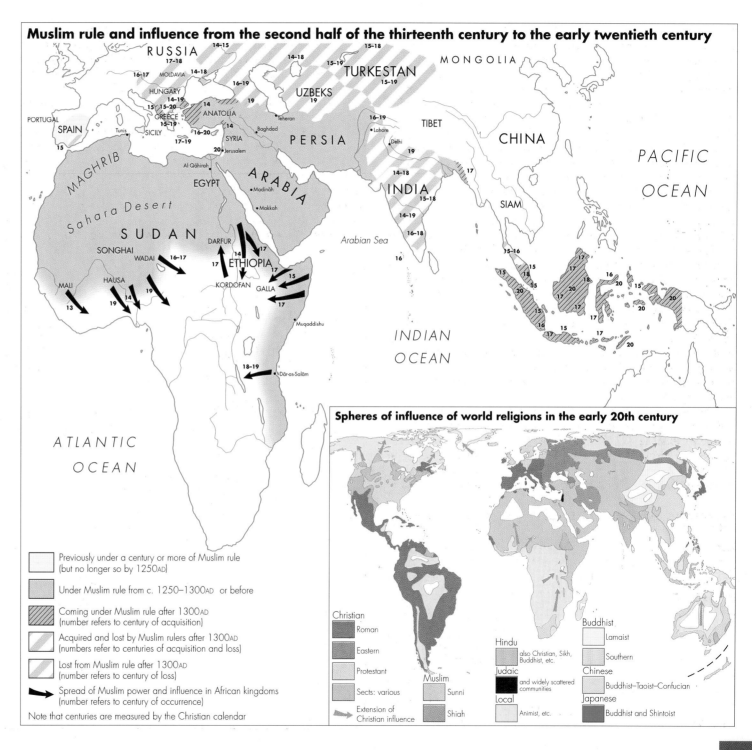

Muslim rule and influence from the second half of the thirteenth century to the early twentieth century

Spheres of influence of world religions in the early 20th century

Previously under a century or more of Muslim rule (but no longer so by 1250AD)

Under Muslim rule from c. 1250–1300AD or before

Coming under Muslim rule after 1300AD (number refers to century of acquisition)

Acquired and lost by Muslim rulers after 1300AD (numbers refer to centuries of acquisition and loss)

Lost from Muslim rule after 1300AD (number refers to century of loss)

Spread of Muslim power and influence in African kingdoms (number refers to century of occurrence)

Extension of Christian influence

Note that centuries are measured by the Christian calendar

Christian
Roman
Eastern
Protestant
Sects: various

Muslim
Sunni
Shiah

Local
Animist, etc.

Hindu
also Christian, Sikh, Buddhist, etc.

Judaic
and widely scattered communities

Buddhist
Lamaist
Southern

Chinese
Buddhist-Taoist-Confucian

Japanese
Buddhist and Shintoist

Many great empires have accumulated wealth through the plunder of civilizations which they could subdue. Alexander, for example, is believed to have collected booty worth about £80 million (at late nineteenth century prices)[1] from Asia in 323 BC. The expansion of European control over the world, beginning in 1492, was not unique in this respect, but Europe's explorers, merchants, rulers and settlers brought new mechanisms to their plunder and carried it out on a much larger scale than their predecessors.

The map opposite illustrates the extent and variety of the pillage associated with the expansion of Europe. It attempts to quantify the better documented examples.

The essence of 'pillage' or 'plunder' is the accumulation of resources with little or no exchange: resources, goods and labour are taken by force. No regard is paid to the subsistence needs of those whose labour accumulated or made the goods plundered, nor to those left behind after a labour force has been extracted. Several of the resource flows depicted on the map were unquestionably plunder: the slave trade and the Spanish looting of Aztec and Inca civilizations, for example. Forced labour in the Latin American metal mines and the use of slave labour in sugar production also fall into this category, although here the subsistence of the labour force was not *totally* ignored. Nevertheless, dramatic population declines in many areas reflected the brutality of labour conditions (along with the spread of European diseases and conscious attempts to wipe out indigenous populations).

With these clear examples of pillage have been included two major 'trades' which depended on the use of force or drugs – the Dutch spice trade and the (primarily British) opium trade – and one 'plunder' in which British rule drained the wealth from Bengal through harsh taxation.

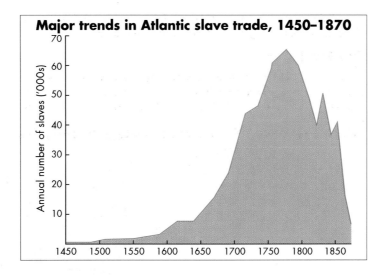

Major trends in Atlantic slave trade, 1450–1870

Annual number of slaves ('000s)

Silver and gold from the Americas

Only a small proportion of the huge bullion haul which accrued to the Spanish crown from its American possessions came from the looting of pre-existing civilizations. Most came from highly productive silver mines discovered in the mid-sixteenth century: Potosi in Peru, Zacatecas and Guanajuato in New Spain. These mines were worked primarily by forced labour. It has been estimated that the mine at Potosi and its associated work (bringing food, fuel, and mercury for processing the silver) required, at any one time, the forced labour of one seventh of the adult male population of Peru.

Between 1600 and 1810, at least 22,000 tons of silver and 185 tons of gold were transferred to Spain.[2] From 1750 to 1810, Portuguese mines in Brazil produced some 800 tons of gold.[3] The total value is difficult to determine – not least because of the effect on prices in Europe – but it was certainly more than £300 million.[4] (This estimate omits metal diverted by piracy and fraud. A nineteenth-century scholar put the overall total at £1700 million.[5]) The amount of silver in circulation tripled, at a time when much of Europe recognized silver as its money standard.

The influx of American treasure caused an historic price inflation in Europe and, in the words of Keynes, a resulting 'profit inflation', particularly in England, France and northern Europe: 'high prices and low wages meant high profits. From the high profits came high savings and a strong incentive to their investment … It was thus that American money and the resulting inflation assisted at the birth of European capitalism.'[6]

The slave trade and slave production

In the fifteenth century, a small slave trade took Africans to Europe. Spanish and Portuguese traders extended this to the Atlantic islands, the Caribbean and then to mainland South America. They created what has been termed 'the South Atlantic system', an economy using the labour of Africans to produce tropical crops in America for consumption in Europe.

Sugar was the main slave crop. The processing of sugar cane – the most nearly 'industrial' crop for several centuries – required careful timing of labour tasks and a large disciplined labour force. Up to the eighteenth century these requirements could be met most cheaply by using slave labour.

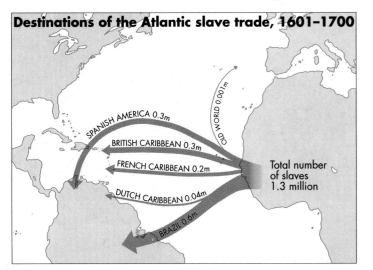

Destinations of the Atlantic slave trade, 1601–1700

SPANISH AMERICA 0.3m
BRITISH CARIBBEAN 0.3m
FRENCH CARIBBEAN 0.2m
DUTCH CARIBBEAN 0.04m
OLD WORLD 0.001m
BRAZIL 0.6m

Total number of slaves 1.3 million

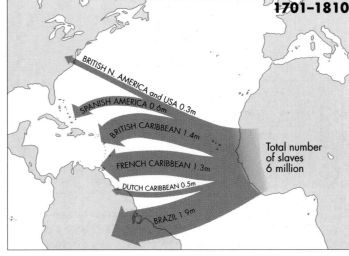

1701–1810

BRITISH N. AMERICA and USA 0.3m
SPANISH AMERICA 0.6m
BRITISH CARIBBEAN 1.4m
FRENCH CARIBBEAN 1.3m
DUTCH CARIBBEAN 0.5m
BRAZIL 1.9m

Total number of slaves 6 million

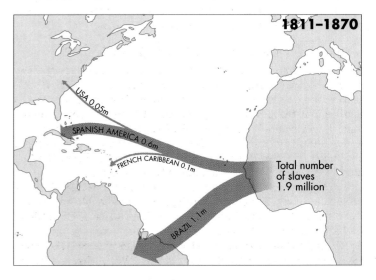

1811–1870

USA 0.05m
SPANISH AMERICA 0.6m
FRENCH CARIBBEAN 0.1m
BRAZIL 1.1m

Total number of slaves 1.9 million

In total, the Atlantic slave trade carried some 9.6 million Africans to the Americas.[7] A much smaller trade in African slaves to Arabia continued simultaneously.

It is estimated that the eighteenth-century British and French slave trades created profits of the order of £75 million[8] and £50 million[9], respectively, and together constituted approximately one third of the total slave trade. Profits from the use of slave labour in production (primarily of sugar) in the British West Indies are estimated at £200–300 million.[10] Again, this is only part of the whole; production methods relying on slave labour were used more extensively and for longer in Portuguese Brazil.

The profits of the Dutch East Indies

During the seventeenth century, the operations of European powers in the East were checked by the remaining Eurasian land empires (Ottoman, Safavid and Mogul), except in the Spice Islands (now Indonesia, Malaysia and the Philippines). The spice trade, before European expansion the world's major high-value trade, was very profitable providing production could be restricted. With government support, rival European companies fought to establish a monopoly. The Portuguese were first but, after a long struggle, the Dutch acquired control. Production was ruthlessly controlled, and the Dutch East India Company extracted remittances, dividends and spices worth an estimated £60 million between 1650 and 1780.[11]

India's 'tribute' to Britain

In the second half of the eighteenth century, exports from British India to European merchants in China and to Europe dramatically exceeded imports. This imbalance of trade was financed ultimately by the land revenue payments of the Indian peasantry. Again, the estimation of the amount so 'drained' from India is controversial, but for the whole half-century £100 million seems plausible.[12]

Opium, tea and the 'opening' of China

At the end of the eighteenth century, the English East India Company needed to expand its tea trade, to replace the profits lost when British textile manufacturers stopped the Company from importing Indian textiles. But tea could only be procured in China, and China wanted almost nothing the Company could offer. China's agrarian economy was self-sufficient, and its textiles superior to those of England. But a demand *could* be generated illegally for opium. From the late eighteenth century opium dominated China's imports.

The profits of the opium trade are estimated at more than £1 million per year.[13] More significantly, once it was established traders could sell British manufactures as well. The huge market of China had been 'opened' to trade.

In 1839, China's rulers tried to stop opium imports. The three-year 'Opium Wars' with Britain followed. With victory, Britain gained five trading ports (the Treaty Ports shown on the map, in effect mini-colonies) and the territory of Hong Kong.

The total sum

In total the various forms of plunder must have concentrated the equivalent of more than £850 million at late-nineteenth century prices (£60,000 million in 1991 prices) of 'liquid resources' in Europe.

Economist Ernest Mandel pointed out that this exceeded the cost of most of the world's industrial plant in 1800. However, although coercive accumulation of wealth impoverished those whose labour produced it, its effect in Europe was not uncomplicatedly to spur the industrial revolution. Much boosted the fortunes of rich landowners and merchants and may have postponed the rise of industrial capitalism.

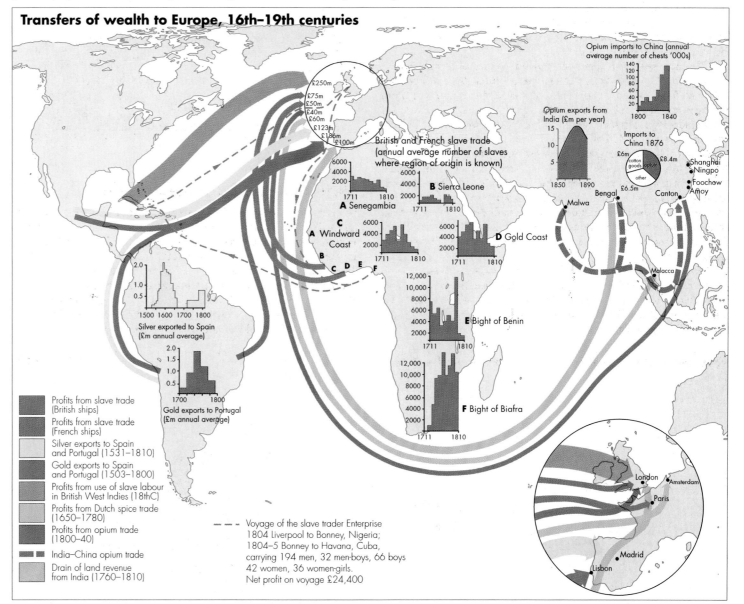

Transfers of wealth to Europe, 16th–19th centuries

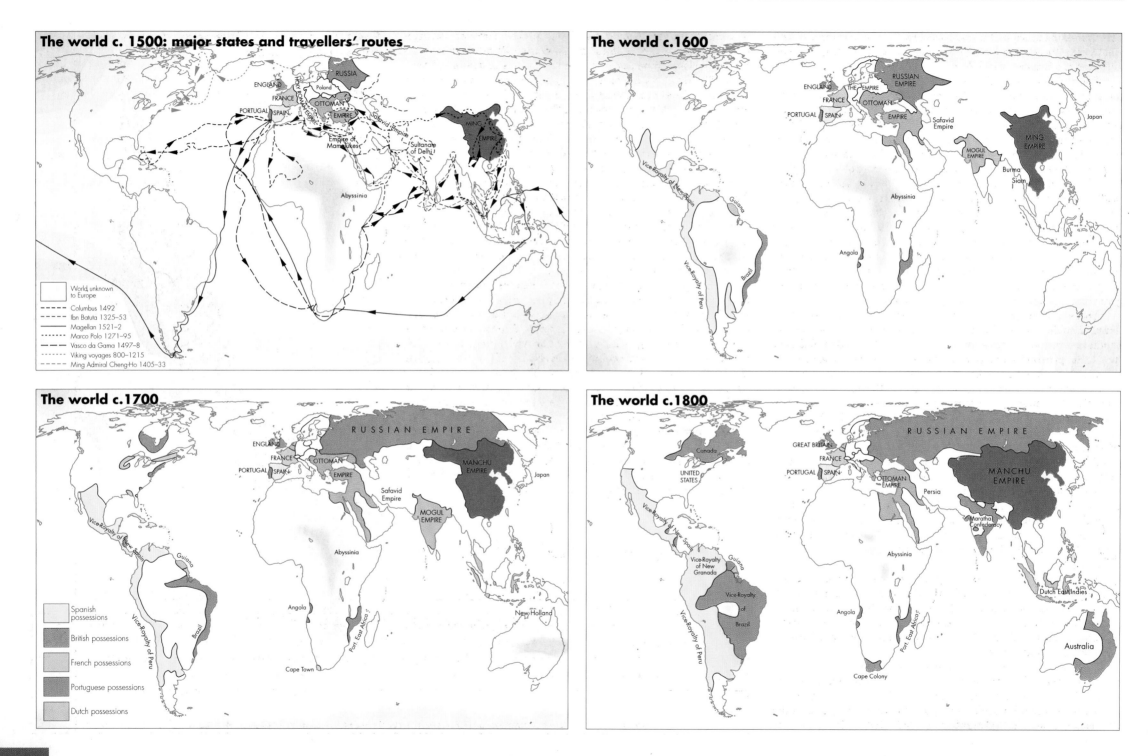

The world c. 1500: major states and travellers' routes

Key:
- World unknown to Europe
- --- Columbus 1492
- --- Ibn Batuta 1325–53
- — Magellan 1521–2
- ···· Marco Polo 1271–95
- — Vasco da Gama 1497–8
- ···· Viking voyages 800–1215
- – – Ming Admiral Cheng-Ho 1405–33

RUSSIA, ENGLAND, Poland, FRANCE, PORTUGAL, SPAIN, OTTOMAN EMPIRE, Safavid Empire, Empire of Mamelukes, Sultanate of Delhi, MING EMPIRE, Abyssinia

The world c.1600

ENGLAND, THE EMPIRE, FRANCE, RUSSIAN EMPIRE, PORTUGAL, SPAIN, OTTOMAN EMPIRE, Safavid Empire, Japan, MOGUL EMPIRE, MING EMPIRE, Burma, Siam, Vice-Royalty of New Spain, Guiana, Vice-Royalty of Peru, Brazil, Abyssinia, Angola

The world c.1700

Key:
- Spanish possessions
- British possessions
- French possessions
- Portuguese possessions
- Dutch possessions

ENGLAND, FRANCE, PORTUGAL, SPAIN, OTTOMAN EMPIRE, RUSSIAN EMPIRE, MANCHU EMPIRE, Japan, Safavid Empire, MOGUL EMPIRE, Vice-Royalty of New Spain, Guiana, Vice-Royalty of Peru, Brazil, Abyssinia, Angola, Port. East Africa, Cape Town, New Holland

The world c.1800

GREAT BRITAIN, FRANCE, PORTUGAL, SPAIN, OTTOMAN EMPIRE, RUSSIAN EMPIRE, MANCHU EMPIRE, Persia, Maratha Confederacy, Canada, UNITED STATES, Vice-Royalty of New Spain, Vice-Royalty of New Granada, Guiana, Vice-Royalty of Peru, Vice-Royalty of Brazil, Abyssinia, Angola, Port. East Africa, Cape Colony, Dutch East Indies, Australia

The figures and maps on this and the following four pages and on p.43 summarize the expansion of European political control between 1492 and the Second World War.

The diagrams on this page measure the overall extent and duration of the major colonial empires. The upper diagram (with inset) shows the proportion of the world's population under European political control for the nearly five centuries of the colonial experience. The inset provides the context: how world, European and colonial populations changed between 1500 and 1980. The main graph indicates the relative populations of the different colonial empires (plotted cumulatively, with Europe's population shown at the base). The lower diagram indicates the rough duration of Europe's empires (classified by continent) during the same period, with continuous lines representing 'major' empires and dotted lines representing 'minor' empires (smaller populations or only partial control). This distinction is not based on a theoretical divide, but rather is intended to allow a rough and ready overview of when, where and by which powers, colonial control was exercised. Much more precise dates are given on the maps in the following four pages.

These two diagrams indicate the early expansion, and long duration, of the 'old' empires of Spain and Portugal, but also that the population ruled by these empires was relatively small (and that of the 'old' empires of Britain and Holland even smaller). The increase in population under European control after 1750 corresponds roughly with the onset of the era we have denoted as the 'rise of industrial capital' and the marked acceleration in the late nineteenth century coincides with the 'new imperialism' of the period denoted 'monopoly capitalism'. Both of these changes in the graph are, however, primarily determined by the expansion of British control in India (with a population of 290 million in 1900). The vertical lines at the right of the population graph indicate the independence of colonies.

World maps on the next page and on p.43 show the extent of European empires in 1714 (just after the Peace of Utrecht, which ended the War of Spanish Succession and confirmed Britain's economic and military predominance in Europe) and in 1914 (the start of the First World War and the end of the most hectic period of imperial expansion).

In 1714, although the 'old' empires had been receiving settlers for 200 years, the possessions of Europe amounted to less than 10% of the world's land area and only 2% of the world's population. In the period between these two maps, much of Northern Europe industrialized, the balance of power in Europe changed, and Europe's imperial quest was renewed.

The maps on pp.33–35 show the processes of expansion in Latin America, Asia and Africa, over periods when each continent was undergoing most change of control. Page 33 describes the expansion of the Spanish and Portuguese empires in Latin America and the Caribbean from 1492 (Columbus) to 1810 (when independence

movements and the Napoleonic subjection of Spain and Portugal started the rapid contraction of these empires). Page 34 summarizes part of the longer and less complete European subjugation of Asia, from 1800 (at the start of a century of expansion) till 1939 (the beginning of the Second World War, during which Japan took brief control of many European colonies). Page 35 focuses on the concise period of African history from 1880 to 1914, when seven European powers moved from mainly coastal settlements and trading stations to divide the whole continent between them.

On each of the maps on pp.33–35 we have tried to adopt a consistent set of conventions: pre-existing states are shown by dashed outlines; European empires at the beginning of the period shown by the darker colours; routes of expansion where relevant by arrows; and acquisitions during the period by lighter colours. The dates are either those of first occupation/date of formal acquisition (as 1804/1815) or a period of possession (as 1804–1815). In many cases the dates of first occupation are a matter of conjecture.

Although these maps appear to be dense with historical detail, they are nevertheless an enormously simplified representation. Details are omitted where territories changed hands more than once during periods of prolonged struggles for trade and power (such as the worldwide struggles between Britain and France in the mid-eighteenth century, or those between Holland and Portugal over the 'East Indies' in the seventeenth century). Many dates of acquisitions have been omitted. Most of the Pacific islands (held in great blocks by Germany and now still largely colonies of France and the USA) have been omitted. These maps also do not describe the settlement of 'empty lands', an important aspect of the expansion of Europe. You will have to look elsewhere for maps showing the march westwards of the colonists in North America, the march eastwards of the Russian Empire, and the settlement of the 'white dominions' of Britain, such as Australia and New Zealand.

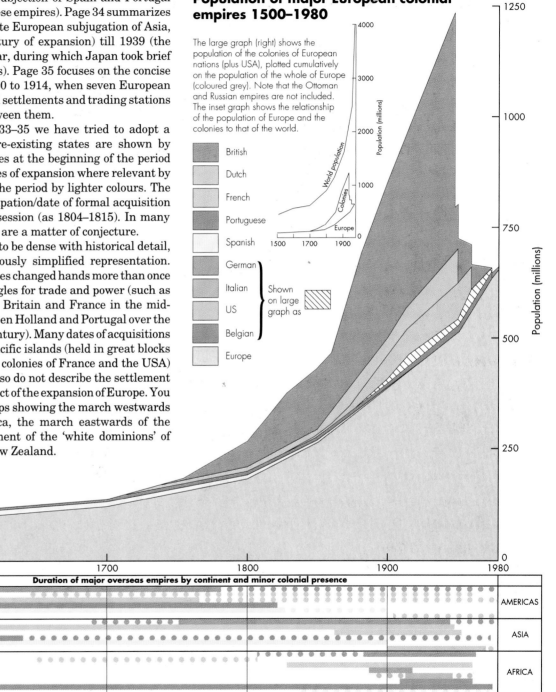

Population of major European colonial empires 1500–1980

The large graph (right) shows the population of the colonies of European nations (plus USA), plotted cumulatively on the population of the whole of Europe (coloured grey). Note that the Ottoman and Russian empires are not included. The inset graph shows the relationship of the population of Europe and the colonies to that of the world.

- British
- Dutch
- French
- Portuguese
- Spanish
- German ⎫
- Italian ⎬ Shown on large graph as ▨
- US ⎪
- Belgian ⎭
- Europe

Duration of major overseas empires by continent and minor colonial presence

AMERICAS

ASIA

AFRICA

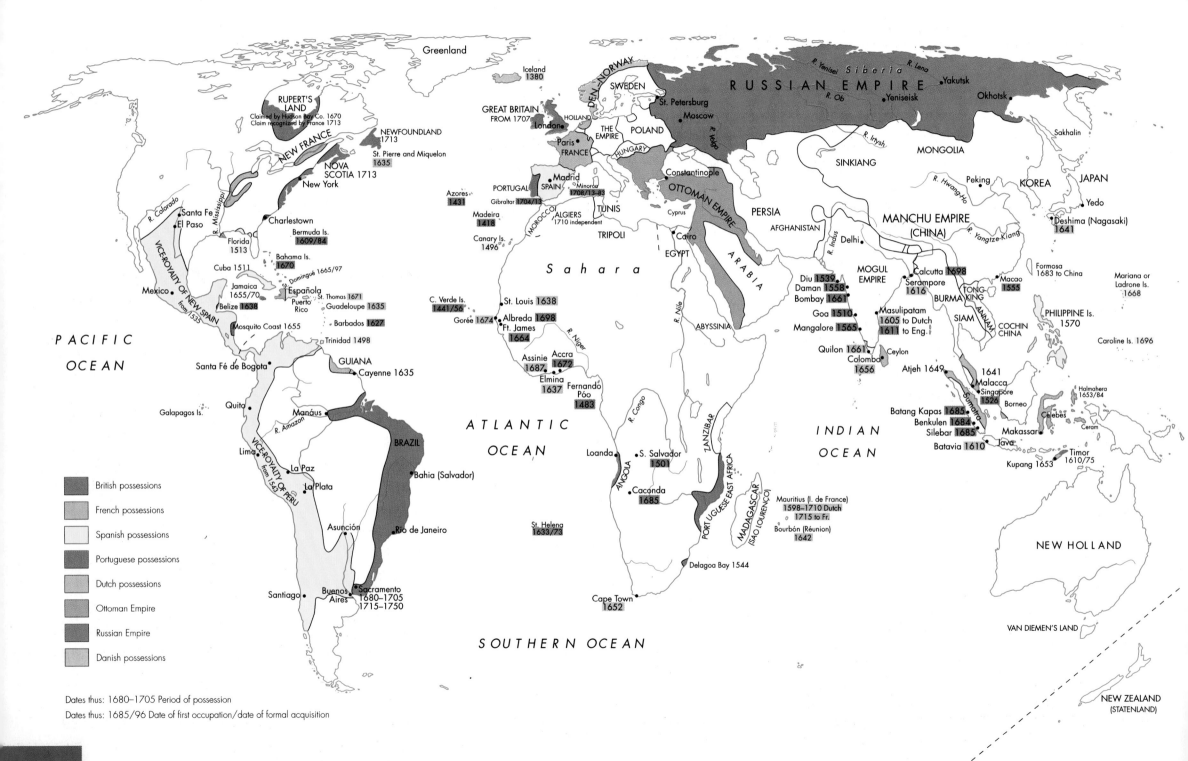

Greenland

Iceland
1380

DEN–NORWAY

SWEDEN

RUSSIAN EMPIRE

Siberia

R. Yenisei
R. Lena

Yakutsk

RUPERT'S
LAND
Claimed by Hudson Bay Co. 1670
Claim recognized by France 1713

St. Petersburg
Moscow

R. Ob
Yeniseisk

Okhotsk

NEW FRANCE

NEWFOUNDLAND
1713

St. Pierre and Miquelon
1635

NOVA
SCOTIA 1713

New York

GREAT BRITAIN
FROM 1707

HOLLAND

London

THE
EMPIRE

POLAND

FRANCE
Paris

HUNGARY

Constantinople

MONGOLIA

SINKIANG

R. Irtysh

R. Volga

Sakhalin

R. Hwang-Ho
Peking

KOREA

JAPAN

Santa Fe
El Paso

R. Colorado

R. Mississippi

Charlestown

VICEROYALTY OF NEW SPAIN
from 1535

Florida
1513

Bermuda Is.
1609/84

Azores
1431

PORTUGAL
SPAIN
Madrid

Minorca
1708/13–83

Gibraltar 1704/13

MANCHU EMPIRE
(CHINA)

Deshima (Nagasaki)
1641

Bahama Is.
1670

Madeira
1418

MOROCCO

ALGIERS
1710 independent

TUNIS

Cuba 1511

Jamaica
1655/70

St. Domingue 1665/97

Belize 1638
Española
Puerto
Rico

St. Thomas 1671

Guadeloupe 1635

Canary Is.
1496

TRIPOLI

Cairo

EGYPT

Sahara

R. Nile

ARABIA

PERSIA

AFGHANISTAN

R. Indus

Delhi

R. Yangtze-Kiang

Macao
1555

Formosa
1683 to China

Mariana or
Ladrone Is.
1668

Mexico

Barbados 1627

Trinidad 1498

Mosquito Coast 1655

C. Verde Is.
1441/56

St. Louis 1638

Gorée 1674

Albreda 1698
Ft. James
1664

R. Niger

ABYSSINIA

MOGUL
EMPIRE

Diu 1539
Daman 1558
Bombay 1661

Goa 1510

Mangalore 1565

Calcutta 1698

Serampore
1616

Masulipatam
1605 to Dutch
1611 to Eng.

BURMA

TONG
KING

ANNAM

COCHIN
CHINA

PHILIPPINE Is.
1570

PACIFIC

OCEAN

Santa Fé de Bogota

GUIANA

Cayenne 1635

Galapagos Is.

Quito

Manáus

R. Amazon

ATLANTIC

OCEAN

Assinie
1687

Accra
1672

Elmina
1637

Fernando
Póo
1483

Quilon 1661
Colombo
1656

Ceylon

Atjeh 1649

1641
Malacca
1526
Singapore

Borneo

Halmahera
1653/84

Ceram

Caroline Is. 1696

INDIAN

OCEAN

Batang Kapas 1685
Benkulen 1684
Silebar 1685

Makassar

Celebes

Batavia 1610
Java

Sumatra

Timor
1610/75

Kupang 1653

Lima

La Paz

Asunción

La Plata

VICEROYALTY
OF PERU
from 1543

BRAZIL

Rio de Janeiro

Bahia (Salvador)

Loanda

ANGOLA

R. Congo

S. Salvador
1501

Caconda
1685

ZANZIBAR

PORTUGUESE EAST AFRICA

MADAGASCAR
(SÃO LOURENÇO)

St. Helena
1633/73

Mauritius (I. de France)
1598–1710 Dutch
1715 to Fr.

Bourbón (Réunion)
1642

NEW HOLLAND

Santiago

Buenos
Aires

Sacramento
1680–1705
1715–1750

Delagoa Bay 1544

Cape Town
1652

SOUTHERN OCEAN

VAN DIEMEN'S LAND

British possessions

French possessions

Spanish possessions

Portuguese possessions

Dutch possessions

Ottoman Empire

Russian Empire

Danish possessions

Dates thus: 1680–1705 Period of possession

Dates thus: 1685/96 Date of first occupation/date of formal acquisition

NEW ZEALAND
(STATENLAND)

Soon after Columbus' first voyage in 1492 to America, the Castilian (Spanish) monarchy opened negotiations with the Pope and the Portuguese monarchy to secure a monopoly of navigation and settlement in the newly discovered lands. Initially the Pope granted the Spanish crown a legal claim to the whole of the New World; but the 1494 Treaty of Tordesillas between Portugal and Spain established exclusive Portuguese rights to the then unexplored Brazil.

Columbus' first voyage discovered the Caribbean islands of Española (now Haiti and Dominican Republic) and Cuba. His second voyage brought 1200 settlers to Española, aiming to set up self-sufficient colonies which could export gold to Spain. The islands' inhabitants were subjugated and employed as forced labour. This, together with smallpox and measles, caused a marked population decline. In a search for labour, gold and converts, Spanish settlement proceeded to Jamaica, Cuba, other islands and the mainland.

On the mainland, in little more than thirteen years, three great civilizations, Aztec, Inca and Mayan, were dominated by Spanish adventurers. The ease of conquest owed much to the alienation of the labourers and peasant producers from their priestly rulers. The new rulers initially stepped into the tribute-receiving or forced-labour-organizing role of their predecessors. But such feudal production forms were already anachronistic in Europe, and the Castilian crown soon replaced the private commanders with lawyers and ecclesiastics.

The administration of Spanish America consisted of an elaborate structure of royal patronage, headed by Viceroys for New Spain, New Granada, Peru and La Plata. The object, in addition to maintaining control, was to maximize revenue. In 1585, a peak year, nearly a quarter of the total revenue of the Spanish state came from its American colonies. Ultimately, this revenue depended upon the labour of native Indians. Throughout the sixteenth century, the Indian population declined while that of Spaniards demanding labour increased. By the late 1600s, food shortages were common. Indian villages, depopulated and deprived of labour power by the demands of forced labour, were unable to produce surplus food either for sale or as tribute.

Portuguese expansion in the Americas started later than Spain's. Serious settlement of Brazil began in 1533 when the territory was divided into twelve captaincies and granted to proprietary landlords with administrative, fiscal and judicial powers similar to those denied to the Spanish *conquistadores*. Portugal's major imperial interests lay in the East, the spice trade and African coastal settlement; gold was not found in Brazil until the 1690s.

The map shows the extent of European imperial control in 1650, after more than 150 years of settlement, and its subsequent expansion up to 1810, when the emancipation of Latin America began. The inset map shows only some of the frequent changes of imperial control which resulted from buccaneer battles and inter-imperialist wars for the control of territory, labour and production in the Caribbean.

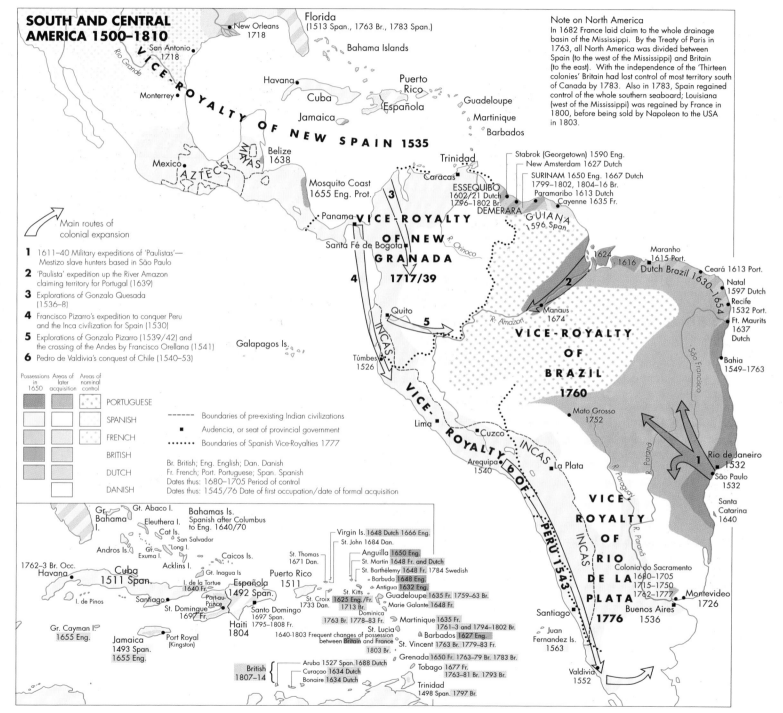

SOUTH AND CENTRAL AMERICA 1500–1810

Note on North America
In 1682 France laid claim to the whole drainage basin of the Mississippi. By the Treaty of Paris in 1763, all North America was divided between Spain (to the west of the Mississippi) and Britain (to the east). With the independence of the 'Thirteen colonies' Britain had lost control of most territory south of Canada by 1783. Also in 1783, Spain regained control of the whole southern seaboard; Louisiana (west of the Mississippi) was regained by France in 1800, before being sold by Napoleon to the USA in 1803.

Main routes of colonial expansion

1 1611–40 Military expeditions of 'Paulistas'—Mestizo slave hunters based in São Paulo
2 'Paulista' expedition up the River Amazon claiming territory for Portugal (1639)
3 Explorations of Gonzalo Quesada (1536–8)
4 Francisco Pizarro's expedition to conquer Peru and the Inca civilization for Spain (1530)
5 Explorations of Gonzalo Pizarro (1539/42) and the crossing of the Andes by Francisco Orellana (1541)
6 Pedro de Valdivia's conquest of Chile (1540–53)

Possessions in 1650	Areas of later acquisition	Areas of nominal control	
			PORTUGUESE
			SPANISH
			FRENCH
			BRITISH
			DUTCH
			DANISH

------ Boundaries of pre-existing Indian civilizations
■ Audencia, or seat of provincial government
•••••• Boundaries of Spanish Vice-Royalties 1777

Br. British; Eng. English; Dan. Danish
Fr. French; Port. Portuguese; Span. Spanish
Dates thus: 1680–1705 Period of control
Dates thus: 1545/76 Date of first occupation/date of formal acquisition

Florida (1513 Span., 1763 Br., 1783 Span.)
New Orleans 1718
Bahama Islands
San Antonio 1718
Rio Grande
Monterrey
Havana
Cuba
Puerto Rico
Española
Guadeloupe
Martinique
Jamaica
Barbados
VICE-ROYALTY OF NEW SPAIN 1535
Mexico
AZTECS
MAYAS
Belize 1638
Trinidad
Mosquito Coast 1655 Eng. Prot.
Caracas
Stabrok (Georgetown) 1590 Eng.
New Amsterdam 1627 Dutch
SURINAM 1650 Eng. 1667 Dutch 1799–1802, 1804–16 Br.
Paramaribo 1613 Dutch
Cayenne 1635 Fr.
ESSEQUIBO 1602/21 Dutch 1796–1802 Br.
DEMERARA
GUIANA 1596 Span.
Panama
VICE-ROYALTY OF NEW GRANADA 1717/39
Santa Fé de Bogota
Quito
INCAS
Galapagos Is.
Túmbes 1526
VICE-ROYALTY OF BRAZIL 1760
R. Orinoco
R. Amazon
Manáus 1674
Maranho 1615 Port.
Ceará 1613 Port.
Natal 1597 Dutch
Dutch Brazil 1630–1654
Recife 1532 Port.
Ft. Maurits 1637 Dutch
São Francisco
Bahia 1549–1763
Mato Grosso 1752
Lima
Cuzco
Arequipa 1540
VICE-ROYALTY OF PERÚ 1543
INCAS
La Plata
R. Paraná
R. Paraguay
Valdivia 1552
Santiago
Juan Fernandez Is. 1563
Rio de Janeiro 1532
São Paulo 1532
Santa Catarina 1640
VICE-ROYALTY OF RIO DE LA PLATA 1776
Colonia do Sacramento 1680–1705 1715–1750 1762–1777
Montevideo 1726
Buenos Aires 1536

Gr. Bahama I.
Gt. Abaco I.
Eleuthera I.
Cat Is.
San Salvador
Andros Is.
Gr. Exuma I.
Long I.
Caicos Is.
Acklins I.
Gt. Inagua Is.
Bahamas Is. Spanish after Columbus to Eng. 1640/70
1762–3 Br. Occ. Havana
Cuba 1511 Span.
I. de Pinos
Santiago
I. de la Tortue 1640 Fr.
Port-au-Prince
St. Domingue 1697 Fr.
Gr. Cayman I. 1655 Eng.
Jamaica 1493 Span. 1655 Eng.
Port Royal (Kingston)
Española 1511
Santo Domingo 1697 Span.
Haiti 1795–1808 Fr. 1804
Puerto Rico 1511
Virgin Is. 1648 Dutch 1666 Eng.
St. John 1684 Dan.
St. Thomas 1671 Dan.
Anguilla 1650 Eng.
St. Martin 1648 Fr. and Dutch
St. Barthélemy 1648 Fr. 1784 Swedish
Barbuda 1648 Eng.
Antigua 1632 Eng.
St. Kitts
St. Croix 1625 Eng./Fr. 1733 Dan.
1713 Br.
Dominica 1763 Br. 1778–83 Fr.
Marie Galante 1648 Fr.
Guadeloupe 1635 Fr. 1759–63 Br.
Martinique 1635 Fr. 1761–3 and 1794–1802 Br.
St. Lucia 1640–1803 Frequent changes of possession between Britain and France 1803 Br.
Barbados 1627 Eng.
St. Vincent 1763 Br. 1779–83 Fr.
British 1807–14 { Aruba 1527 Span. 1688 Dutch
Curaçao 1634 Dutch
Bonaire 1634 Dutch
Tobago 1677 Fr. 1763–81 Br. 1793 Br.
Grenada 1650 Fr. 1763–79 Br. 1783 Br.
Trinidad 1498 Span. 1797 Br.

In Asia the dominance of the European powers was never as complete as in the Americas or Africa. Little of Asia was 'settled'; instead the pattern was largely one of economic infiltration and political control of existing societies, starting in the seventeenth and eighteenth centuries in the East Indies, as Holland thwarted Portuguese attempts to control the spice trade. Trading posts were established by the Dutch East India Company, providing the basis for future Dutch colonies.

Similarly, in India the French and English East India Companies struggled for control of the eastern ports. The English East India Company subsequently established itself as the major administrative power, and was the agent of British expansion until the British government took over after the Indian Revolt of 1857–58. Even after 1858, Britain ruled large parts of India indirectly through the princely states.

The spread of British control, as well as bringing rich economic rewards, was partly motivated by the fear of Russian expansion further into Central Asia and, later, French colonization of Indo-China. The independence of Afghanistan and Siam was agreed by Anglo-Russian and Anglo-French concords of 1907 and 1904, to maintain buffer zones between the rival powers.

At the height of its control of Asia, Britain controlled one-fifth of the area of the world and a quarter of the population. Earlier in the nineteenth century, Manchu China was the world's largest empire, with influence in Korea, Indo-China, Siam, Burma and Nepal. During the period depicted, this empire gradually collapsed, though little territory was lost from China itself. However, persistent and eventually successful foreign attempts were made to gain entry to Chinese markets. British victory in the Opium Wars of 1839–42 opened up China to foreign powers, with the cession of Hong Kong and the first five Treaty Ports. Subsequently, influence in Indo-China was lost after war with France (1884–85) and in Burma in 1886.

In the case of Japan, by contrast, rapid industrialization was followed by overseas expansion. Conflict with China and Russia led to the acquisition of Taiwan (1895), Korea (1910) and part of Manchuria (1905). Further unrest in China led to the autonomy of Tibet and Mongolia, under British and Russian influence respectively.

There were many nationalist uprisings throughout Asia in the 1920s and 1930s, forcing more local participation in government. Britain moved towards the establishment of dominion status in India, with the administrative separation of Burma and Aden from India in 1935. Also in India, pressure was growing for a separate Muslim state (eventually resulting in the emergence of Pakistan). Revolutionary movements in the Dutch East Indies were resisted until the Second World War. The lack of concessions by the French in Indo-China led to disturbances in the 1930s and the formation of the Viet Minh in 1939. Pages 44–45 give more on the struggles to end foreign domination.

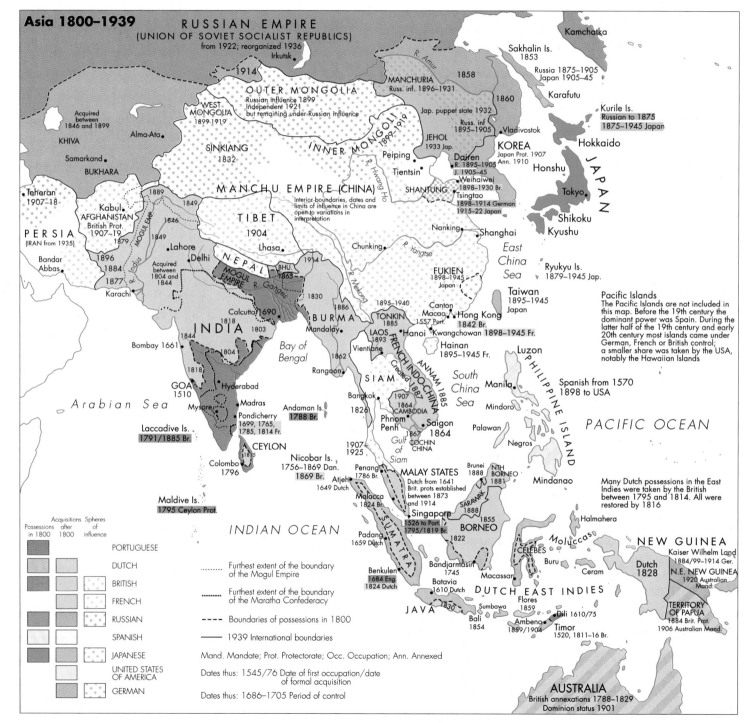

In the history of European expansion, the partition of Africa stands out as an episode of high drama. Seven European powers took simultaneous military action; in just over twenty years Africa was carved up and subjugated.

Until 1880, little of Africa was under direct European rule. In what is now South Africa, Britain possessed the Cape Colony and Natal, and Dutch settlers had established the Boer republics; in the north, France had conquered Algeria; there were small European settlements scattered mainly near the coasts. By 1902 the political boundaries of modern Africa had been defined, and thirty-six of the forty political units into which it had been divided were ruled by Britain, France, Portugal, Germany, Belgium, Italy or Spain.

The map shows the extent of European imperial control in 1880 and 1914, and European advances between those dates. The pattern is dominated by British actions in the north and south, and French in the west.

The British expansions were linked to material financial interests. Britain occupied Egypt in 1882, partly to defend the Suez Canal and the route to India, but primarily to maintain financial control. In the south, Britain's acquisition of the Boer Republics in 1899 was in defence of investors' interests in Transvaal gold, which had been discovered in 1886, as much as for the Cape sea routes. 'Britain's stake in controlling these resources was manifest: gold reserves underwrote her capacity to finance free trade on a global scale; British investors supplied 60–80% of foreign investment on the Rand by 1899; and economic growth centred on the Transvaal provided a rich and rapidly growing market for British goods.'[14]

The conquest of west and north Africa is dominated by three French advances: up the river Senegal and down the Niger; into the Sahara from the north; and into central Africa and Gabon. These substantial military interventions occurred in the context of relatively modest strategic ambitions, but were spurred by intense inter-imperialist rivalry and by an army unwilling to be halted by Muslim resistance.

In this same period, Germany occupied territories in south-west, east and central Africa, Belgium followed Stanley into the Congo, Italy established a presence in the Horn of Africa, the Portuguese settlements in Angola and Mozambique were expanded, and Spain's occupation of 'Spanish Sahara' began.

Historical explanations for the scramble for Africa, this last rush to complete the seizure of the world, are hotly contested. The strategic aims of governments and local rivalry between merchants undoubtedly shaped the immediate pattern. But it is important to note that the four main European actors involved, Britain, France, Germany and Belgium, had just achieved roughly comparable levels of industrialization, and Africa offered the last chance to extend political dominion over resources, labour and markets on a large scale.

Africa 1880–1914

Note that the information for the Middle East covers the period 1880–1920

Routes of colonial expansion

1 Rhodes' British South Africa Company 'Pioneer Column' 1890, crushing Matabele and Mashona opposition

2 Stanley's exploration, 1877, and colonial claim (1879) on behalf of Belgium

3 French expansion from Gabon (1888) into equatorial Africa and on to Fashoda (1898) and Lake Chad

4 1880–1902 British expansion into Nigeria

5 Advance of French army 1883 and 1890–6 crushing Islamic states in its path

6 French military expeditions 1898–1906

7 British invasion and occupation of Egypt in 1882

8 Kitchener's military conquest of Mahdist Sudan in 1898

9 Anglo–Boer Wars. South African Republic (Transvaal) and Orange Free State were independent Boer republics from 1853 and 1854 respectively. Transvaal annexed by Britain 1876–81 then fell to Britain with Orange Free State in Boer War of 1899–1902

Acquisitions after in 1880	Possessions 1880	Spheres of influence	
			FRENCH
			BRITISH
			SPANISH
			PORTUGUESE
			GERMAN
			BELGIAN
			ITALIAN
			RUSSIAN

L. Lebanon (Fr. Mand. 1920)
P. Palestine (Br. Mand. 1920)
T. Transjordan (Br. Mand. 1920)
B. Basutoland
S. Swaziland

········· Pre-existing African states
----- European colonial boundaries 1880
——— European colonial boundaries 1914
ooooooo Boundary of the Mahdist State 1881–1898
---- 1880 boundaries of Ottoman and Egyptian Empires

Prot. Protectorate   Mand. Mandate
Occ. Occupation   Indep. Independent

Dates thus: 1545/76 Date of first occupation/ date of formal acquisition
Dates thus: 1680–1705 Period of control

One of the main consequences of the expansion of Europe and the rise of capitalism was the gradual incorporation of much of the world's agriculture into a world economy. European discoverers were aware that new crops and products would, in the long term, be more lucrative than the plunder of gold and silver. Agricultural change has had enduring economic and social consequences for developing societies.

The main map on this page shows the main areas of cultivation and husbandry of the most important crops and domestic animals, and the main modes of subsistence in the world, at the beginning of the sixteenth century, the start of the era of European expansion. It can be compared with the similar map showing world agriculture at AD 0 which appears on p.26. The change over fifteen centuries can be interpreted as the cumulative effect of gradual and mainly local shifts. The changes to come over the following five centuries would include more severe, radical dislocations, requiring interpretation at the level of the global control of crops, labour and trade in food products.

Food crop transfers

Although many crop transfers have occurred slowly for thousands of years, European expansion led to an unprecedented movement of new plants to and from the Old World. Superimposed on the main map on this page are estimated dates and directions of transfer of some of the main staple food crops, showing how they spread from

Transfer of selected staple crops until AD 1800 and main modes of subsistence AD 1500

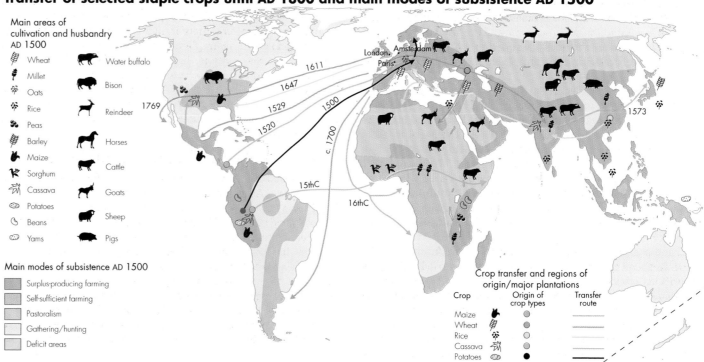

Main areas of cultivation and husbandry AD 1500

- Wheat
- Millet
- Oats
- Rice
- Peas
- Barley
- Maize
- Sorghum
- Cassava
- Potatoes
- Beans
- Yams

- Water buffalo
- Bison
- Reindeer
- Horses
- Cattle
- Goats
- Sheep
- Pigs

Main modes of subsistence AD 1500

- Surplus-producing farming
- Self-sufficient farming
- Pastoralism
- Gathering/hunting
- Deficit areas

Crop transfer and regions of origin/major plantations

Crop	Origin of crop types	Transfer route
Maize		
Wheat		
Rice		
Cassava		
Potatoes		

European agriculture, c. 1700

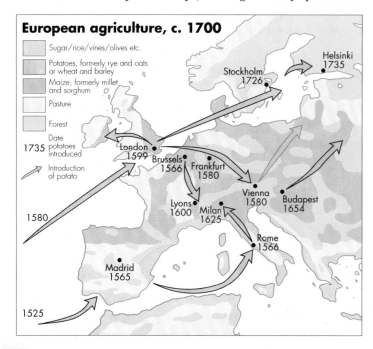

- Sugar/rice/vines/olives etc.
- Potatoes, formerly rye and oats or wheat and barley
- Maize, formerly millet and sorghum
- Pasture
- Forest
- 1735 Date potatoes introduced
- Introduction of potato

Helsinki 1735
Stockholm 1726
London 1599
Brussels 1566
Frankfurt 1580
Lyons 1600
Milan 1625
Vienna 1580
Budapest 1654
Rome 1566
Madrid 1565
1580
1525

local origins to large parts of the world. For instance, maize, which has been described as 'the Americas' gift to mankind', was probably taken back with Columbus on his first voyage, and quickly spread both to the Mediterranean and to North Africa. Potatoes, which also originated in the Andes, revolutionized European agriculture in the two centuries after they were introduced by the Spanish conquistadores (see the map of European agriculture, left). Potatoes and maize produced between four and five times as much carbohydrate per hectare as the wheat, oats, rye and barley which had been the previous staples. This dietary transformation had profound economic consequences. Fewer people were needed to produce the same energy value of food, thereby freeing labour to work in industry, a pre-condition for the Industrial Revolution.

Important foods were also introduced from one tropical environment to another. Cassava, sweet potato and maize were taken from Latin America to West Africa, possibly by returning slaves. They soon became integrated into farming systems across the continent, a testimony to the adaptability of local communities, long before the advent of formal agricultural extension systems. Rice, on the other hand, spread from China west to India and then further afield.

Plantation crops and production

Western control of commercial agriculture involved three primary factors: the movement of crops; control over trade; and the availability of and control over a labour force. These conditions were met in a variety of ways. In the case of spices an existing trade was taken from Arab merchants. In the case of sugar, production was moved to new locations (the Caribbean, South and Central America) and labour was brought from Africa to produce it. In the case of tea, cocoa and rubber, production had to be transformed out of the hands of monopoly producers before these products could become important world commodities.

Colonial powers often went to great lengths to ensure monopoly control. The Dutch destroyed spices on islands that they could not control. The Spanish kept the 'secret' of chocolate production for almost a hundred years until the Dutch smuggled cocoa from plantations in what is now Venezuela into nearby Curaçao, then on to their other possessions, Ceylon and Java.

Perhaps the most characteristic and enduring feature of colonial agriculture was the plantation: a large-scale, European-owned and -managed enterprise, producing single crops for the world market with local or imported labour. Sugar plantations, for example, were established only 22 years after Columbus's first voyage. Four centuries later, towards the end of the colonial period, they were still being planted (though not with slave labour) in Africa and East Asia. Islands such as Java, Sri Lanka, Jamaica and Fiji became a particular focus for plantation development, presumably because they were more easily controlled than larger land masses with stronger governments.

Some key plant transfers of the colonial era are mapped on these pages. The map opposite shows transfers of food crops. The three maps on this page show transfers of some plantation and commercial crops. Other important crops have been omitted for simplicity, including those which were transferred through the auspices of 'colonial botanic gardens', such as Kew in London. The role of these gardens was often crucial to new introductions. In 1706 the botanical gardens of Amsterdam received some coffee plants from Java, of which only one tree fruited. The descendants of this plant were the basis of plantations all over the tropical Americas and as far away as the Philippines.

The types of crop required by Europe, together with their relative profitability and vulnerability to disease, often led to changing compositions of crops. An example is shown in the graph below. Ceylon (now Sri Lanka) was a leading coffee producer until its plantations were devastated by the disease 'coffee rust' in the late nineteenth century. The economy was saved by the establishment of tea plantations, and for a short while by cinchona bark (a source of quinine), used as a treatment for malaria (cinchona is a high-value low-tonnage crop, therefore shown on a different scale: pounds sterling.)

Not all tropical crop production in the colonial era came from plantations. By the end of the nineteenth century, many smallholders were competing on world markets: for example, with cocoa in West Africa, coffee in Brazil and rubber in Malaysia. A wide variety of production forms representing many millions of households, thousands of miles from Europe, became integrated into the world economy.

Until the nineteenth century, colonial agriculture provided mainly condiments and quasi-drugs for Europe (spices, sugar, tea, coffee, tobacco). Demand for these products rose dramatically: world coffee production increased tenfold in the second half of the nineteenth century and sugar consumption in the UK went up five times in the same period (see diagram, below centre). Demand also steadily increased for industrial raw materials (rubber, sisal, cotton) and for grain and meat in the European market. From the late nineteenth century, areas of European settlement in temperate climates, such as Argentina, USA, Australia and New Zealand, became important sources of food.

Ecological effects of agricultural change

The expansion of capitalist agriculture had unfavourable ecological consequences. As already mentioned, plantation monocultures were highly susceptible to disease, but more fundamentally, the new international division of labour created by capitalism has disrupted whole ecological cycles. In most parts of the world before the sixteenth century, crops were harvested and eaten near to the areas where they were grown. Sewage and other wastes could then be returned to the ground, maintaining the organic content and trace minerals in the soil. The organization of agriculture over the last five centuries has given rise to the transport of agricultural surpluses for many thousands of miles. Organic wastes are rarely returned to the soil, but dumped in rivers and oceans. Although industrial fertilizers are used to maintain soil fertility, it is argued by some that soils are being irreversibly 'mined' or impoverished.

The global commercialization of agriculture, a central part of colonial policies, has had enduring effects on both the economies and the environments of many developing countries. For example, in Section 1 (p.18) we saw how many countries are still heavily dependent on exports of one or two plantation crops. In such cases increased revenue can hardly be achieved without further intensifying what has already been monoculture production for decades or centuries. Such effects are described further in Section 3 (pp.52–53).

Transfer of selected crops, 500 – 1900

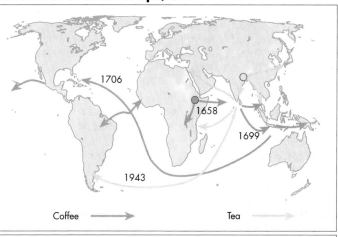

Coffee   Tea

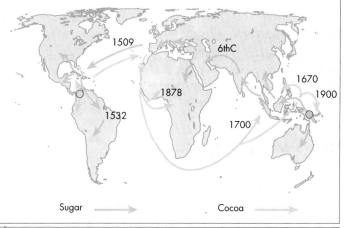

Sugar   Cocoa

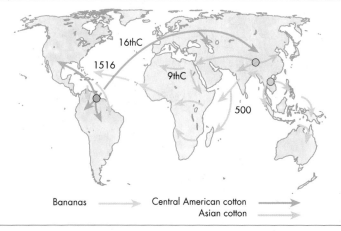

Bananas   Central American cotton
Asian cotton

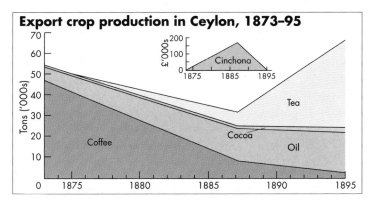

Export crop production in Ceylon, 1873–95

Consumption of sugar in the UK, 1700–1937

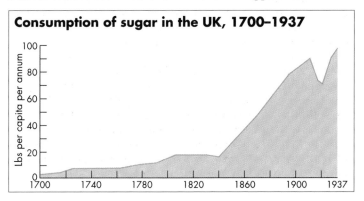

37

The establishment and expansion of capitalist industry in Western Europe during the nineteenth century led to an unprecedented growth in world trade (see pp.40–41). Along with European political control, trade and the control of labour through capital investment were major forces changing the objects and processes of production in the Third World. On these two pages are various measures of the changes in Third World industrial production.

Generally, but not everywhere, the expansion of capitalism led to the decline of the handicrafts industries (small-scale production using local resources to make directly used goods) and, somewhat later and to a lesser extent, the rise of 'machinofacture' (factories employing wage labour to operate machines producing goods for sale). There was a corresponding tendency for the Third World to provide the raw materials for European capitalism rather than finished goods: to provide raw cotton, for example, rather than textiles or clothing. These were general but not universal changes; they occurred in different regions at different times and in diverse ways. Thus the crucial questions with respect to industrial change for any country in the Third World are these: When and to what extent did handicraft production decline? When and to what extent has capitalist industry been substituted? Was that industry producing for export or for local consumption? Historical statistics can provide

Distribution of world's industrial production, 1870–1971

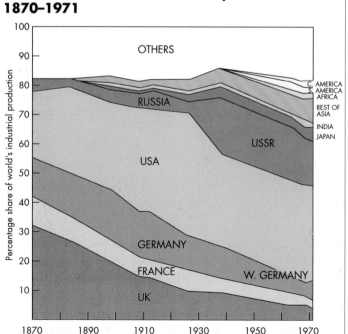

Rise of productivity in the textile industry, 1750–1970

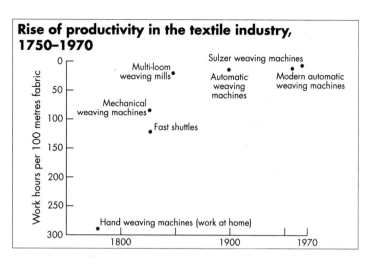

only glimpses of the world-scale answers to these questions. Cumulatively, the processes involved amount to the subordination of world industrial production to capitalism.

The graph (below left), showing distribution of world industrial production between 1870 and 1971, indicates the continuing importance of countries like the USA, the UK and Germany where industrialization began early, the post-revolution growth of the USSR and the relatively small share of industrial production located in the Third World, even by 1970.

The chronology (right), concentrating on China, India and Latin America, provides an indication of when these changes occurred. The pie charts (opposite) show the composition of exports from eight countries at two dates, generally at the end of the nineteenth century.[15] There is a marked contrast between the exports, predominantly of manufactured goods, from the UK, and the primary products dominating the exports of the other countries. The exported primary products are particularly characteristic of trade during the colonial era: opium and cotton are significant Indian exports, cotton dominates exports from Egypt, silk and tea from China, coffee from Brazil, silver from Mexico, grain from Argentina. Note that the exports of the former white settler colony, USA, are also primary agricultural produce early in the nineteenth century, but toward the end of the century are dominated by 'sundries' (not distinguished in these statistics but undoubtedly consisting mostly of manufactured goods).

Putting together the pie charts and the chronology, three phases of industrial transformation can be identified: destruction of handicraft production; processing of primary products; and production of manufactured goods for world markets. The third phase appears in only a few countries before 1920 and is not discussed further in these pages.

A chronology of industrial change, 1800–1940

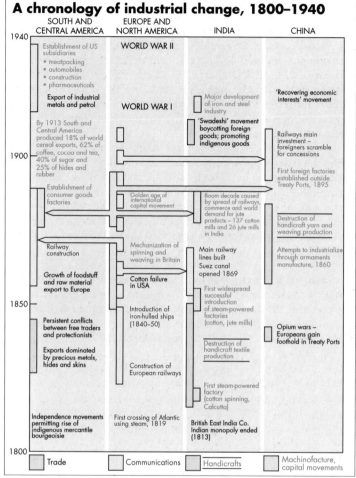

The destruction of handicraft production

The classic example of this first phase is the Indian cotton spinning and handloom weaving industry. The pie charts indicate that cotton goods were a significant proportion of Indian exports in 1814–15, but by 1851 they had become negligible, replaced by increased exports of raw cotton. Imports of cloth to India went up 12.5 times between 1849 and 1889. The graph (above centre) of historical productivity in weaving indicates how European manufacturers were able to 'undercut' handicraft produce. Hand spinning and handloom weaving were unable to compete against the products of steam-powered machinery. In remote areas, some spinning and weaving persisted (and Gandhi attempted to rally nationalist forces to buy this *swadeshi* or Indian produce in 1919), but the major urban manufacturing centres, producing textiles which had made India famous for centuries, such as Murshidabad and Dacca muslins, were 'de-industrialized'.

Something similar happened to India's metallurgical industry, which had been producing iron plough shares, hoes, sickles and weapons (for example) for many centuries before Mogul or British rule. These industries, and India's ceramics, all lost their markets to British manufactured imports. The founder of Grindlays Bank wrote in 1837: 'India can never again be a great manufacturing country, but by cultivating her connection with England she may be one of the greatest agricultural nations.'[16]

In Latin America, indigenous industry declined similarly after 1785 (the manufacture of cotton cloth was prohibited by law in Portuguese Brazil). In China, the continuing opposition of the Manchu state to foreign economic influence (even after the Opium Wars) and a series of nationalist economic revival movements provided a measure of protection to Chinese production, but textile and metallurgical industries suffered major declines. In Africa, only Egypt was at all changed industrially, until the late nineteenth century.

In all continents, throughout the phase of destruction of handicraft production there was a rise in exports of agricultural and mineral primary products to European capitalist industry.

The processing of primary products

At the end of the colonial period in Latin America there were very few factories, but during the second half of the nineteenth century the first textile (machino-) factories were established, and the preliminary processing of mineral ores began (with a notable switch from precious metals to industrial metals for export). During the early years of the twentieth century, many meat-packing factories were opened. In China, foreign factories were confined to the areas of the Treaty ports (established as free trade zones but effectively almost mini-colonies of the European powers, as a result of the Opium Wars) until the very end of the nineteenth century. This pattern of export production can be seen to this day in Hong Kong, Shanghai and other peripheral Chinese territories. Elsewhere a nationalist response to European expansion – 'Learn the strong techniques of the barbarians in order to control them' – brought a measure of industrialization through investment in armament manufacture.

The map (above right) indicates the uneven levels of industrialization in the world in 1930. It uses two measures of industrial development: (a) the percentage of the population in non-agricultural employment (which aggregates employment in service and industrial sectors); and (b) the net income produced by manufacturing. (Estimated GNP per capita is also shown, for comparison with the 1988 data on pp.14–15.) This data should be considered with that on p.42, which shows further historical measures of Third World industrialization.

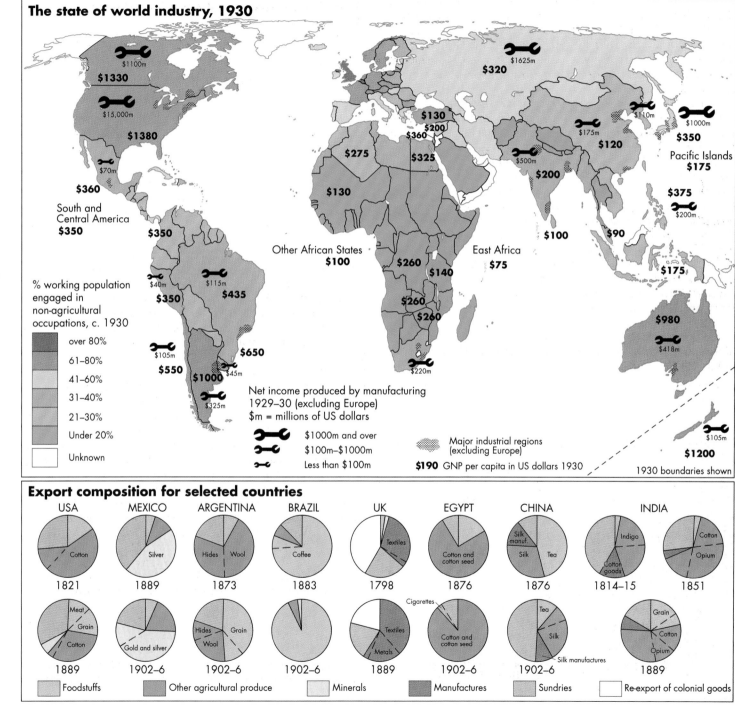

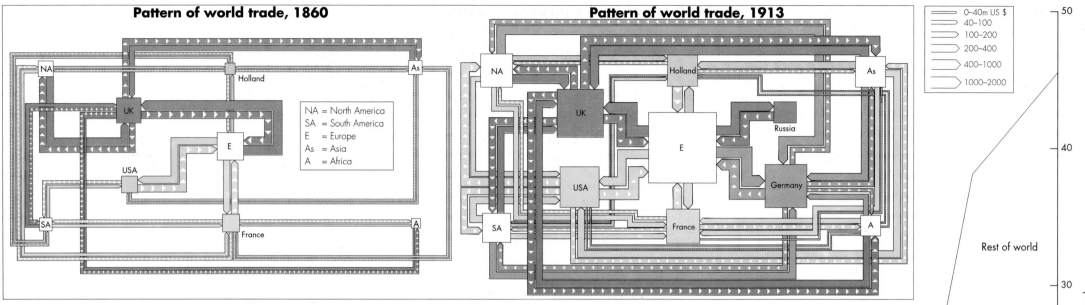

Pattern of world trade, 1860

Pattern of world trade, 1913

0–40m US $	
40–100	
100–200	
200–400	
400–1000	
1000–2000	

NA = North America
SA = South America
E = Europe
As = Asia
A = Africa

'Britain's industries were reared behind protective walls, nourished on imperial tribute and encouraged by the destruction of all competition from the East. But once established, they needed protection, plunder and protected markets no more … the factory product could undersell the work of handicraftsmen in any country. All the industrialists asked was the freedom to trade – to obtain food and raw materials wherever they were most cheaply produced and to open up the whole of the world as markets for their wares.'[17]

During the late eighteenth century and through the nineteenth century, world trade grew dramatically. Somewhat later, Europe began directly organizing colonial production on a large scale by investing overseas. These two economic changes remoulded much of the world's production and distribution into an interconnected capitalist economy centred on Europe.

The growth of world trade

During the four and a half centuries of European expansion, the centre of world trade moved successively from Venice (until the sixteenth century) to Amsterdam (during the seventeenth) to London (the eighteenth and nineteenth) and then to the USA and, to a lesser extent, to Germany. As the centre of world trade moved, its nature and scale were transformed. Venetian trade included notable (small volume, high value) exchanges with most of Eurasia and Northern Africa, but was predominantly an exchange of goods produced and consumed in the Mediterranean region. With the rise of Dutch influence and naval power, the merchants of Amsterdam were able

to command the produce of a wider area, including the Caribbean, coastal India and Africa, and the (Dutch) East Indies. Even then, most of the world's produce was exchanged and consumed near its area of production. During the eighteenth and nineteenth centuries, British naval power and the march of imperial expansion into Africa and Asia brought the rise of a market centred on London encompassing the whole world and influencing the production of most of its goods.

The graph of world trade between 1750 and 1938 shows the early and continuing dominance of British trade until the latter part of the nineteenth century, when the shares of US, German and French merchants together began to exceed those of British.

The complex flow diagrams at the top of this page depict the pattern of world trade in 1860 and 1913, showing the relative importance of each continent to the trade of the major imperial nations. The width of each arrow is proportional to the value of the total trade between the two areas it connects, the direction indicating either import or export trade. To reduce the complexity of the pattern, the diagrams do not show separately trade between individual nations or between continents. For example, the arrows linking France and Europe represent trade between France and all the rest of Europe (including Britain, Holland, etc.). In these diagrams, the

■	Russia
□	USA
▨	Holland
▨	Germany
░	France
■	UK

Growth and distribution of world trade, 1750 – 1938

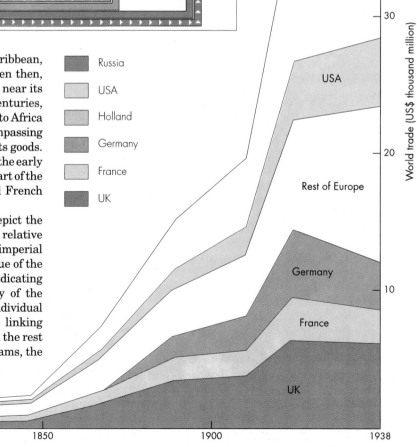

Rest of world

USA

Rest of Europe

Germany

France

UK

World trade (US$ thousand million)

1750   1800   1850   1900   1938

dominance of British trade in 1860 is again apparent, as is the challenge from the USA and other European nations by 1913.

For Britain, cotton goods led the growth of trade (from a negligible amount in the early 1700s to 50% of exports by the early 1900s). The British Empire, particularly India, took a substantial proportion of these exports: in 1800–20, India took 10% of British textile exports, the rest of the Empire 14%; by 1914 the figures were 25% and 19%, respectively. As British trade grew, the Empire took over from Europe as Britain's chief foreign market, and remained so until the middle of the twentieth century.

The opening of the Suez Canal in 1869, making a faster, cheaper route to the markets, food and raw materials of Asia and the Pacific, was only one of several technological changes promoting the expansion of capitalism. In Britain, in 1855, ten times as much of the shipping capacity constructed was powered by sail as by steam; from the 1880s, more steam than sail was constructed. More important than either Suez or the steamship, however, in opening world markets to European manufacturers, was the railway, and for that heavy capital investment was required.

The beginning of overseas investment

Until about 1770, Britain imported wealth from the rest of the world. Thenceforth, much of that wealth was invested overseas. The rest of the industrialized world was importing capital until the early twentieth century.[18] From the early 1800s, as the graph (right) shows,[19] Britain invested overseas to an ever increasing extent (until the depression of the 1930s). Initially this capital went to Europe, but by the 1880s, 40% was going to the Empire. There it was invested in railways, canals, cotton mills and jute mills, and plantations. The pie chart of British overseas investment in 1913 shows how large a factor railway investment remained at the beginning of this century.

The map (below) shows the density of railways constructed by 1880, the railway network at about 1914 (in Asia, Africa and Latin America, where known) and foreign investment by continent and investing power in 1900 and 1914. Railway provision corresponds with the extension of world trade to that country, but also generally with overseas investment. The pattern of railways generally serves seaborne, international trade rather than intra-regional trade.

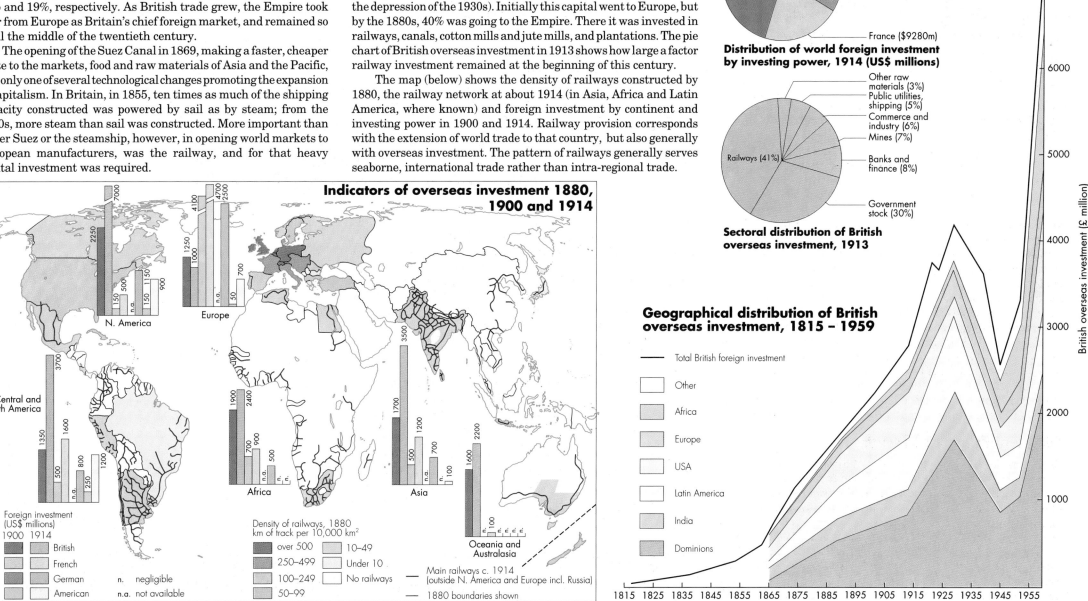

Distribution of world foreign investment by investing power, 1914 (US$ millions)

Russia ($500m)
Belgium ($900m)
USA ($3510m)
Holland ($4100m)
UK ($19,935m)
Germany ($5650m)
France ($9280m)

Sectoral distribution of British overseas investment, 1913

Railways (41%)
Other raw materials (3%)
Public utilities, shipping (5%)
Commerce and industry (6%)
Mines (7%)
Banks and finance (8%)
Government stock (30%)

Indicators of overseas investment 1880, 1900 and 1914

N. America
Europe
Central and South America
Africa
Asia
Oceania and Australasia

Foreign investment (US$ millions)
1900 1914
British
French
German
American

n.   negligible
n.a. not available

Density of railways, 1880 km of track per 10,000 km²
over 500
250–499
100–249
50–99
10–49
Under 10
No railways

Main railways c. 1914 (outside N. America and Europe incl. Russia)
1880 boundaries shown

Geographical distribution of British overseas investment, 1815 – 1959

Total British foreign investment
Other
Africa
Europe
USA
Latin America
India
Dominions

British overseas investment (£ million)

1815 1825 1835 1845 1855 1865 1875 1885 1895 1905 1915 1925 1935 1945 1955

On pp.16–17, three tests of industrialization were used. The map on p.39 used a different set of measures to show the enormous differences in levels of industrialization between parts of the world in 1930. For example, in terms of production, India had the largest manufacturing sector in the Third World, but was still producing only 3% of the manufactures produced in the USA.

Data allowing a long historical view of all the measures used on pp.16–17 and p.39 does not exist. However, different ways of measuring changes in the labour force appear in both those presentations. The governments of major states have, since the late nineteenth century or early twentieth centuries, been concerned to collect census statistics which show the size and sectoral distribution of the labour force. This data provides the most useful single indicator of long-term changes in the economy such as industrialization. As industrialization proceeds, the industrial labour force expands (and the number employed in or subsisting by agriculture falls). The industrial sector may become the largest in terms of labour force, and within it the labour force in manufacturing becomes a significant proportion of the total.

In the USA, the UK and Japan, the pattern of growth in manufacturing employment and decline in agriculture is very clear and consistent, showing the steady progress of industrialization in these countries (though for the UK the agricultural decline occurred before the start of these statistics). This characteristic feature of industrialization is shown particularly by the ratio of the agricultural to the industrial labour forces (a falling ratio indicating industrialization). The graph (below left) depicting changes in this ratio indicates a steady fall for Japan as it industrialized and a faster fall for the rapid industrialization of the USSR. (Presumably a curve similar to that for Japan could have been drawn for the USA over the preceding century and for the UK much earlier than that, if statistics had been collected.)

The Third World countries shown, with the exception of Chile, are distinguished by the larger proportion of their labour forces in agriculture. The map on p.39 reinforces this point: in 1930 most countries in Africa had over 80% of the labour force employed in agriculture, whereas most European countries had less than 40%. In most cases the situation has not changed much since then. The graph on this page (bottom left) confirms that the Third World countries represented have exhibited very little consistent progress towards industrialization in terms of change in labour force. (Note that the ratio exaggerates small variations in the industrial labour force when the agricultural sector is large.)

Historical changes in GNP per capita

The map on p.39 showed estimated gross national product (GNP) per capita in 1930. The graph (right) on this page shows how GNP per capita for different world regions changed over a long period before and after that date. GNP per capita is an indicator of income levels rather than directly of industrialization, but rises in the income levels or living standards of countries or world regions have in the past been associated strongly with the productivity increases resulting from large-scale industrialization.

The data for the GNP graph is obtained from a systematic survey of historical data on production and standard of living by Paul Bairoch[20]. It provides a rough indication of changes in regional productivity. Bairoch cautions that: 'pre-1900 data [for the Third World regions] should be regarded as very conjectural'.

Bairoch's study suggests that in the mid-eighteenth century the average standard of living in Europe was a little lower than that in the rest of the world. At the beginning of the nineteenth century the ratio of productivity (and wealth) between the richest and poorest regions of the world was about 1.5:1 . The rise of capitalist industry in Western Europe transformed this rough parity into a large disparity (at least 7:1) by 1975. Between the poorest classes of one region and the richest of Western Europe, the disparity would be much greater. Bairoch's figures suggest that GNP per capita fell or rose hardly at all in Africa and Asia (except for Japan), rose more in Latin America, rose sharply in Western Europe and North America, and, since 1950, rose sharply in Eastern Europe and Japan (although more recent data would show a big difference between the last two – see graph on p.72).

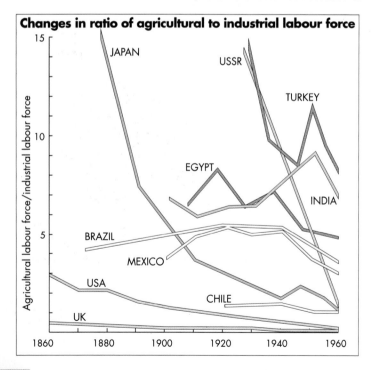

Changes in ratio of agricultural to industrial labour force

Agricultural labour force/industrial labour force

JAPAN · USSR · TURKEY · EGYPT · INDIA · BRAZIL · MEXICO · USA · CHILE · UK

1860 · 1880 · 1900 · 1920 · 1940 · 1960

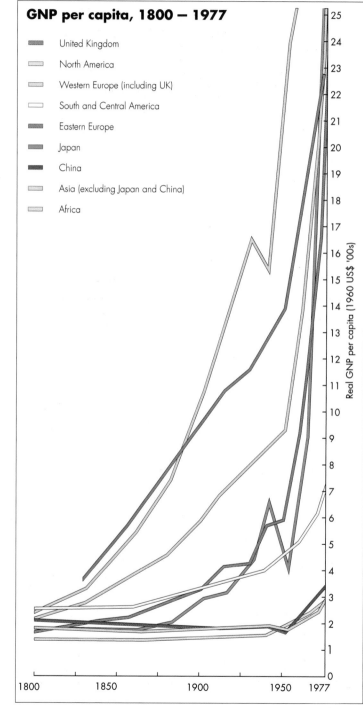

GNP per capita, 1800 – 1977

- United Kingdom
- North America
- Western Europe (including UK)
- South and Central America
- Eastern Europe
- Japan
- China
- Asia (excluding Japan and China)
- Africa

Real GNP per capita (1960 US$ '00s)

1800 · 1850 · 1900 · 1950 · 1977

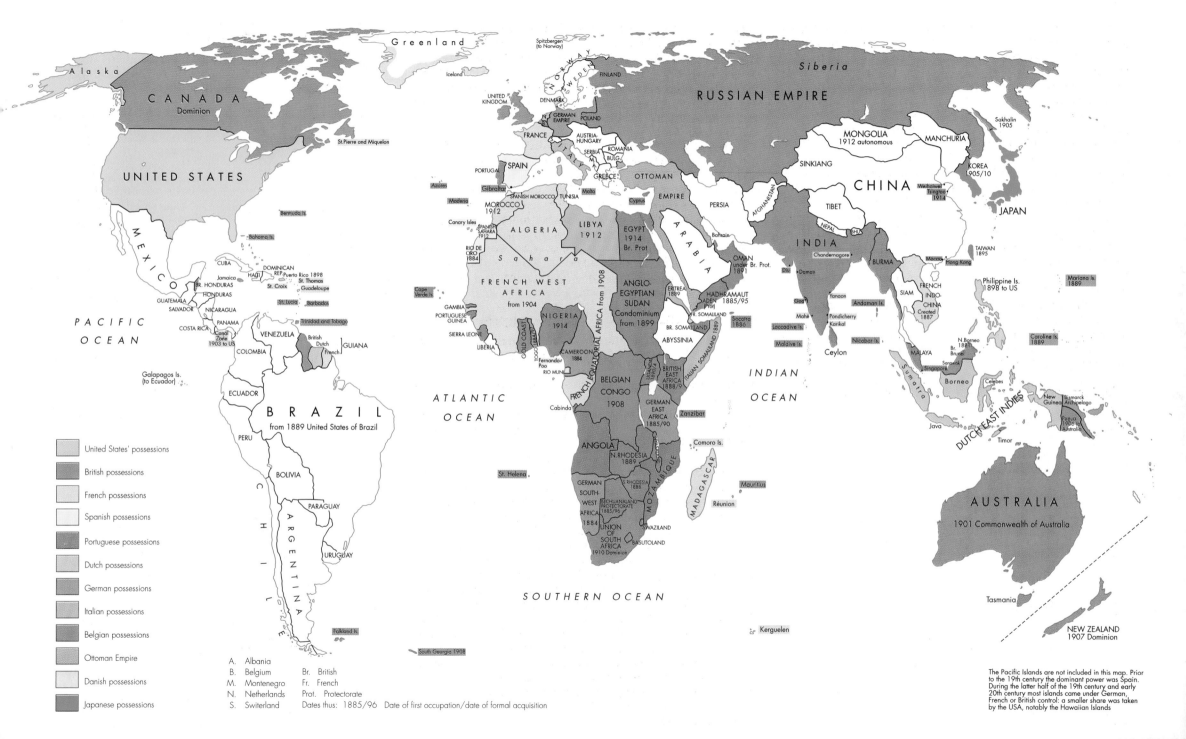

Greenland

Spitzbergen
(to Norway)

Iceland

Alaska

C A N A D A
Dominion

St.Pierre and Miquelon

Bermuda Is.

UNITED STATES

M
E
X
I
C
O

Bahama Is.

CUBA
DOMINICAN
REP. Puerto Rico 1898
HAITI   St. Thomas
Jamaica   St. Croix
BR. HONDURAS   Guadeloupe
GUATEMALA   St. Lucia   Barbados
HONDURAS
SALVADOR   Trinidad and Tobago
NICARAGUA
COSTA RICA   British
PANAMA   Dutch
Canal   French
Zone   GUIANA
1903 to US

PACIFIC
OCEAN

VENEZUELA

COLOMBIA

Galapagos Is.
(to Ecuador)

ECUADOR

B R A Z I L
from 1889 United States of Brazil

PERU

BOLIVIA

PARAGUAY

C
H
I
L
E

A
R
G
E
N
T
I
N
A

URUGUAY

Falkland Is.

South Georgia 1908

NORWAY
SWEDEN
FINLAND

UNITED
KINGDOM
DENMARK
GERMAN
EMPIRE   POLAND
FRANCE
AUSTRIA-
HUNGARY
SPAIN   SERBIA   ROMANIA
PORTUGAL   BULG.
GREECE
Azores
Madeira   Gibraltar   TUNISIA   Malta
SPANISH MOROCCO   Cyprus
Canary Isles   MOROCCO
1912
SPANISH
SAHARA   ALGERIA   LIBYA   EGYPT
1912   1912   1914
Br. Prot
RIO DE   Sahara
ORO
1884
FRENCH WEST
AFRICA
from 1904   ANGLO-
EGYPTIAN
Cape   SUDAN
Verde Is.   Condominium
GAMBIA   NIGERIA   from 1899
PORTUGUESE   1914
GUINEA
SIERRA LEONE
LIBERIA   GOLD COAST
TOGO
Fernando
Poo   CAMEROON
RIO MUNI   1884

RUSSIAN EMPIRE

Siberia

Sakhalin
1905

MONGOLIA
1912 autonomous   MANCHURIA

SINKIANG   KOREA
1905/10

CHINA   Weihaiwei
Tsingtao
1914
JAPAN

OTTOMAN   PERSIA   TIBET
EMPIRE   AFGHANISTAN
NEPAL   BHUTAN
ARABIA   INDIA
Bahrein   Chandernagore   BURMA   TAIWAN
1895
OMAN
under Br. Prot.   Diu   Daman   Macao   Hong Kong
1891
Goa
ERITREA   FR. SOMALILAND   Yanaon
HADHRAMAUT   Mahé   Pondicherry   Andaman Is.   SIAM   FRENCH
ADEN   1885/95   Karikal   INDO-
BR. SOMALILAND 1884/86   Socotra   CHINA
ABYSSINIA   1886   Laccadive Is.   Nicobar Is.   Created
1887
ITALIAN SOMALILAND
Maldive Is.   Philippine Is.
1898 to US

FRENCH EQUATORIAL AFRICA from 1908

BELGIAN
CONGO
1908

Cabinda

GERMAN
EAST
AFRICA
1885/90

UGANDA
1890/94
BRITISH
EAST
AFRICA
1888/9

Zanzibar

Ceylon

INDIAN
OCEAN

Mariana Is.
1889

Caroline Is.
1889

N. Borneo
1881
Br.
Brunei
Sarawak

MALAYA
Singapore
Borneo

Celebes

Sumatra

DUTCH EAST INDIES

Java

Timor

New
Guinea   Bismarck
Archipelago

Papua
1906 to
Australia

ATLANTIC
OCEAN

ANGOLA

N. RHODESIA
1889

St. Helena

GERMAN
SOUTH-
WEST
AFRICA
1884   S. RHODESIA
1888

BECHUANALAND
PROTECTORATE
1885/96

UNION
OF
SOUTH
AFRICA
1910 Dominion

SWAZILAND
BASUTOLAND

M
O
Z
A
M
B
I
Q
U
E

Comoro Is.

M
A
D
A
G
A
S
C
A
R

Réunion

Mauritius

SOUTHERN OCEAN

Kerguelen

AUSTRALIA
1901 Commonwealth of Australia

Tasmania

NEW ZEALAND
1907 Dominion

United States' possessions

British possessions

French possessions

Spanish possessions

Portuguese possessions

Dutch possessions

German possessions

Italian possessions

Belgian possessions

Ottoman Empire

Danish possessions

Japanese possessions

A.   Albania
B.   Belgium   Br.   British
M.   Montenegro   Fr.   French
N.   Netherlands   Prot.   Protectorate
S.   Switerland   Dates thus: 1885/96   Date of first occupation/date of formal acquisition

The Pacific Islands are not included in this map. Prior
to the 19th century the dominant power was Spain.
During the latter half of the 19th century and early
20th century most islands came under German,
French or British control: a smaller share was taken
by the USA, notably the Hawaiian Islands

These two pages attempt to identify the main concerted responses to European rule, ranging across three continents and two hundred years. With such a canvas, only the main features can be shown, and although the maps are cluttered, they are very selective. As Low wrote of Kenya, 'Any map which outlined the operational theatres of the many small British military expeditions during the first fifteen years of British rule ... would exhibit few interstices'.[21]

We have categorized the struggles as follows:

1 *Resistance to conquest*: wars of response to European penetration.

2 *Rebellions against European rule*: violent responses to the bedding down of imperial authority.

3 *Movements of religious revivalism*: expressions of religious discontent.

4 *Outbreaks of guerrilla radicalism*: liberation struggles.

A fifth category of response, *constitutional moves toward decolonization*, can also be identified, but it is not mapped here.

This typology suggests that there is a range of actions between primary resistance (resistance to conquest) and modern mass nationalism (expressed either as constitutional opposition or as guerrilla radicalism). Nevertheless, these categories cross widely separated periods and include very different types of struggle. Resistance to conquest includes wars between professional armies as well as battles between European armies and ill-armed bands of mass resistance. Movements of religious revival may make appeals to 'traditional' values but may also contain elements of a vision of the future. Even within one subcontinent, India, 'rebellions against European rule' just before the end of British rule varied from mass non-violent 'civil disobedience', in which hundreds of thousands were jailed, to acts of individual violence (in the Quit India movement) and the recruitment of an Indian National Army making common cause with Japan.

The maps focus primarily on major incidents of violent action which demanded immediate response from the colonial state. However, strike waves and slave revolts, of which there were many in the sugar regions of Central America and particularly the Caribbean (see diagram below) have generally been excluded. The maps do not show Russian expansion into Central Asia nor Chinese opposition to Japanese rule (with the exception of the Long March, which was partly a mobilization of anti-Japanese feeling).

The map below covers the period of Latin American independence and the main expansion of Europe after the industrial revolution. The map opposite covers the independence of much of Asia and Africa. In both Asia and Africa, the two World Wars diverted the attention of the European rulers and raised the expectations of the ruled (particularly those enlisted), providing a significant boost to many nationalist movements. Nevertheless, the nature and timing of independence depended primarily on local conditions. Jeffrey[22] has suggested a rough guide to the conditions which were associated with evolutionary (constitutional) and revolutionary (guerrilla radicalism) paths to independence in Asia:

Evolutionary

1 Long period of rule, which grudgingly fostered education and participatory government

2 Large Westernized elite, sympathetic to existing government structure.

3 Small proportion of Europeans (e.g. 1 : 1600 in Philippines, 1 : 3700 in India in 1930s).

4 Large locally staffed colonial bureaucracy and army.

5 Colonial power willing to release its grip.

Revolutionary

1 Short period of colonial rule. Little Western-style education

2 No nationwide Westernized elite until well into the twentieth century.

3 Larger proportion of Europeans (e.g. 1 : 200 in Indonesia, 1 : 475 in Vietnam).

4 Heavy colonial economic interest in country, with little participatory government.

5 Colonial power unwilling to release its grip.

These distinctions (developed specifically to summarize Asian experience) form part of an explanation of the diversity of anti-colonial struggles in the later period, but only part.

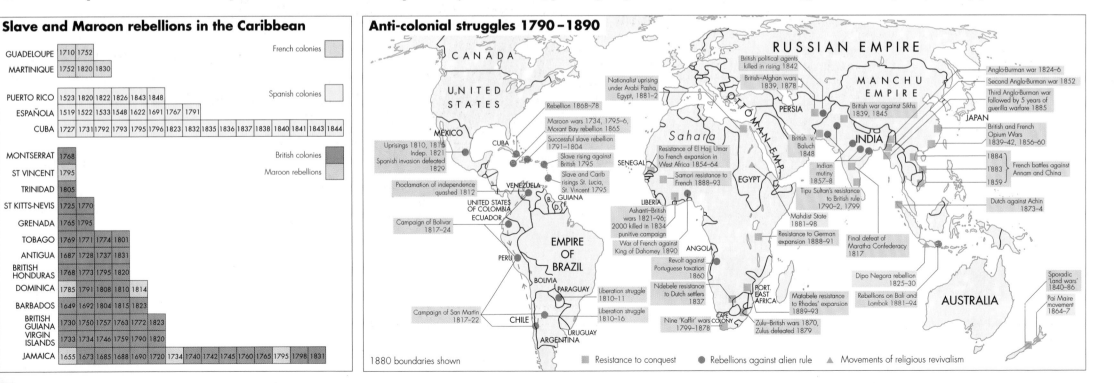

Slave and Maroon rebellions in the Caribbean

GUADELOUPE	1710	1752															French colonies			
MARTINIQUE	1752	1820	1830																	
PUERTO RICO	1523	1820	1822	1826	1843	1848								Spanish colonies						
ESPAÑOLA	1519	1522	1533	1548	1622	1691	1767	1791												
CUBA	1727	1731	1792	1793	1795	1796	1823	1832	1835	1836	1837	1838	1840	1841	1843	1844				
MONTSERRAT	1768											British colonies								
ST VINCENT	1795											Maroon rebellions								
TRINIDAD	1805																			
ST KITTS-NEVIS	1725	1770																		
GRENADA	1765	1795																		
TOBAGO	1769	1771	1774	1801																
ANTIGUA	1687	1728	1737	1831																
BRITISH HONDURAS	1768	1773	1795	1820																
DOMINICA	1785	1791	1808	1810	1814															
BARBADOS	1649	1692	1804	1815	1823															
BRITISH GUIANA	1730	1750	1757	1763	1772	1823														
VIRGIN ISLANDS	1733	1734	1746	1759	1790	1820														
JAMAICA	1655	1673	1685	1688	1690	1720	1734	1740	1742	1745	1760	1765	1795	1798	1831					

Anti-colonial struggles 1790–1890

1880 boundaries shown   ■ Resistance to conquest   ● Rebellions against alien rule   ▲ Movements of religious revivalism

Anti-colonial struggles 1890–1990

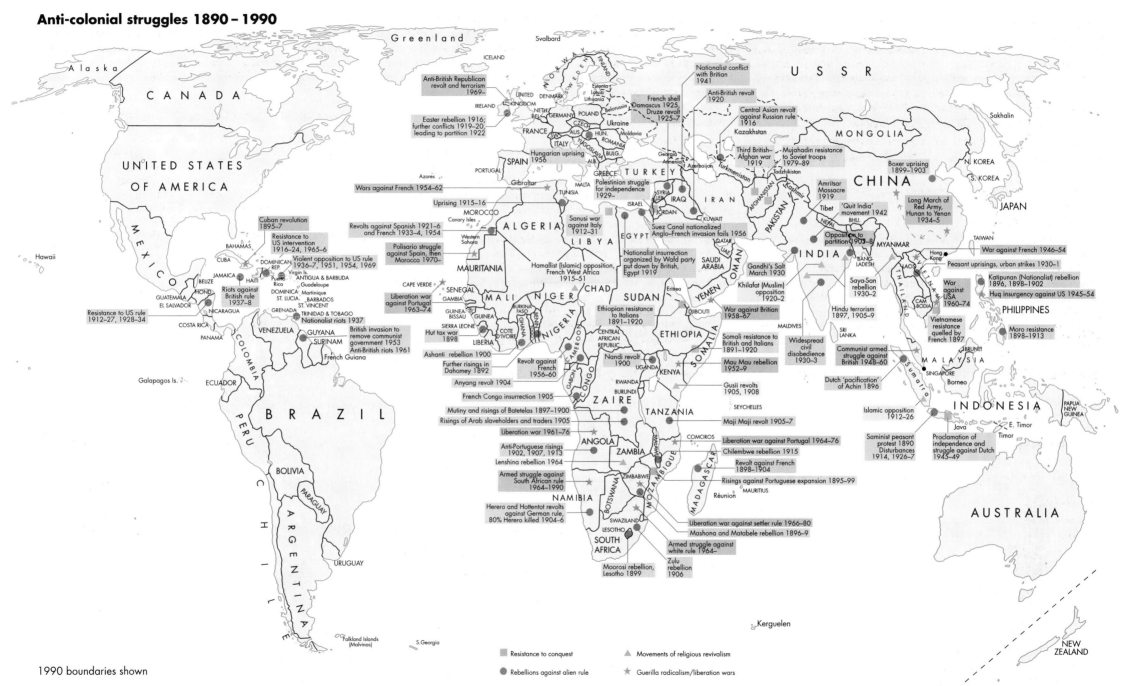

Greenland

Svalbard

ICELAND

Alaska

CANADA

UNITED STATES

OF AMERICA

Hawaii

MEXICO

BAHAMAS

CUBA
DOMINICAN REP.
Virgin Is.
Puerto Rico
JAMAICA HAITI
Guadeloupe
ANTIGUA & BARBUDA
Dominica
St. Lucia
Martinique
BARBADOS
St. Vincent
GRENADA
TRINIDAD & TOBAGO

Cuban revolution 1895–7

Resistance to US intervention 1916–24, 1965–6

Violent opposition to US rule 1936–7, 1951, 1954, 1969

Riots against British rule 1937–8

Resistance to US rule 1912–27, 1928–34

BELIZE
GUATEMALA
EL SALVADOR
HOND.
NICARAGUA
COSTA RICA
PANAMA

Nationalist riots 1937

British invasion to remove communist government 1953
Anti-British riots 1961

Galapagos Is.

ECUADOR
COLOMBIA
VENEZUELA
GUYANA
SURINAM
French Guiana

PERU
BRAZIL
BOLIVIA

PARAGUAY

CHILE
ARGENTINA
URUGUAY

Falkland Islands (Malvinas)

S.Georgia

NORWAY SWEDEN FINLAND
DENMARK
Estonia
Latvia
Lithuania
UNITED KINGDOM
IRELAND
NETH.
BEL.
GERMANY POLAND
Belorussia
CZECH.
Ukraine
AUS. HUN.
Moldavia
FRANCE
ITALY
YUGOSLAVIA
ROMANIA
BULG.
ALB.
SPAIN
PORTUGAL
Azores
Gibraltar
MALTA

Anti-British Republican revolt and terrorism 1969–

Easter rebellion 1916; further conflicts 1919–20; leading to partition 1922

Hungarian uprising 1956

Nationalist conflict with Britian 1941

French shell Damascus 1925, Druze revolt 1925–7

Anti-British revolt 1920

Wars against French 1954–62

TUNISIA

Uprising 1915–16

MOROCCO
Canary Isles
Western Sahara

Revolts against Spanish 1921–6 and French 1933–4, 1954

Polisario struggle against Spain, then Morocco 1970–

ALGERIA
LIBYA

Sanusi war against Italy 1912–31

EGYPT

Suez Canal nationalized Anglo–French invasion fails 1956

Nationalist insurrection organized by Wafd party put down by British, Egypt 1919

GREECE TURKEY
Georgia
Armenia
Azerbaijan

SYRIA
LEB.
ISRAEL
JORDAN
IRAQ
KUWAIT
QATAR
UAE
SAUDI ARABIA
YEMEN
OMAN

Palestinian struggle for independence 1929–

USSR

Central Asian revolt against Russian rule 1916

Kazakhstan
Turkmenistan
Tadzhikistan

MONGOLIA

N. KOREA
S. KOREA

CHINA

JAPAN

Sakhalin

Boxer uprising 1899–1903

Third British–Afghan war 1919

Mujahadin resistance to Soviet troops 1979–89

AFGHANISTAN
Kashmir
PAKISTAN
IRAN

Amritsar Massacre 1919

Tibet
Nepal
BHU.

'Quit India' movement 1942

Long March of Red Army, Hunan to Yenan 1934–5

TAIWAN

Hong Kong

MAURITANIA
CAPE VERDE
SENEGAL
GAMBIA
GUINEA BISSAU
GUINEA
SIERRA LEONE
LIBERIA
COTE D'IVOIRE
MALI
BURKINA FASO
NIGER
GHANA
TOGO
BENIN
NIGERIA
CHAD
CAMEROON
CENTRAL AFRICAN REPUBLIC
SUDAN

Hamallist (Islamic) opposition, French West Africa 1915–51

Liberation war against Portugal 1963–74

Hut tax war 1898

Ashanti rebellion 1900

Further risings in Dahomey 1892

Anyang revolt 1904

French Congo insurrection 1905

Mutiny and risings of Batetelas 1897–1900

Risings of Arab slaveholders and traders 1905

Revolt against French 1956–60

Ethiopian resistance to Italians 1891–1920

Eritrea
DJIBOUTI

ETHIOPIA

Nandi revolt 1900

UGANDA
RWANDA
BURUNDI
GABON
CONGO
ZAIRE

KENYA

War against Britian 1958–67

Somali resistance to British and Italians 1891–1920

SOMALIA

Mau Mau rebellion 1952–9

Gusii revolts 1905, 1908

TANZANIA

Maji Maji revolt 1905–7

MADIVES

MYANMAR

War against French 1946–54

Peasant uprisings, urban strikes 1930–1

Katipunan (Nationalist) rebellion 1896, 1898–1902

War against USA 1960–74

Huq insurgency against US 1945–54

PHILIPPINES

Moro resistance 1898–1913

INDIA

Opposition to partition 1905–8

Gandhi's Salt March 1930

Khilafat (Muslim) opposition 1920–2

Saya-San rebellion 1930–2

Hindu terrorism 1897, 1905–9

BANG-LADESH

SRI LANKA

Widespread civil disobedience 1930–3

Communist armed struggle against British 1948–60

Dutch 'pacification' of Achin 1896

LAOS
VIETNAM
THAILAND
CAM-BODIA
BRUNEI
MALAYSIA
Borneo
SINGAPORE
Sumatra

Vietnamese resistance quelled by French 1897

Islamic opposition 1912–26

INDONESIA

PAPUA NEW GUINEA

E. Timor

Java
Timor

Saminist peasant protest 1890
Disturbances 1914, 1926–7

Proclamation of independence and struggle against Dutch 1945–49

AUSTRALIA

Liberation war 1961–76

Anti-Portuguese risings 1902, 1907, 1913

Lenshina rebellion 1964

Armed struggle against South African rule 1964–1990

ANGOLA
ZAMBIA

ZIMBABWE
BOTSWANA
NAMIBIA
SOUTH AFRICA
SWAZILAND
LESOTHO

MOZAMBIQUE
MALAWI
COMOROS
MADAGASCAR
SEYCHELLES
Réunion
MAURITIUS

Liberation war against Portugal 1964–76

Chilembwe rebellion 1915

Revolt against French 1898–1904

Risings against Portuguese expansion 1895–99

Herero and Hottentot revolts against German rule, 80% Herero killed 1904–6

Liberation war against settler rule 1966–80

Mashona and Matabele rebellion 1896–9

Armed struggle against white rule 1964–

Moorosi rebellion, Lesotho 1899

Zulu rebellion 1906

Kerguelen

NEW ZEALAND

1990 boundaries shown

■ Resistance to conquest
● Rebellions against alien rule
▲ Movements of religious revivalism
★ Guerilla radicalism/liberation wars

USA

During the nineteenth century, while European powers built worldwide empires, the new republic on the Atlantic seaboard of North America focused on westward expansion across the continent (1783–1850). The indigenous Indians were conquered and their way of life destroyed. The local culture of native Americans was replaced with an integrated capitalist economy. The abundance of physical resources across the American continent (combined with other factors such as the freeing of slave labour for capitalist industries and immigrants from Europe) led to increased agricultural and industrial productivity in the USA. By 1890, the USA had become the world's leading industrial power (see graphs on p.38, bottom left, and on p.42).

After the occupation of the country from the Atlantic to the Pacific, US energies were directed (1867–1917) towards the acquisition of colonies and consolidation of influence in South-east Asia, Latin America and the Caribbean, and trading interests in China, as the map below indicates.

In an attempt to exert influence on international affairs and to protect democracy in Europe against 'German autocracy', the USA entered the First World War. The years between the First and Second World Wars were marked in the USA by the Great Depression and isolationism on the international front. With the rise of Hitler and fascism in Europe, however, isolationism was eroded. Japan, an ally of Germany and Italy in the Second World War and an imperial rival of the USA in the Pacific, attempted to consolidate its imperial perimeter by attacking the US fleet at Pearl Harbor in the Hawaiian islands in 1941. This brought the USA into the Second World War as an ally of Britain and the USSR.

Japan

In less than half a century (1868–1912), Japan transformed itself from a secluded feudal society to a world power that was determined to gain equality with Western nations. It built up the infrastructure of a modern industrial nation, including a modern army and navy. The need for raw materials led to expansionist wars with China (1895) and Russia (1905). Japan's victory over Russia in 1905 provoked the interest of the USA and Britain. Korea was ruled by Japan from 1910. Between the First and Second World Wars, Japan continued to expand into northern China. In 1931 Japan occupied Manchuria, thus eroding the influence there of Britain, the USA and the USSR.

Japanese expansion into South-east Asia during the Second World War was checked by the Allied forces, and the war was brought to a swift conclusion in 1945 when the USA dropped atomic bombs on Hiroshima and Nagasaki.

The Cold War in Asia

After the Second World War, the USA and the USSR emerged as the two leading rival world powers. The Russian Revolution of 1917 not only transformed the USSR from a feudal society to an industrial and military power but also fundamentally altered the pattern of international relations. It inspired the formation of socialist and revolutionary governments and nationalist movements all over the world.

The USA also experienced tremendous economic growth after the Second World War. As a result of wealth and success, many Americans were convinced about the universal validity of the Anglo-Saxon way of life and their own zealous mission to carry it to the rest of humanity.

'The Cold War' is a term which refers to the strategic and political struggle after the Second World War between the two 'superpowers': the USA with its Western European allies, and the USSR and communist countries. The conflict was based on mutual suspicion: the American conviction that the USSR was intent on expansion and world conquest and Soviet antagonism to Western imperialism and capitalism, which, it was believed, would inevitably seek the destruction of the Soviet system.

Starting as a conflict over a divided Germany and Central Europe, the Cold War spread to Asia after the Chinese Communist victory in 1949. The future of East and South-east Asia was uncertain after the withdrawal of Japan from the territories it had occupied. The likelihood of a Communist government in Korea brought US involvement in a land war there in 1950, resulting in partition of that country which persists to this day.

In South-east Asia, France was never able to regain full control over its colonies. Whereas in the cases of India, Pakistan, Sri Lanka, Indonesia and the Philippines there was a relatively peaceful transition to independence, the Vietnamese had to wage a protracted guerrilla war, first against the French and then against the USA, before defeating the latter and achieving independence in 1971.

In the meantime, after its defeat in the Second World War, Japan resumed full sovereignty in 1952 and economic development became a priority of government policy. By the 1970s, Japan had become the world's third largest economy, and also a bastion for the USA against Communist China.

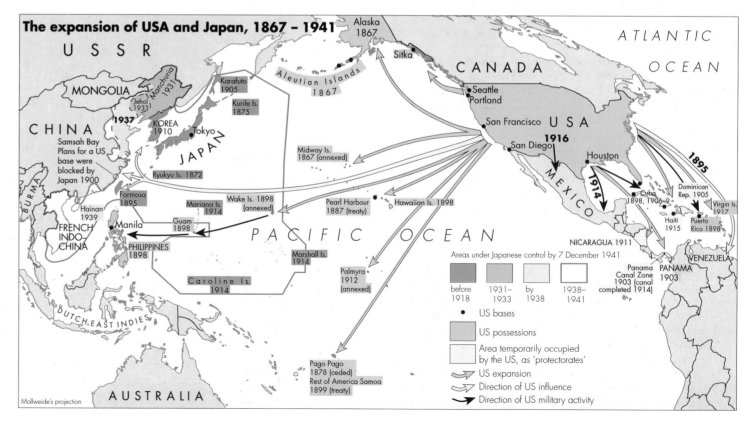

The expansion of USA and Japan, 1867 – 1941

In the fifties, after the stalemates in Central Europe and Korea, the USA devised the strategy of 'containment' which involved anticipating and preventing further Soviet gains by maintaining overwhelming military superiority. This was achieved by forming military alliances in Asia and the Middle East and extending economic and military assistance to any country thought to be in danger of communist subversion. The USSR responded by economic and military competition with the USA in the Middle East, Africa and elsewhere, including support for nationalist movements, some of the newly independent states such as Nkrumah's Ghana, and Castro's revolution in Cuba.

The sixties saw the height of the Cold War, with the two superpowers racing to develop and deploy nuclear missiles against each other. This resulted in the Berlin crisis of 1961 and the Cuban missile crisis of 1962. US military intervention in Laos, Cambodia and Vietnam in the 1960s led to a change in focus of the Cold War to South-east Asia.

The Nuclear Test Ban Treaty of 1963 was a turning point in the Cold War, and in the 1970s East and West were able to negotiate their differences in a spirit of 'détente'. However, US military intervention continued in the 1970s (e.g. the US-backed military coup in Chile in 1973). In 1979, the installation of a Soviet puppet regime in Afghanistan and the extension of Soviet influence in Central Asia served to undermine the détente process.

Throughout the period of détente and the more confrontational early 1980s, it can be argued that the Cold War was fought largely by proxy in the regional wars of the Middle East, South Asia, South-east Asia, Latin America and the Horn of Africa. The late 1980s brought large-scale movements of social and political protest in Eastern Europe as well as in the Republics of the USSR. In 1989 the two superpowers declared the end of the Cold War; Germany was reunified in 1990; and the USSR itself broke up into its constituent Republics in 1991. However, despite this apparent victory for the capitalist side in the Cold War, several of the 'proxy' disputes continue as protracted civil wars, wreaking havoc on development prospects.

The Non-aligned Movement

The Non-aligned Movement was a response to the tension, hostility and rivalry generated by the Cold War. From its inception at Belgrade (1961), the Movement has taken an anti-colonial and anti-racist stance. Founder members were mostly newly independent countries who did not want to become client states of the superpowers after the decolonization process, plus Cuba and Yugoslavia.

The Movement was characterized by triennial meetings and conference diplomacy. In the 1960s and 1970s, the Non-aligned states combined their voting power into blocs and commanded effective working majorities in organizations such as the UN. Until the Algiers meeting of 1973, political concerns predominated, such as disarmament, prevention of the use of force in international conflicts, support for national liberation movements, including that of the Palestinian people, opposition to apartheid in South Africa, and staying clear of the military alliances built by the two superpowers.

In the 1970s, attention was focused, among other things, on the call for a New International Economic Order, with the formation of associations of producers of raw materials to obtain more favourable rates for Third World products. By 1979, although the Movement had 100 members, it had weakened, partly due to heightened tension between the two major blocs and internal divisions within the Movement itself, including armed confrontations between member states.

More recently, the Movement has taken on the role of the 'trade union of the poor'. Grave concern has been expressed at the deteriorating political and economic conditions globally, particularly the unequal distribution of the world's wealth and resources between the rich North and the poor South, the debt crisis which is slowly eroding the sovereignty of debtor nations, hunger and famine in Africa, and the unwillingness of the major world powers to entertain the notion of global negotiations. In 1986, the Movement specifically condemned US aggression against Libya and Nicaragua, and Israeli bombing of Iraqi nuclear installations.

The map shows the world's main military and trading blocs in 1981 and how the Non-aligned Movement sat between (and slightly overlapping) them. Since then the Eastern bloc has dissolved. It is difficult to maintain a unifying identity for Third World countries in terms of non-alignment or a positive 'third way', but in the 'New World Order' with the USA as the sole superpower such an identity is perhaps needed more than ever.

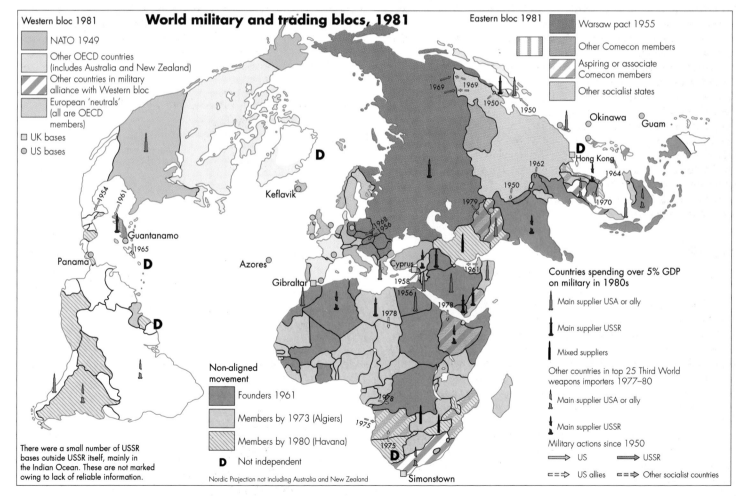

World military and trading blocs, 1981

Western bloc 1981
- NATO 1949
- Other OECD countries (includes Australia and New Zealand)
- Other countries in military alliance with Western bloc
- European 'neutrals' (all are OECD members)
- □ UK bases
- ○ US bases

Eastern bloc 1981
- Warsaw pact 1955
- Other Comecon members
- Aspiring or associate Comecon members
- Other socialist states

Non-aligned movement
- Founders 1961
- Members by 1973 (Algiers)
- Members by 1980 (Havana)
- D Not independent

Countries spending over 5% GDP on military in 1980s
- Main supplier USA or ally
- Main supplier USSR
- Mixed suppliers

Other countries in top 25 Third World weapons importers 1977–80
- Main supplier USA or ally
- Main supplier USSR

Military actions since 1950
- ⇒ US
- ⇒ USSR
- ⇢ US allies
- ⇢ Other socialist countries

There were a small number of USSR bases outside USSR itself, mainly in the Indian Ocean. These are not marked owing to lack of reliable information.

Nordic Projection not including Australia and New Zealand

ISSUES AND CHALLENGES IN CONTEMPORARY DEVELOPMENT

This section maps some of the more dramatic current changes in developing countries and their growing diversity. Some of the major challenges for the twenty-first century are outlined.

Industrial Transformation (pp.49–51) illustrates the highly variable extent of recent industrialization. The dramatic transformation of some South-east Asian nations contrasts with the lack of progress in Sub-Saharan Africa.

Changes on the Land (pp.52–53) have been a major feature of post-war development. Agriculture remains the chief source of livelihood for many in developing countries.

Hunger and Famine (pp.54–55) goes beyond the simplistic idea of food scarcity causing widespread starvation. Food shortages can be managed without unusually large numbers of deaths; even in the context of sufficient overall food famine can affect particular groups.

Disease and Health Care (pp.56–57) shows the stark differences between North and South in types and causes of disease and access to health provision.

Children and Development (pp.58–59). International efforts to improve the chances of the next generation have had variable results.

Gender and Development (pp.60–61) illustrates the continuing gap between women and men in health, work and education.

Environmental Degradation (pp.62–63) is now a global concern, though Southern priorities differ from those in the North.

Arms and the Military (pp.64–65). Military spending is a constant drain on scarce resources while armed conflict continues unabated in many places, particularly in the developing world.

Migration and Refugees (pp.66–67) shows population movements and their economic, environmental and political causes.

International Debt (pp.68–69). The threat of large-scale defaults in Latin America and elsewhere has receded, but for many developing countries debt servicing is still a huge problem.

Finally, **Towards the Twenty-first Century** (pp.70–73) outlines some global trends in population and in economic and human development.

Manufacturing is the most important part of industrial production. The processing of raw materials such as cotton, wood, iron and petroleum dramatically increases their value. Most world manufacturing takes place in developed countries. In fact this in part accounts for their developed status (see pp.16–17). Although developing countries have increased their share of world manufacturing in the last three decades, growth has been largely confined to Hong Kong, Taiwan, South Korea and Singapore (collectively known as the Asian Tigers) The pie diagram below shows that the four Asian Tigers export a higher value of manufactured goods than the other 100 or so developing nations put together. Hong Kong, an island of fewer than six million people, exports more manufactures than China and India combined. Japan's manufacturing output (not shown on the chart) is greater than that of all other South-east Asian countries put together.

The graphs (right) plot the relationship between manufacturing as a percentage of gross domestic product (GDP) and the wealth of a country, as measured by gross national product (GNP) per capita. The lower graph demonstrates that the relationship between the two variables is generally positive: countries with low per capita incomes tend to have small manufacturing sectors; wealthier countries have larger manufacturing sectors. However, the relationship is not linear, since some of the wealthiest countries in the world have experienced a drop in the relative importance of manufacturing in the last two decades. This decline in Northern Europe, North America and Australia has been described as de-industrialization. The trend is due to the increase in service industries (finance,

banking, leisure), which are increasingly important in affluent societies.

Vehicle production and ownership serve to demonstrate some global contrasts. The table above shows that in the late 1980s the USA had one vehicle for every 1.4 people, the lowest ratio in the world. By contrast, Ethiopia had one vehicle for every 1000 people and China one for every 1400. One-third of all cars in the world are in the USA.

The most spectacular entrant in the automobile industry in the last three decades has been Japan, which now produces almost a quarter of world production.[2] The graph (below centre) shows the increase of Latin American and Asian car manufacturing in the 1980s. Asian producers, such as South Korean Hyundai and the Malaysian producers of the Proton, look set to gain a foothold on international markets. Production by Brazil and Mexico has been more problematic as these countries have grappled with foreign debt repayments and rising import costs.

Manufacturing wages vary considerably between countries. The bar chart below shows that, in 1986, wages for car workers in Brazil and Korea were a quarter of those in Europe and almost a

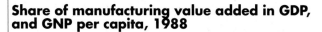

Share of manufacturing value added in GDP, and GNP per capita, 1988

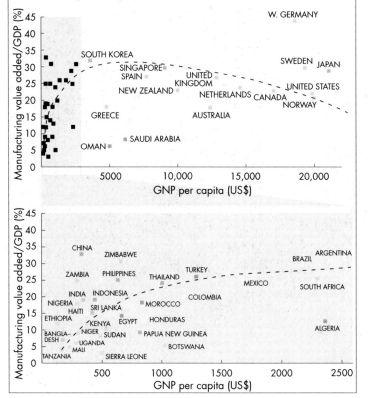

Vehicles per person, 1985–87[1]

	Vehicles per 1000 people	People per car
Ethiopia	1	1000.0
Uganda	3	333.3
Argentina	172	5.8
Colombia	43	23.3
China	0.7	1428.6
Indonesia	13	76.9
Japan	408	2.5
UK	373	2.7
Poland	137	7.3
Australia	575	1.7
USA	728	1.4

Manufacturing exports from developing countries, by country or region of origin, 1988 (US$ millions)

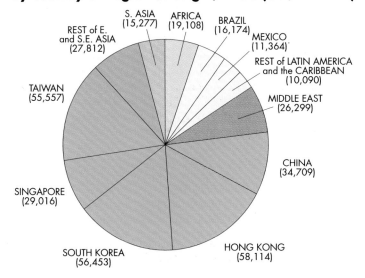

Latin American and Asian car production in selected countries, late 1980s

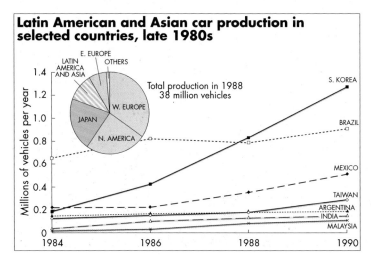

Hourly wages in the car industry, 1986

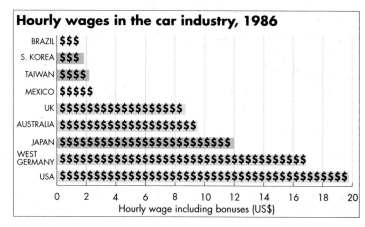

tenth of those in the USA. You might think that it would be comparatively easy for countries with low wage costs to produce competitively. However, this is not the case because, ominously for developing nations, only 20% of the cost of a finished high technology product such as cars relates to its wage component.[3] Low wages are insufficient to attract computer-age industries. Very large investment in modern machinery and a skilled labour force are needed.

The role of the state as financier and regulator in the industrialization process has been the subject of much scrutiny by industrial strategists. A general conclusion has now been reached that countries which have made headway as industrial nations have done so through a strict balance between state intervention and private enterprise.[4] Contrary to popular myth, Korea, Taiwan and Singapore shielded their infant industries from global competition until the mid-1960s and have since played a central role in stimulating and guiding the direction of industrial investments. In the 1970s the South Korean government, going against world trends, made large investments in heavy industries such as iron and steel and shipbuilding. Today, South Korea is one of the world's most efficient steel producers and leading ship builders.

The colours on the map opposite show manufacturing growth rates during the 1980s. The fastest growth occurred in South-east Asia and the Middle East. From the traditional industrial powers output was generally steady, while in Africa performance was patchy but generally poor. In Latin America the debt-induced shortage of funding for long-term industrial development has checked ambitious industrialization plans. Manufacturing actually declined in Argentina and Uruguay. In Brazil, despite a large internal market, manufactured goods are increasingly being exported to the USA, to earn the foreign exchange to service its debts.

The pie charts on the map illustrate the value of manufacturing per person in selected economies; the segments show the composition of manufacturing industry. Note the very small value of manufacturing per person in Bangladesh (US$9) and Ethiopia ($15) compared with the USA ($4608) and Japan ($5708). The bar graph on the map divides world manufacturing into nine sectors and shows the extent of production from the Third World. The most valuable manufacturing industry in the world in 1990 was machinery, yet this is where developing nations have their smallest share, 8%. Developing countries contribute to a significant proportion (about one-fifth) of global manufacturing in three sectors: food, beverages and tobacco; textiles, clothing and footwear; and chemicals and petroleum.

In the last 30 years there have been changes in the international division of labour. Industries and parts of industries that were once located in the West have been relocated in developing countries. The bar graph below (left) illustrates how employment in the USA in the mid-1980s changed as a consequence of production in developing countries. High-technology, capital-intensive industries such as those producing machinery expanded, but simpler manufacturing operations such as food processing and clothing manufacture declined, unable to compete with cheaper imports, mainly from Asia.

Sources of foreign investment capital in Thailand, 1985–87

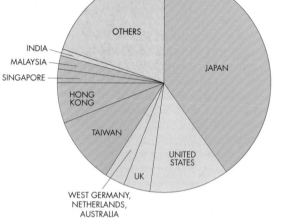

Shoe production is a relatively straightforward industrial process in which South-east Asian nations gained an increased proportion of world market in the 1980s (see pie diagram left). Taiwan is the largest exporter: 744 million pairs in 1987.[5] Western production has declined as major manufacturers such as Nike and Reebok have moved production to South-east Asia. Taiwan and Hong Kong are increasingly subcontracting less sophisticated product lines to a second generation of newly industrializing nations, including Thailand, Malaysia, Indonesia and the Philippines.

The comparative advantage of one trading bloc over another is a constant source of friction in international trade. The undermining of textile industries in the European Community and North America has led to calls for 'home' industries to be increasingly 'protected' from cheaper imports. Although Western industrialized countries appear to be forceful advocates of free trade, it is claimed that 'while the gospel of liberal trade is spreading, its apostles are sinning more grievously'.[6] During the 1980s, 'protective' measures such as quotas, subsidies and anti-dumping measures increased, to the extent that developing countries lost almost as much revenue as they received through official development aid.[7]

In the 1990s, there is growing evidence of three regional trading blocs: the Americas, East and South-east Asia and Europe. The Asian success stories (dominated by Japan) are likely to more than hold their own and provide important investments for other countries in the region (see chart of investments in Thailand above). Latin American industrial effort will be linked to debt arrangements and the formation of a pan-American trading bloc. Sub-Saharan Africa, however, falls outside all of the major regional groupings.

Net employment gains and losses in the USA as a result of trade with developing countries, 1983

World shoe production by region, 1978 and 1987

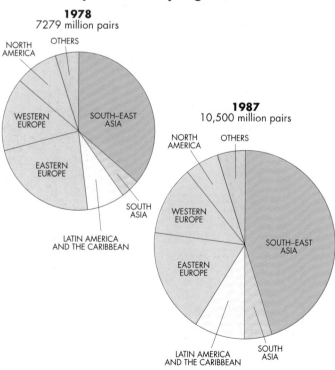

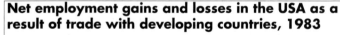

Manufacturing production: value and growth rate

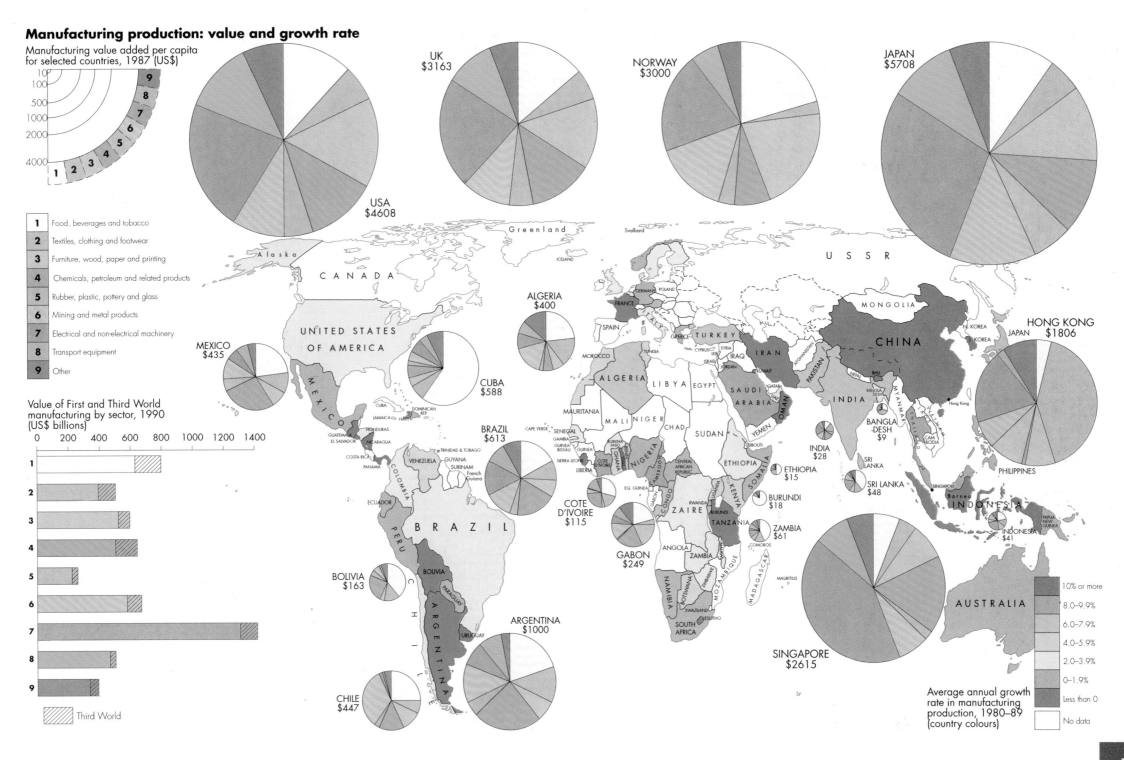

Manufacturing value added per capita for selected countries, 1987 (US$)

10
100
500
1000
2000
4000

1 Food, beverages and tobacco
2 Textiles, clothing and footwear
3 Furniture, wood, paper and printing
4 Chemicals, petroleum and related products
5 Rubber, plastic, pottery and glass
6 Mining and metal products
7 Electrical and non-electrical machinery
8 Transport equipment
9 Other

Value of First and Third World manufacturing by sector, 1990 (US$ billions)

0   200   400   600   800   1000 1200 1400

1
2
3
4
5
6
7
8
9

Third World

USA $4608
UK $3163
NORWAY $3000
JAPAN $5708

MEXICO $435
ALGERIA $400
CUBA $588
HONG KONG $1806

BRAZIL $613
BOLIVIA $163
COTE D'IVOIRE $115
GABON $249
ETHIOPIA $15
BURUNDI $18
ZAMBIA $61
INDIA $28
SRI LANKA $48
BANGLA-DESH $9
INDONESIA $41

ARGENTINA $1000
CHILE $447
SINGAPORE $2615

Average annual growth rate in manufacturing production, 1980–89 (country colours)

10% or more
8.0–9.9%
6.0–7.9%
4.0–5.9%
2.0–3.9%
0–1.9%
Less than 0
No data

Agriculture remains the chief source of income for most people in developing countries. The map (top right) on the opposite page shows the percentage of the economically active population dependent on agriculture. Although a very small proportion of the population in developed countries depends on agriculture for a living, OECD countries produce the largest share of the world's food (see pie diagrams below). Even though many millions of people are undernourished, the west in general and Europe, in particular, produces food surplus to requirements. At the end of the 1990s the European Community amassed a surplus of over 16 million tonnes of grain, one and a half million tonnes of butter and 620,000 tonnes of beef.[8]

The value of agricultural production per worker varies greatly between continents. In 1988, output per worker in industrialized countries was valued at US$23,300; in Latin America and the Caribbean $2704, in Sub-Saharan Africa $510 and in China just $228. The histogram (right) contrasts the average cereal yields, fertilizer consumption and tractor usage of selected countries. The UK is typical of western European countries in that it has high yields, high fertilizer inputs and a high level of mechanization. An analysis reveals some interesting comparisons: 28 kg of cereal are produced

Regional shares of world food production, 1987–88 (proportions of world totals)

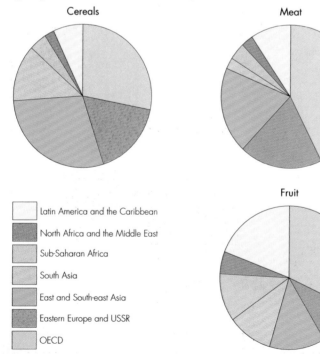

Cereals

Meat

Fruit

- Latin America and the Caribbean
- North Africa and the Middle East
- Sub-Saharan Africa
- South Asia
- East and South-east Asia
- Eastern Europe and USSR
- OECD

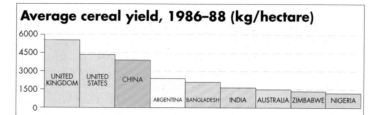

Average cereal yield, 1986–88 (kg/hectare)

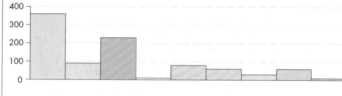

Fertilizer consumption of arable land, 1987–88 (kg per hectare of arable land)

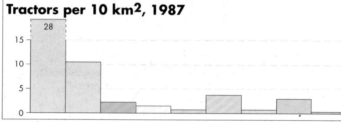

Tractors per 10 km², 1987

from each kilogram of fertilizer in Bangladesh while in the UK the figure is below 16 kg. Similarly, although the UK has 280 times as many tractors per unit land area as Nigeria, output per tractor in Nigeria is 60 times greater.

The examples above demonstrate that although Third World production systems such as subsistence farming and pastoralism may look unproductive compared with agriculture in temperate regions, they are often remarkably efficient when comparing energy inputs and returns. Furthermore, modern farming methods of wide-scale land clearance, mono-cropping and mechanization have often proved unsustainable in the environments of developing countries, and cannot be considered a passport to increased production.

The graph on the right shows the relationship between food grain production and population growth in India since the Second World War. In 1950 the population of India was 350 million; 40 years later it was 850 million. The most important line on the graph is the one which shows per capita food grain production. The amount of cereal produced per person changed little between 1950 and 1981. The graph also shows that in the mid-1960s India experienced a near-famine situation. In response to this grain shortage, India embarked on a now legendary programme of introducing new

high-yielding varieties of rice and wheat, which has come to be known as the green revolution. Together with irrigation and chemical fertilizers the new high-yielding varieties resulted in a steady increase in food grain production per head over the next five years. Unfortunately this success was limited to the more affluent farmers who could afford all the necessary inputs. Improved production was confined to the north-western states of India, and to rice and wheat, rather than other important food crops like beans and pulses.

In the 1990s new scientific methods of manipulating the genetic make-up of plants and animals are creating a potential 'biotechnological revolution' in agriculture. Plant scientists are now able to take specific genetic features from one organism and place them in another. Although developing countries contain the areas of natural vegetation with the largest pool of genetic material, only large biotechnology companies can afford the huge investments needed for research.

In the nineteenth century Europe underwent a remarkable transformation. As the industrial revolution transformed society, fewer people produced more agricultural output. The decline was accompanied by an exodus of 40 million people to the newly settled territories of North and South America, Australia and southern Africa. Until the 1960s it was widely held that developing countries would undergo a similar structural transformation of society. The map opposite (middle right) shows that this has not been so. In nearly

India: grain production and population growth, 1949–81

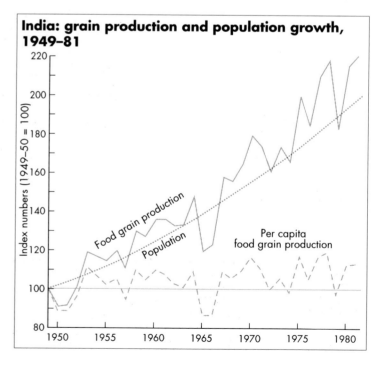

all of Africa and South Asia, the absolute numbers of people reliant on agriculture increased in the 1980s, in many cases by over 25%.

The map below is a 'proportional base' map where the size of each country is proportional to population. The inset grids are proportional to the total amount of cultivated land. Mauritania, for example, is a very large country, more than four times the area of the UK. Only a small part of Mauritania, however, is cultivated, not enough to show up on the map. Nevertheless, Mauritania's small population means that in terms of cultivated land per person it is in the same range as the UK.

In the 1970s and 1980s, in both developing and developed countries, protected areas of outstanding flora and fauna increased. The map (bottom right) shows the percentage of land excluded from general commercial exploitation. It is now recognized that, as well as their intrinsic value, areas protected from logging and mechanized agriculture have a valuable role in maintaining the environment, supporting a tourist industry and providing an on-going livelihood for local people. In many countries over 10% of land has been protected, yet some countries with unique environmental heritages still have no protected sites, including Jamaica, Laos and Burundi.

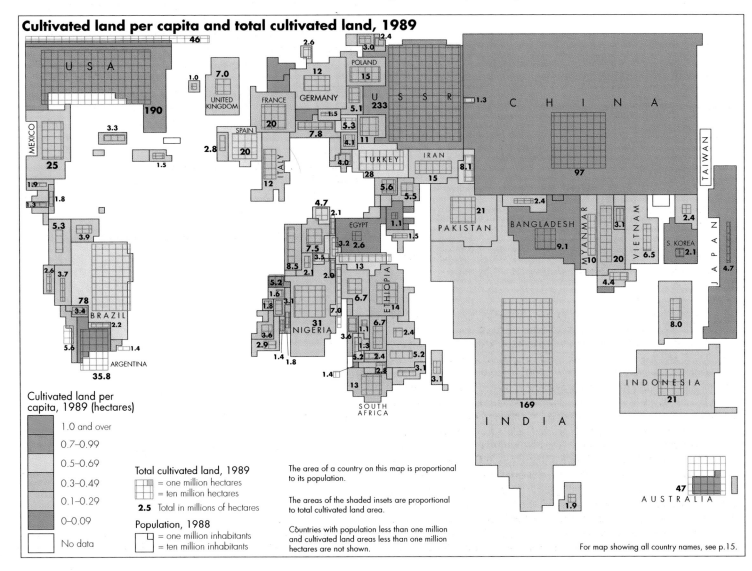

Cultivated land per capita and total cultivated land, 1989

Cultivated land per capita, 1989 (hectares)
- 1.0 and over
- 0.7–0.99
- 0.5–0.69
- 0.3–0.49
- 0.1–0.29
- 0–0.09
- No data

Total cultivated land, 1989
- = one million hectares
- = ten million hectares
- 2.5 Total in millions of hectares

Population, 1988
- = one million inhabitants
- = ten million inhabitants

The area of a country on this map is proportional to its population.

The areas of the shaded insets are proportional to total cultivated land area.

Countries with population less than one million and cultivated land areas less than one million hectares are not shown.

For map showing all country names, see p.15.

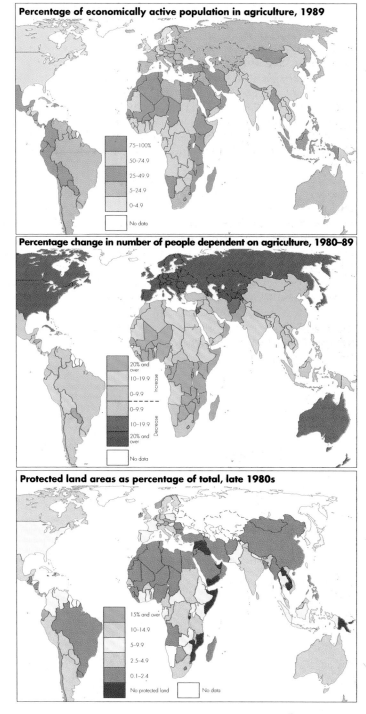

Percentage of economically active population in agriculture, 1989
- 75–100%
- 50–74.9
- 25–49.9
- 5–24.9
- 0–4.9
- No data

Percentage change in number of people dependent on agriculture, 1980–89
- 20% and over / 10–19.9 / 0–9.9 (Increase)
- 0–9.9 / 10–19.9 / 20% and over (Decrease)
- No data

Protected land areas as percentage of total, late 1980s
- 15% and over
- 10–14.9
- 5–9.9
- 2.5–4.9
- 0.1–2.4
- No protected land
- No data

Entitlement Curtin with endowment.

Hunger and famine have always been a part of human history. The map opposite shows the extent of deaths from starvation throughout the world this century. Despite the ubiquity of famine, its causes are still often misunderstood. Perhaps the most enduring fallacy is the Malthusian view that famines are a positive check on population arising from natural disasters in societies where food production lags behind population growth. Indian experience refutes this hypothesis. Between 1951 and 1991 India's population grew from 360 to 860 million, yet food production kept pace with population growth and the country has witnessed its longest period without significant famine. Many developing countries are food exporters, yet it is farming families who are malnourished. Famine and hunger do not just happen, they affect specific social groups at particular times and are avoidable.

Hunger, in its chronic form, refers to sustained nutritional deprivation. Unlike famine it is common among certain groups in most Third World countries. The map on the opposite page shows food availability per capita. This indicator does not, however, take into account the crucial question of how food is distributed within societies. Using India as an example again, UNICEF reported in 1989 that some three and a half million children died from the debilitating effects of malnutrition and disease. Yet India has grain reserves of 20 million tons. The problem is not a shortage of food, but one of poverty, which prevents people from buying the food available.

Famine is understood as acute starvation associated with a sharp increase in mortality. In the last two decades the Sahelian countries have experienced both widespread hunger and periodic food crisis (see map opposite). Natural causes are frequently cited as the sole contributors to famine but, more often than not, a natural event such as rain failure is only the final trigger for famine. In the late 1980s drought conditions occurred in the USA and Australia, causing significant reductions in cereal production. Yet while many farmers lost their businesses, the population of these countries experienced neither hunger nor famine. In the West, unlike the Sahel, most farmers had formal insurance against losses and received State assistance, while consumers' demands were met through accumulated stockpiles.

Food systems and their failure (which may result in famine) can be seen as consisting of four elements:

The market enables producers to sell their products or their labour in exchange for other commodities. The Great Bengal Famine of 1943–44 is a good example of a man-made famine. As a result of war and price speculation by rice traders, the cost of the basic staple was driven beyond the reach of the poor. One and a half million people died. In the Sahel pastoralist producers are 'twice hit' in times of crisis. As the unmitigated effect of drought takes place herders are

forced to sell their stock. It is a buyers' market. More livestock enters the market, so prices go down. Conversely, as more pastoralists become reliant on grain for survival the market price rises.

Nutritional deprivation can follow from market speculation, the forcible settlement of pastoral communities, or a decline in producer prices. Famines may occur when one mechanism, such as agricultural prices, breaks down completely and is not compensated by other support mechanisms, such as state intervention or the pooling of community resources.

The community. This term encompasses both relations within social groups in any given community and those between one community and another. The relationships between landowners and landless labourers are particularly important in determining access to food. In addition a common denominator in many recent famines has been civil war (Ethiopia, Sudan, Somalia, Angola and Mozambique).

War is often the ultimate breakdown in the relationship between competing communities. The effects of such conflicts are a disruption of agriculture, transport and service networks and a diversion of scarce resources to produce weapons of destruction.

The state has been responsible for providing services and infrastructure in exchange for taxes on production and consumption. State policies can alleviate potential famine situations or aggravate them. In Ethiopia in 1973 Haile Salassie denied the existence of famine, for fear that it would harm the tourist industry; one million people died. In China, during the Great Leap Forward (1959–61), communes came under pressure to fabricate production targets. Shortfalls caused by poor weather were not acknowledged, or acted upon. As many as 25 million people died.

The environment rarely causes famines by itself. Even the worst natural disasters only lead to famine if exacerbated by other elements. For example, in 1974 floods covered nearly half of Bangladesh. Stockpiles of rice, controlled by the government, were not made available to flood victims, but exported to India instead. Repeated shortages of rain in the Sahel over the last two decades have undoubtedly exacerbated the problem of providing all its people with food and a means of earning a living.

The international economy often has direct relevance to hunger and famine. Farmers throughout the developing world have become increasingly dependent upon world rather than local markets. Cash crop production *per se* does not cause famine but it may aggravate nutritional deprivation if scarce resources are being diverted away from food production towards crops for export.

A particularly useful concept in understanding famine is the different entitlement of social groups to food. Entitlement[9] is the

command that people can exert over goods in two ways: by using their own resources in direct production; and/or by using their labour or produce to buy and sell on the market. This concept captures the combined effect of owning resources and being able to use them, in production or in trade, to gain access to food and other goods. Agricultural societies are highly differentiated: some people own land; some work as labourers; some provide services. A crisis such as rain failure may be catastrophic for one group (such as landless farm workers) but beneficial for others (merchants selling grain or buying cheap land). An increase in the price of basic foods relative to wages can be as devastating as a natural disaster (see graph of the 1974 Bangladesh famine below). Repeated famines may permanently change social relationships. The livelihoods of the poor may become more marginal, ultimately resulting in destitution and migration.

An understanding of the multiple causes of famine may shed some light on the best policies for their alleviation. Improved entitlement to food may be achieved through agrarian reform, increased employment, promotion of local organizations or the establishment of small-scale lending banks. The state has a role in providing technical support for agriculture and making food stocks available to those who need it most in deficit years.

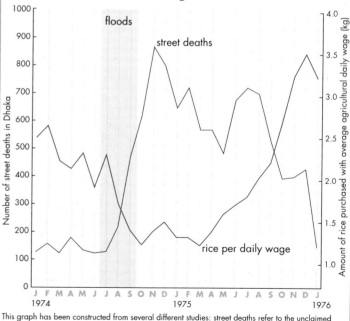

Relationship between rice prices, agricultural wages and deaths in Bangladesh, 1974–75

This graph has been constructed from several different studies: street deaths refer to the unclaimed bodies collected by the Muslim burial society in Dhaka, agricultural wages are based on those of agricultural labourers at Gopalganji Faridpur.

Famines, 1900-91, and dietary energy supply per capita, 1988

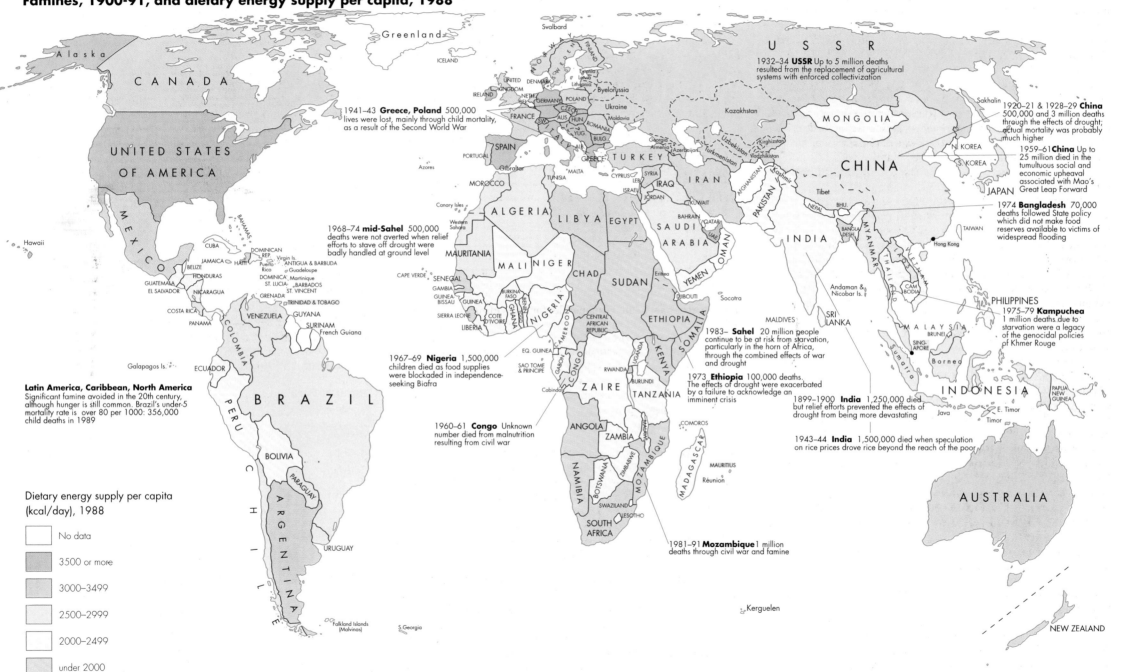

1932–34 USSR Up to 5 million deaths resulted from the replacement of agricultural systems with enforced collectivization

1941–43 Greece, Poland 500,000 lives were lost, mainly through child mortality, as a result of the Second World War

1920–21 & 1928–29 China 500,000 and 3 million deaths through the effects of drought; actual mortality was probably much higher

1959–61 China Up to 25 million died in the tumultuous social and economic upheaval associated with Mao's Great Leap Forward

1974 Bangladesh 70,000 deaths followed State policy which did not make food reserves available to victims of widespread flooding

1968–74 mid-Sahel 500,000 deaths were not averted when relief efforts to stave off drought were badly handled at ground level

1967–69 Nigeria 1,500,000 children died as food supplies were blocked in independence-seeking Biafra

1983– Sahel 20 million people continue to be at risk from starvation, particularly in the horn of Africa, through the combined effects of war and drought

1973 Ethiopia 100,000 deaths. The effects of drought were exacerbated by a failure to acknowledge an imminent crisis

PHILIPPINES

1975–79 Kampuchea 1 million deaths due to starvation were a legacy of the genocidal policies of Khmer Rouge

1899–1900 India 1,250,000 died but relief efforts prevented the effects of drought from being more devastating

1943–44 India 1,500,000 died when speculation on rice prices drove rice beyond the reach of the poor

1960–61 Congo Unknown number died from malnutrition resulting from civil war

Latin America, Caribbean, North America Significant famine avoided in the 20th century, although hunger is still common. Brazil's under-5 mortality rate is over 80 per 1000: 356,000 child deaths in 1989

1981–91 Mozambique 1 million deaths through civil war and famine

Dietary energy supply per capita (kcal/day), 1988

- No data
- 3500 or more
- 3000–3499
- 2500–2999
- 2000–2499
- under 2000

55

At the end of the 1980s an estimated 50 million deaths occurred in the world each year. Although mortality rates in both First and Third World are about 9.9 per 1000, the ages at which deaths occur are markedly different. In developed countries two-thirds of all deaths occur among those over 65, whereas in developing countries 40% of deaths are of children under 15 years old; i.e. ten times as many as in developed countries (see also pp.58–59).

The graph below shows the general improvement in life expectancy for all regions of the world between 1960 and 1990. The map opposite shows life expectancy for each country of the world. In the late 1980s life expectancy for 24 countries (21 of them African) was still below 50 years.

The pie diagrams on the right show the causes of death in developed and developing countries. A major difference is that infectious and parasitic diseases are the chief killers in the Third World, while in developed counties half of all deaths are due to circulatory diseases.

Over two billion people, the vast majority in developing countries, are at risk from malaria; every year between one and two million die. Nutritional anaemia is estimated to affect between 30 and 50% of all women in Africa and Asia. Trachoma, a chronic eye infection, is endemic amongst 500 million people in the Third World, and is estimated to have permanently blinded at least six million.

Acquired immune deficiency syndrome (AIDS) is likely to be a central health problem for many Third World countries in the 1990s and beyond. Difficulties in diagnosing AIDS in developing countries mean that official figures of its incidence are likely to be inaccurate. The World Health Organization estimates that in 1990 8.8 million people had the HIV virus, which leads to AIDS, and that 5.8 million

Distribution of deaths in developed and developing countries by cause, 1985

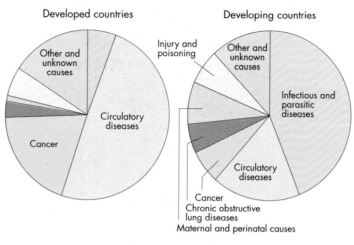

of these were in Sub-Saharan Africa; by the year 2000 they estimate that these figures will have risen to 26 million and 12 million, respectively.[10]

The relative importance accorded to health care varies widely in national budgets (see symbols on map). In the late 1980s Scandinavian countries devoted up to 8% of their GNPs to health care; in Somalia and Uganda the figure was just 0.2%. On average in 1987 developing countries spent four times as much money paying interest on debts as they did on health care.

There were also wide global differences in the availability of health service personnel worldwide. Italy has the highest ratio of doctors to people in the world, 1 : 230; Ethiopia has the lowest, one doctor for every 78,970 people. In many countries, particularly in the Middle East and South-east Asia, the ratio of doctors to people has increased greatly in the last three decades, although in some war-torn African countries the situation has deteriorated (see histogram right).

The total number of doctors in a country does not, however, indicate how accessible they are to the population as a whole. India has almost doubled the ratio of doctors to people since the mid-1960s, but currently 80% of practitioners work in cities, while 80% of the population lives in the countryside.

The developing world is often under pressure to buy products from multinational pharmaceutical companies. The WHO has listed 250 essential drugs which are sufficient for virtually all health needs, but the Indian market alone has 65,000 different medicines. The agenda for health research is set by First World companies where per-capita health research is 100 times greater than in the Third

World. Despite the abundance of 'western' medicines many 'tropical' diseases are under-researched. Companies are concerned that resultant treatments could not be afforded by needy populations and hence the return would not be sufficient to warrant the required investment.

Since 1978 most developing countries have embarked on a programme of primary preventive health care. The focus has been on encouraging good health through community action and education for women, rather than merely 'treating' disease. This may also entail giving more recognition to traditional medical practices, which may be far more common than a visit to a hospital. India has over 300,000 practitioners of traditional medicine who receive training at 250 centres. In China 90% of the 10,000 general hospitals have departments of traditional medicine.

Preventive health care, in theory at least, involves creating healthy living environments, through the promotion of good nutrition, safe water, sanitation and child immunization. In reality, many developing countries still put much of their health resources into technologically advanced curative care as exemplified by the practices in western-style hospitals. This means in practice that a very high proportion of health expenditure may go to benefit a small, already privileged, section of the population.

Life expectancy at birth by region, 1960 – 90

Note: Data for East and South-east Asia 1960 include average life expectancy for China for 1963–67

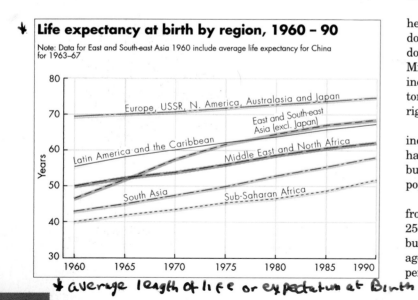

♦ average length of life or expectation at Birth.

Population per doctor for selected countries, 1965 and 1984

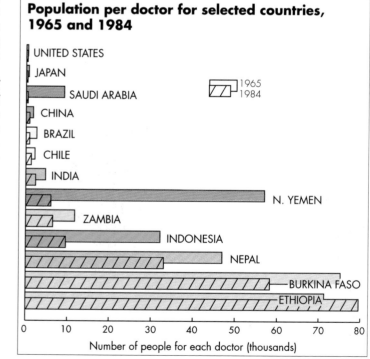

Life expectancy and expenditure on health, late 1980s

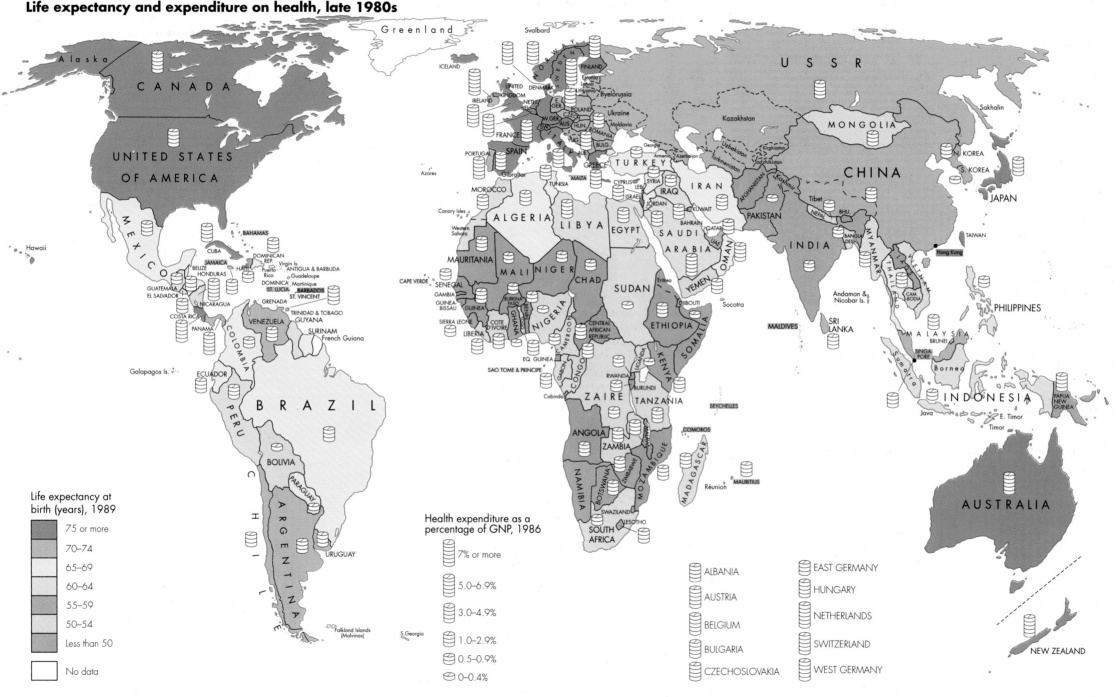

Life expectancy at birth (years), 1989

- 75 or more
- 70–74
- 65–69
- 60–64
- 55–59
- 50–54
- Less than 50
- No data

Health expenditure as a percentage of GNP, 1986

- 7% or more
- 5.0–6.9%
- 3.0–4.9%
- 1.0–2.9%
- 0.5–0.9%
- 0–0.4%

- ALBANIA
- AUSTRIA
- BELGIUM
- BULGARIA
- CZECHOSLOVAKIA
- EAST GERMANY
- HUNGARY
- NETHERLANDS
- SWITZERLAND
- WEST GERMANY

(handwritten: What is meant here? ↑)

Each minute 28 children under five years old die; twenty-seven of these lived in developing countries. For every fatality many more children survive but are underfed, live without shelter or are forced to work for minimal wages.

In September 1990 the governments of 159 countries met at the first World Summit for Children to discuss ways of improving the livelihoods of the next generation. The seven key areas they addressed, which are a useful summary of issues relating to child welfare, are outlined below.

(handwritten: Why is it important? If infant + under 5 is a child it is most likely to be a useful indicator of susceptibility to disease)

Reducing under-five death rates. Currently over 14 million children under five die each year in developing countries. The map opposite is coloured according to under-five mortality. There is a wide variation not only between the First and Third World, but also between developing countries. South Asia has particular contrasts: one in four children die before their fifth birthday in Afghanistan, one in seven in India, but just one in 28 in Sri Lanka.

Although mortality rates are higher in Sahelian Africa, the larger population of South Asia explains why six times as many

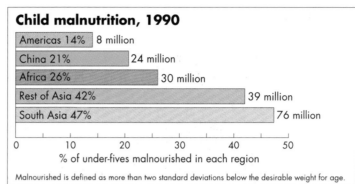

Child malnutrition, 1990

Region	% malnourished	millions
Americas 14%		8 million
China 21%		24 million
Africa 26%		30 million
Rest of Asia 42%		39 million
South Asia 47%		76 million

% of under-fives malnourished in each region

Malnourished is defined as more than two standard deviations below the desirable weight for age.

under-fives die each year in India and Pakistan as in Ethiopia and Sudan.

The pie graphs (below left) show regional trends in child mortality and the chief causes of child deaths. Measles, tetanus, whooping cough, pneumonia and diarrhoea are responsible for 60% of all deaths, yet all are preventable. Diarrhoea alone kills 11,000 children a day, but it can usually be treated with a low-cost mixture of sugar and rehydration salts.

2   Preventing severe and moderate malnutrition among the world's under fives. In 1990 an estimated 177 million children were malnourished. The largest proportion of these children were from South Asia (not Sub-Saharan Africa as is sometimes thought), as shown in the bar chart above. In Africa a quarter of children are malnourished, in South Asia almost half. When China is included, Asia as a whole has three-quarters of the world's under-fed children.

3   Reducing maternal mortality rates. Each year an estimated half a million mothers die from conditions related to childbirth.

4   Safe water and sanitation for all families. In the late 1980s over one-third of rural families in the developing world did not have access to clean water while one-half had inadequate sanitation (see p.21).

5   Basic education for all children. Only a little over half of all children in developing countries complete four years of primary schooling. Gender is important: on average one boy in seven is absent from the classroom, whereas for girls the ratio is one in four (see symbols on the map opposite).

6   Raising adult literacy rates and achieving equal opportunities for women and men. At present 900 million adults worldwide are illiterate, two-thirds of whom are women. For the data used here, the literacy rate is defined as the proportion of the population over the age of 15 who can, with understanding, read and write a short, simple statement on their everyday life. The graph on the right shows the important linkage between female education and child welfare.

7   Protection for the many millions of children in especially difficult circumstances. Worldwide an estimated 80 million children are exploited in the workplace; some 30 million are left to fend for themselves on city streets. Many children are the victims of war: in Africa alone refugee camps are 'home' to seven million children.

The Summit concluded that by the next millennium US$20 billion a year would be necessary to achieve a significant improvement in the livelihoods of children worldwide. Although this figure sounds large, it represents only one eighth of 1% of the world's annual income, or just ten days' military expenditure.

The lives of children are affected not only by health and educational programmes, but also by agricultural practices, the status of women and economic policies. The livelihoods of the next generation depend on trade policies, debt agreements, investment and research. The quality of life for the next generation thus depends on commitments and change in the North as much as the South.

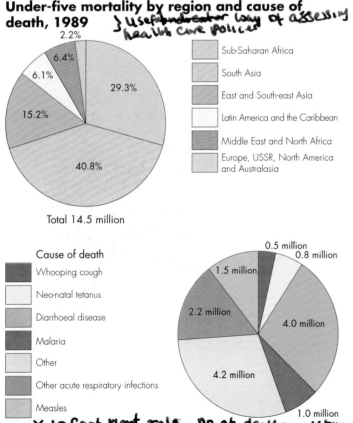

Under-five mortality by region and cause of death, 1989

(handwritten: a useful indicator / way of assessing health care policies)

Total 14.5 million

Cause of death: Whooping cough, Neo-natal tetanus, Diarrhoeal disease, Malaria, Other, Other acute respiratory infections, Measles

*(handwritten: * Infant Mort. rate no of deaths in 1st year of life per 1000 live births. Under 5 mort rate is no of child die before age 5 for every 1000 live birth)*

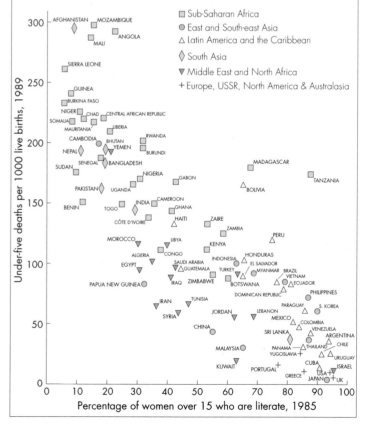

Under-five mortality rates and women's literacy for selected countries, late 1980s

- Sub-Saharan Africa
- East and South-east Asia
- Latin America and the Caribbean
- South Asia
- Middle East and North Africa
- Europe, USSR, North America & Australasia

Under-five deaths per 1000 live births, 1989

Percentage of women over 15 who are literate, 1985

Child under-five mortality rate and primary schooling, late 1980s

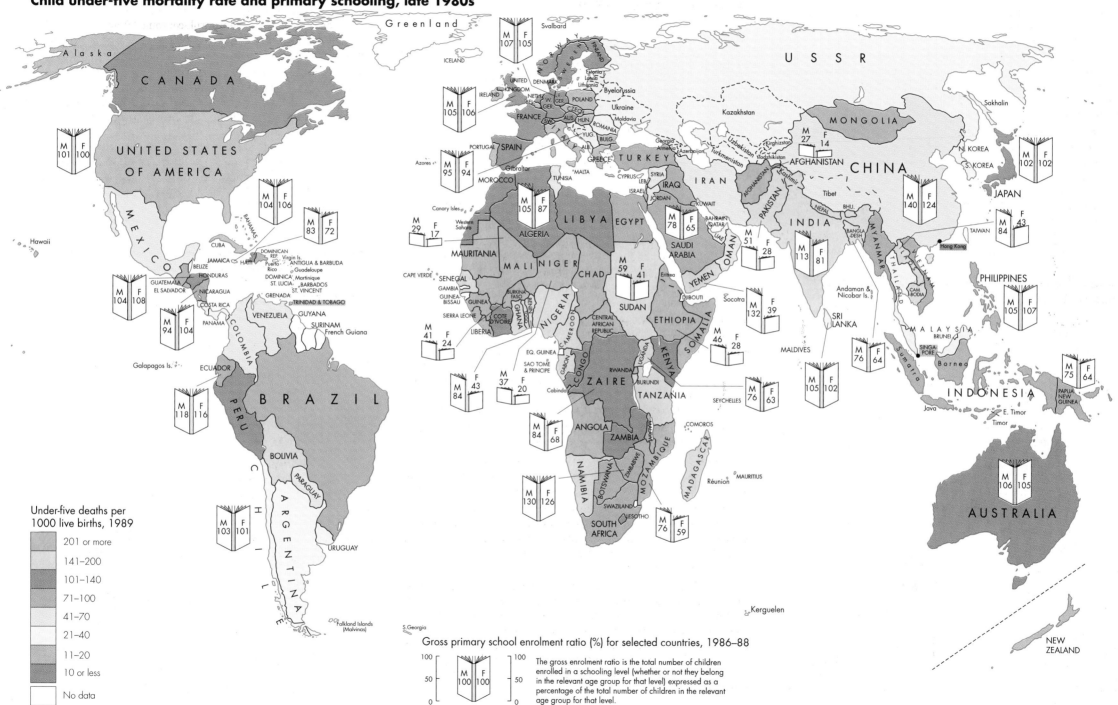

Under-five deaths per 1000 live births, 1989

- 201 or more
- 141–200
- 101–140
- 71–100
- 41–70
- 21–40
- 11–20
- 10 or less
- No data

Gross primary school enrolment ratio (%) for selected countries, 1986–88

The gross enrolment ratio is the total number of children enrolled in a schooling level (whether or not they belong in the relevant age group for that level) expressed as a percentage of the total number of children in the relevant age group for that level.

[Handwritten notes in top margin: "Gender det Soc culture Social relation ♂♀ - Institution form of rel. between ♂♀. Varies between soc include sex div. of lab."]

The UN Declaration of Human Rights of 1948 affirmed the equal rights of men and women. Nearly half a century later, severe gender inequalities persist.

The gap between men and women can been seen in the sketchy and inadequate data available for international cross-comparisons of the situation of women. Gender-differentiated data is particularly difficult to come by in areas such as women's productive roles in their national economies. The lack of data can be attributed to the failure of male 'experts' to conceptualize and account for female economic activity. Women's employment, for example, presents special measurement problems. Many definitions of economic activity do not take into consideration women's work on family farms, or income-generating and reproductive work carried out within the household.

In these two pages we attempt to throw light on some gender issues, bearing in mind the problems of data collection and representation and acknowledging that women are not a homogenous category.

Physical well-being

A widely used indicator for health in global terms is life expectancy. The diagram below (left) shows regional averages for women's life expectancy. The difference between the countries with the highest and the lowest life expectancy for women in 1990 (Japan and Afghanistan) was 38 years. Even then, country averages do not account for internal rural, urban and ethnic differentials. On average women tend to outlive men in the developed countries by about six years. In developing countries, gender differences in life expectancy are narrow. The Third World average in 1990 was 64 for women, 62 for men. In India, Nepal and Pakistan, the difference in life expectancy was in men's favour by an average of two years.

Some factors affecting women's health in the Third World are gender specific. These include poor nutritional status, nutritional anaemia in child-bearing years, pregnancy at an early age, short intervals between births and repeated child bearing. One important measure of women's health is maternal mortality. Serious under-reporting distorts data from some Third World countries but nevertheless the World Health Organization estimates that maternal causes are among the five leading causes of death of women aged

between 15 and 44. The map on this page shows average maternal mortality rates per 100,000 births in 1988.

Women and work

[Handwritten notes: "This explains Sexual div of lab ... of different tasks for ♂♀ Most soc. allocate disproportionate amount to ♀"]

The International Labour Office defines the economically active population as: 'All persons of either sex who furnish the supply of labour for the production of economic goods and services … [The] production of economic goods and services should include all production and processing of primary products whether for market, for barter or for own consumption … the production of all other goods for the market and in the case of households which produce goods and services for the market, the corresponding production for own consumption.'[11] However, data on women's work does not always take into account agricultural work done near the home, on a small-scale, part-time or seasonal basis; production and processing of food for the home; provision of fuel and water for the household; involvement in the informal sector, including markets; piecework contracted to women working at home; or other income-generating activities carried out in the home. So the statistics on which the map opposite (top) is based understate women's contribution to economic activity.

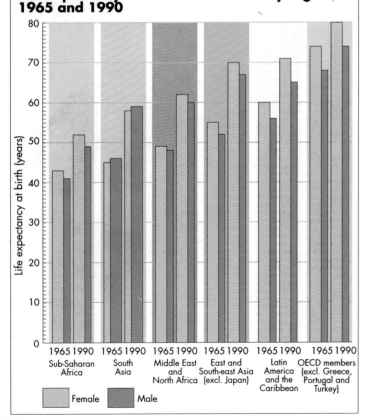

Life expectancy for men and women by region, 1965 and 1990

Life expectancy at birth (years)

	1965	1990
Sub-Saharan Africa		
South Asia		
Middle East and North Africa		
East and South-east Asia (excl. Japan)		
Latin America and the Caribbean		
OECD members (excl. Greece, Portugal and Turkey)		

Female   Male

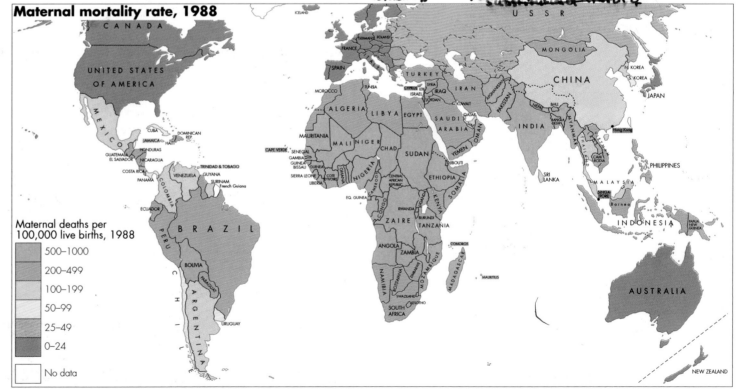

Maternal mortality rate, 1988

Maternal deaths per 100,000 live births, 1988

- 500–1000
- 200–499
- 100–199
- 50–99
- 25–49
- 0–24
- No data

Gender blinds!

Women and education

Education is seen as a vital element for developing human potential. Although many developing countries are committed to the goal of basic education for all, statistics show that they are far from achieving this. Gender-differentiated data reveals that girls and women are generally disadvantaged in relation to boys in many countries.

The disparity in school enrolment between girls and boys was shown on p.59. Another common indicator to gauge women's access to education is the literacy rate. Worldwide literacy rates show large discrepancies, with developed countries having a much higher rate of female literacy than developing countries (see map, bottom right). Furthermore, literacy rates of the world's poorer countries reveal significant gaps between men and women (symbols on the map).

It is now accepted that female education and health are correlated, that female literacy rates have a direct impact on demographic variables such as fertility rates and infant mortality rates. The graph below shows the relationship between female literacy and fertility rates for developing countries. Female education is thus seen as a health issue, a means towards a lower population growth rate and towards achieving other developmental goals as well as an end in itself.

Women's literacy and fertility for selected Third World countries, 1990

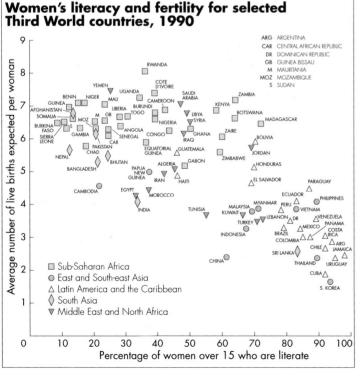

ARG ARGENTINA
CAR CENTRAL AFRICAN REPUBLIC
DR   DOMINICAN REPUBLIC
GB   GUINEA BISSAU
M   MAURITANIA
MOZ MOZAMBIQUE
S   SUDAN

Average number of live births expected per woman (y-axis, 0–9)
Percentage of women over 15 who are literate (x-axis, 0–100)

□ Sub-Saharan Africa
● East and South-east Asia
△ Latin America and the Caribbean
◇ South Asia
▽ Middle East and North Africa

Women in the labour force, 1988–90

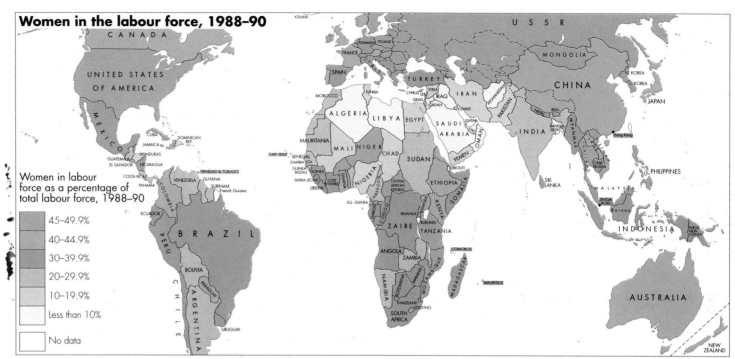

Women in labour force as a percentage of total labour force, 1988–90

- 45–49.9%
- 40–44.9%
- 30–39.9%
- 20–29.9%
- 10–19.9%
- Less than 10%
- No data

Women's literacy and its relation to men's literacy, 1990

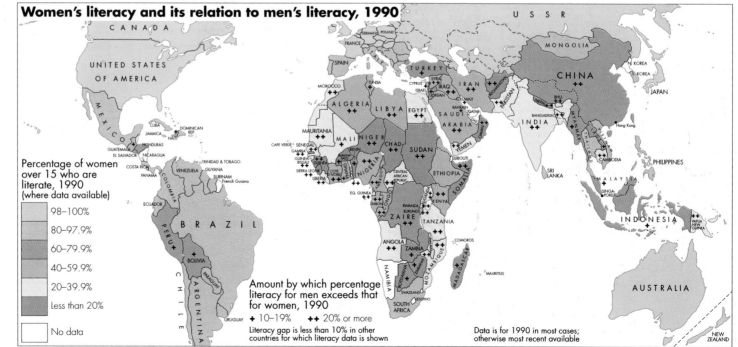

Percentage of women over 15 who are literate, 1990 (where data available)

- 98–100%
- 80–97.9%
- 60–79.9%
- 40–59.9%
- 20–39.9%
- Less than 20%
- No data

Amount by which percentage literacy for men exceeds that for women, 1990
+ 10–19%
++ 20% or more
Literacy gap is less than 10% in other countries for which literacy data is shown

Data is for 1990 in most cases; otherwise most recent available

Concern for the global environment is high on the international political agenda in the 1990s.

Industrialized nations, with a fifth of the world's population, contribute two-thirds of the gases that increase global warming, and emit more than 85% of the chlorofluorocarbon (CFC) gases associated with depletion of the ozone layer (see pie diagram, bottom right). They are also responsible for most of the sulphur dioxide and nitrogen oxide emissions that cause 'acid rain'.

Economic development in the Third World may greatly increase such atmospheric pollution, the regulation of which featured strongly at the UN Conference on Environment and Development (UNCED) at Rio de Janeiro in June 1992. Currently, however, the more significant forms of environmental degradation in the Third World relate to primary commodity production. Production for export or subsistence can lead to over-exploitation of natural resources, and hence problems such as desertification and deforestation.

The map opposite shows how regions at different stages of economic development affect the global environment differently and have different environmental problems: areas affected by acid rain, desertification, deforestation and degradation of the seas are shown.

Acid rain affects large areas, characterized by dead lakes and the gradual destruction of temperate forests. As the map indicates, acid rain is a regional problem, but winds can spread its effects to areas where there are no emissions.

Desertification in the sense of encroachment of sand or irreversible loss of vegetative cover is hard to measure and may occur less than commonly believed. However, widespread over-cultivation of poor

Estimated percentages of world species in tropical forests

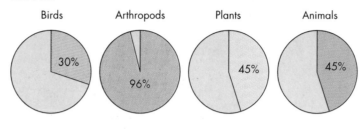

soils, over-grazing by cattle and excessive cutting of fuelwoods have caused a less dramatic gradual deterioration of soils in dryland areas in all continents. A global assessment by the United Nations Environmental Programme (UNEP)[12] estimated that 1.2 billion hectares (about 10% of the earth's vegetated surface) has suffered moderate or severe soil degradation over the 45 years to 1990. UNEP also estimates that an area equivalent to the size of North and South America combined is threatened with desertification.

Deforestation. Tropical moist forests cover an area of about 1.5 billion hectares and are the richest ecosystems in biomass and biodiversity on land. About two-thirds are in Latin America, with the rest split between Africa and Asia. Tropical dryland forests and temperate forests cover similar total areas, but the main concern is with the loss of tropical moist or 'rain' forests. It is estimated that their global rate of clearance increased from 11.4 million hectares per year in the early 1980s to between 17 and 20 million hectares in 1990.[13]

Tropical forests are cleared for a variety of reasons. Felling in Brazil produced 167 million cubic metres (m m³) of timber in 1987, of which 128 m m³ was burnt as fuelwood. Here the causes underlying forest clearance are poverty and landlessness; Brazilian commercial logging accounts for less than 1% both of gross domestic product (GDP) and of export revenues. By contrast, Malaysia produced 42 m m³ in the same year; 36 m m³ was non-fuelwood, of which 75% was exported (see pie diagram, bottom left).

Local problems caused by deforestation include soil erosion and sometimes severe flooding (as in Thailand in November 1988). Long-term global effects may be even more serious. Besides providing hardwood timber and fuelwood, tropical forests produce oxygen and regulate the climate. They also contain around 50% of the world's animal and plant species (see pie diagrams above). Deforestation has already caused the extinction of many species, a loss to global biodiversity. Tropical forests must also contain undiscovered genetic resources of unknown worth for medicine, agriculture and industry. 40% of the world's drugs originate in the wild, but less than 1% of known rainforest plants have been screened for possible medical use.

Environmental degradation of the seas is increasing at an unprecedented rate, through oil pollution, industrial waste dumping, over-exploitation of its resources and other causes. Coral reefs, with nearly one-third of all fish species, are a sensitive indicator of the state of the seas. The map opposite shows the large areas of coral reef under threat, due in part to blast fishing and tourism. In many countries coral is also smothered by silt, often due to deforestation inland, after which soil is washed down rivers into the sea and out to the reefs.

Sustainable development

The UN World Commission on Environment and Development (the Brundtland Commission)[14] defined sustainable development as 'development which meets the needs of the present without compromising the ability of future generations to meet their own needs'. It also provided clear evidence linking poverty, environmental degradation in Third World countries and the structure of the world economy. In many Third World economies people have no choice but to destroy their natural endowments to survive. At a national level, increased production of primary products may be required to repay debts, especially when world prices decrease.

So far there are few examples of international cooperation aimed at counteracting the tendency of the world economy to work against environmental concerns. One is the Montreal Protocol, which aims at eliminating CFC manufacture completely by the year 2000. However, concerted international action on the other problems outlined here lags well behind the rhetoric.

Production of tropical timber in Brazil and Malaysia, 1987 (million m³)

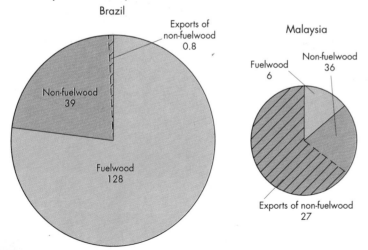

Production of CFC gases by world regions, 1984 (tonnes)

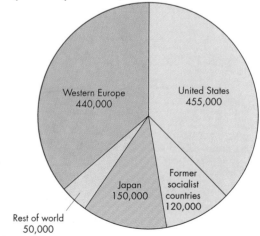

Environmental degradation at land and sea

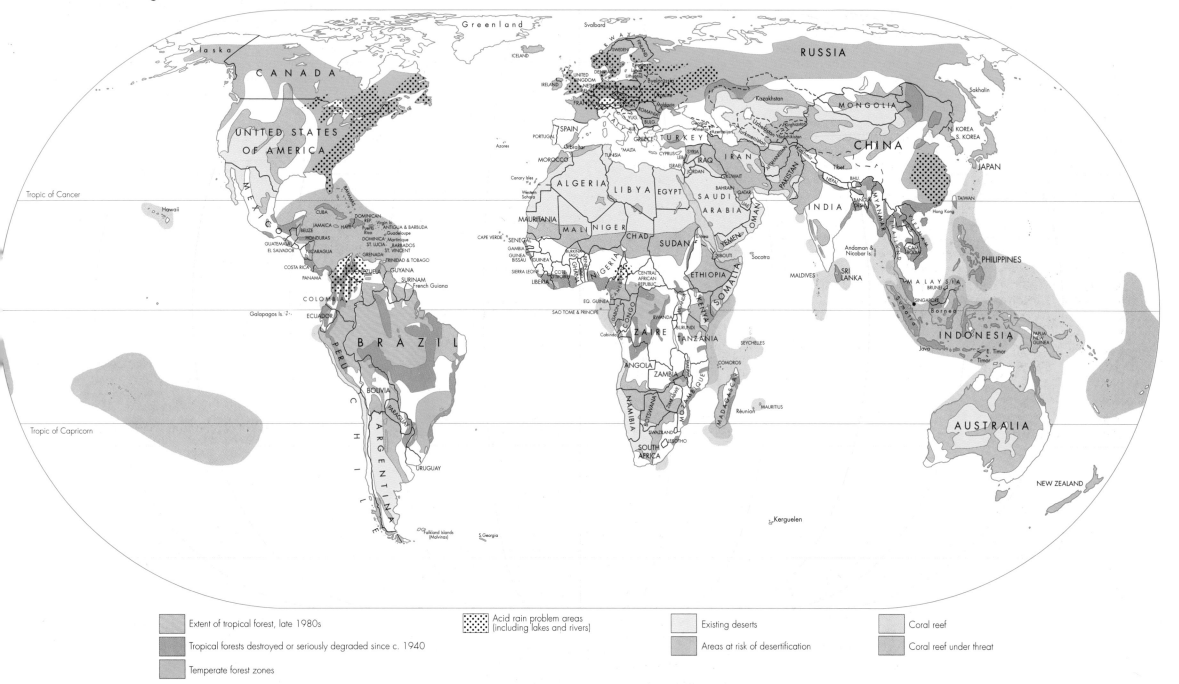

Legend:

- Extent of tropical forest, late 1980s
- Tropical forests destroyed or seriously degraded since c. 1940
- Temperate forest zones
- Acid rain problem areas (including lakes and rivers)
- Existing deserts
- Areas at risk of desertification
- Coral reef
- Coral reef under threat

Third World military expenditure accounts for less than 15% of the world total.[15] However, between 1965 and the mid-1980s it increased faster than that in Western countries and accounted for a greater proportion of gross domestic product (GDP) (on average over 4%), exacerbating economic problems for impoverished societies and preventing resource transfers to areas such as health and education.

The growth in military expenditure in the South began in the 1950s and 1960s when the birth of new Third World states coincided with an unfolding Cold War between the superpowers (see p.47). Throughout this period the USA and the USSR transferred vast quantities of defence equipment to Third World regions. Conflicts fought within and between developing countries became proxy battles between the superpowers. Politically, institutionally and technically, the armed forces of the recipient countries became locked into a dependent relationship with the supplier countries. Breaking those dependent links, as Egypt did in the 1960s and 1970s, was not impossible but extremely difficult and expensive.

Domestically, the military established an influential political base in many developing countries. The map opposite illustrates the experience of many developing countries of 'military rule'.

In the 1970s, after the first oil-price rise, an increase in credit to developing countries facilitated a leap in Third World arms imports. For OECD economies, arms export was a means of recycling petro-dollars and maintaining industrial output despite the threat of recession. Arms sales to the Third World remained buoyant until the mid-1980s. At the end of the 1980s, despite the occurrence or continuation of several major conflicts (Southern Africa, Central America), arms sales to the Third World began to decline. After the end of Cold War hostilities, industrialized countries reduced their

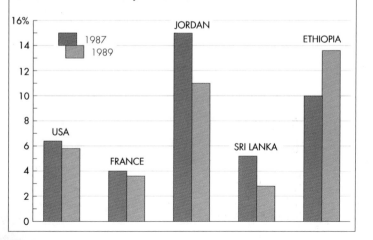

Military expenditure as a percentage of GDP for selected countries, 1987–89

Public expenditure on military, education and health by major arms importers as a percentage of GNP, 1960–88

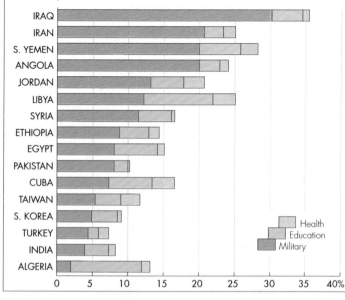

total military spending from a peak of US$838 billion in 1987 to $762 billion in 1990. The potential for resource transfers is high. A 1% reduction in US military expenditure could increase American overseas development aid by 40%; whether this occurs is a matter of political choice.

Although developing countries also reduced military expenditure from a peak of $155 billion in 1984 to $123 billion in 1990, they did so for different reasons. Faced with chronic recession, indebtedness and foreign exchange shortages they could no longer afford the rising cost of defence. The only regions where military spending has not yet started to decline are also the poorest: South Asia and Sub-Saharan Africa.

Military expenditure and its cost can be measured in different ways: in terms of public wealth spent annually, per capita or cumulatively over a period. The bar chart (bottom left) shows this expenditure as a percentage of GDP for selected First and Third World countries; the bar chart above illustrates the big differences in relative expenditure on military, health and education between different Third World arms importers. Since military expenditure, unlike that on education, health and infrastructure, is not 'wealth' producing, the economic burden is cumulative. Even a small but steady use of productive assets for 'unproductive' military hardware becomes a major loss over time. The pie diagrams show the vast sums spent by Third World regions in the past two decades and the income gained by, especially, the two superpowers during the same period.

The map opposite depicts major on-going armed conflicts in the world, as well as selectively revealing their cost in human life. Most contemporary wars take place within or between developing countries. The international community has responded by setting up UN peacekeeping missions, listed opposite up to early 1992, either to monitor a truce or ceasefire or to administer the process of conflict resolution as in Cambodia.

Values of imports of major weapons by Third World region, 1971–90 (cumulative in US$ million)

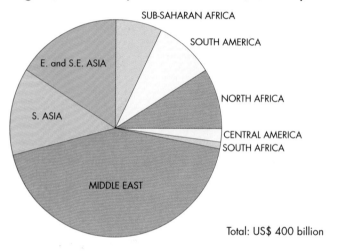

Total: US$ 400 billion

Values of exports of major weapons to Third World regions, by supplier, 1971–90 (cumulative in US$ million)

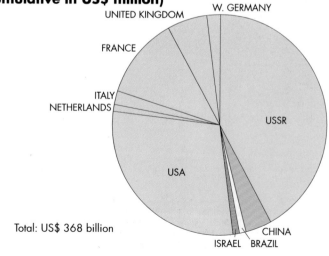

Total: US$ 368 billion

Military governments, armed conflicts and UN peacekeeping, early 1990s

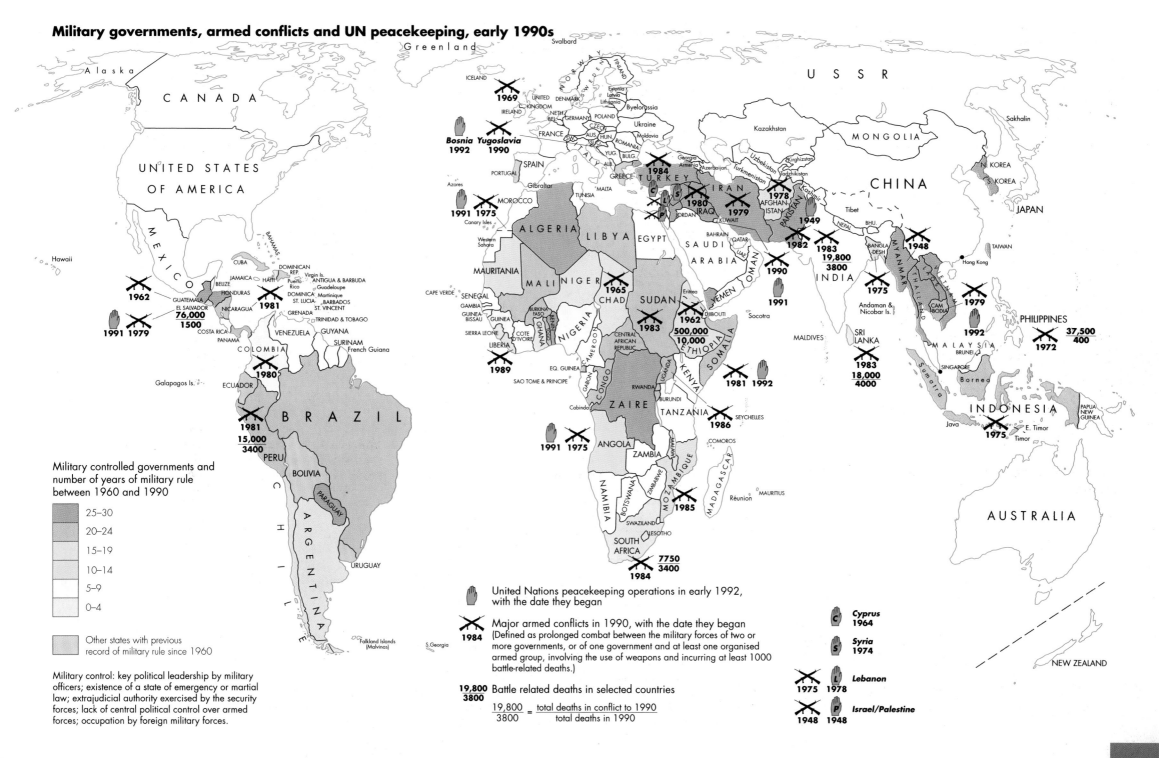

Military controlled governments and number of years of military rule between 1960 and 1990

- 25–30
- 20–24
- 15–19
- 10–14
- 5–9
- 0–4

Other states with previous record of military rule since 1960

Military control: key political leadership by military officers; existence of a state of emergency or martial law; extrajudicial authority exercised by the security forces; lack of central political control over armed forces; occupation by foreign military forces.

United Nations peacekeeping operations in early 1992, with the date they began

1984 Major armed conflicts in 1990, with the date they began (Defined as prolonged combat between the military forces of two or more governments, or of one government and at least one organised armed group, involving the use of weapons and incurring at least 1000 battle-related deaths.)

19,800
3800 Battle related deaths in selected countries

$$\frac{19,800}{3800} = \frac{\text{total deaths in conflict to 1990}}{\text{total deaths in 1990}}$$

C Cyprus 1964

S Syria 1974

L Lebanon 1975 1978

P Israel/Palestine 1948 1948

The UN Population Monitoring Report identifies six main flows of international migration in the 1980s. The first five are flows of international labour or economic migration and are summarized on the map opposite. Patterns and statistics for these flows reflect the trends of an interdependent world economy. The sixth, shown on the map on this page, is the flow of refugees, those who cross international borders as a result of conflict, disaster or fear for personal safety. In this case the figures fail to indicate the political, environmental and social causes underlying the displacement and dislocation of populations and the human suffering involved.

The five flows of international labour migration are:

1   Permanent migration to Australia, New Zealand, Canada and the USA. The pie charts on the map opposite show the total number and origins of such immigrants. The immigration policies of these countries are geared towards attracting, among others, young highly skilled labour and entrepreneurs, well endowed with capital, from the Third World. Statistical data on the capital and brain drain from the Third World is very hard to obtain.

2   Flow of 'temporary' labour to countries of Western Europe. This is reported to have stabilized in the 1980s.

3   Flow of labour from the Third World to the oil-producing countries of the Middle East. Remittances from workers' wages can be significant for the national economies of certain South and South-east Asian and North-east African countries of origin.

4   Migration in Africa. The sizeable population flows between African countries are poorly documented. In West Africa, Côte d'Ivoire and Nigeria have large immigrant populations; countries of origin include Burkina Faso, and Ghana. During the 1980s, Lesotho remained the largest supplier of labour to South Africa, followed by Mozambique.

5   Migration from Latin America and the Caribbean. Host countries include the USA, Argentina and Venezuela; Mexico, Colombia, Chile and Paraguay are countries of origin.

Another important type of economic migration, not included by definition in these five flows, is **rural–urban migration** within national boundaries. The cities with squatter settlements shown on the map opposite are one indication of this movement.

Refugees

The total number of refugees in the world increased by 75% between 1980 and 1989, from 8.5 million to almost 15 million, or 17 million if Palestinian refugees are included (see map on this page). Of these, 87% found asylum in developing countries. The impact of a large refugee population on the economy of a poor host country may be considerable.

A combination of successive droughts and civil strife has resulted in a large concentration of refugees in the north-east of Africa. Some

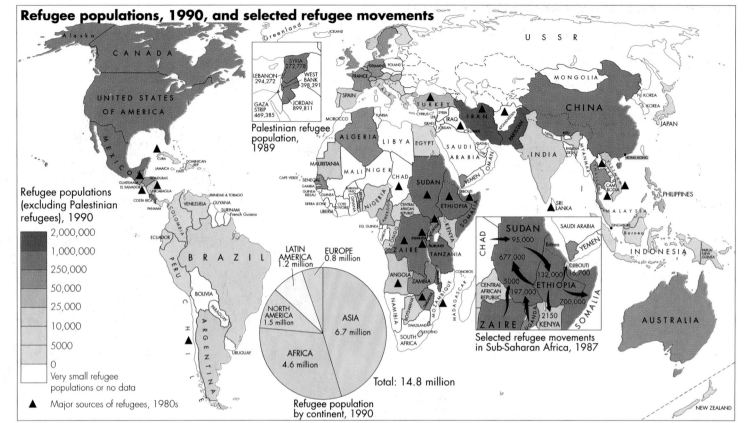

Refugee populations, 1990, and selected refugee movements

Palestinian refugee population, 1989
LEBANON 294,272
SYRIA 272,778
WEST BANK 398,391
GAZA STRIP 469,385
JORDAN 899,811

Refugee populations (excluding Palestinian refugees), 1990
2,000,000
1,000,000
250,000
50,000
25,000
10,000
5000
0
Very small refugee populations or no data
▲ Major sources of refugees, 1980s

Selected refugee movements in Sub-Saharan Africa, 1987
SUDAN 95,000
677,000
132,000
16,700
5000
197,000
2150
700,000

Refugee population by continent, 1990
LATIN AMERICA 1.2 million
EUROPE 0.8 million
NORTH AMERICA 1.5 million
ASIA 6.7 million
AFRICA 4.6 million
Total: 14.8 million

African countries have simultaneous inflows and outflows of refugees (see map). In fact, the same people may cross and re-cross the same border repeatedly, fleeing successively from different versions of repression or conflict. For example, between 1989 and early 1993 some groups may have crossed the Sudan–Ethiopia border five times. Over long periods, this means that the identification of large numbers of people with their 'original' – or any – nation-state becomes uncertain, and the integrity of the nation-state itself is weakened as a result.

However, it is Asia, not Africa, which continues to be the region hosting the largest number of refugees, more than five million of whom are Afghan refugees in Pakistan and Iran.

A note of caution: these maps and data are based on official statistics, which are only an indicator of the number of displaced people around the world. They do not include populations displaced by war, famine or civil conflict within their own countries, which may be very large. For example, in early 1993 some estimates put the numbers of internally displaced people in camps around Khartoum in Sudan as high as two million.

Official figures also do not include returning refugees, who can pose equally serious problems for what is technically these populations' 'home' country. In the 1980s, there were major repatriations, among others, in Zimbabwe, some Central American countries and Uganda. In the 1990s, there may be large-scale repatriations in Eritrea, Afghanistan and any site of ongoing conflict that may be 'solved'.

Although maps of international population movements may not look very different in the mid-1990s, this will probably hide several important new trends which are likely to intensify:

- The potential for an influx of refugees into Western Europe is much increased, particularly since there are now conflicts in former Yugoslavia and some ex-Soviet republics.

- Borders of richer countries are increasingly closed to refugees as well as to labour force movements; human rights which have previously protected refugees are being eroded.

- There is a tendency to discourage international movements by policing borders more heavily and by creating so-called 'safe zones' in war-torn countries (e.g. Somalia, Iraq, Bosnia).

Labour flow and international migration, 1980s

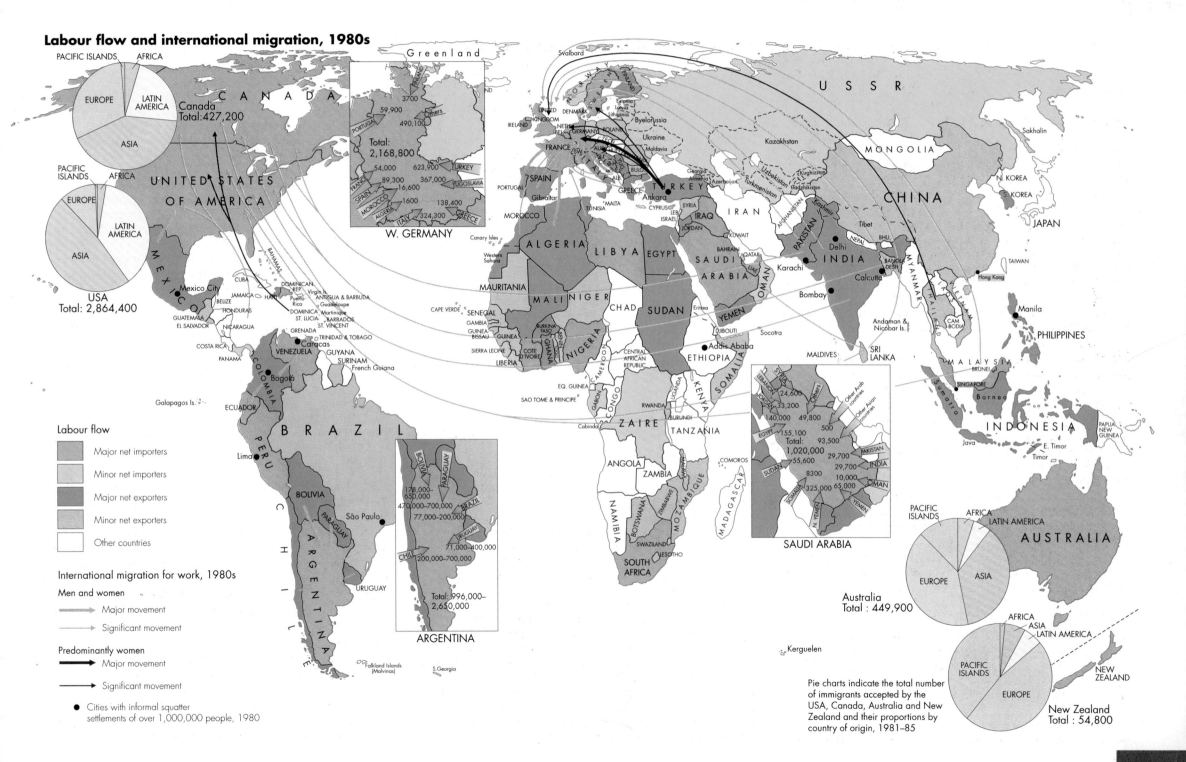

PACIFIC ISLANDS **AFRICA**
EUROPE
LATIN AMERICA
ASIA
Canada
Total: 427,200

PACIFIC ISLANDS **AFRICA**
EUROPE
LATIN AMERICA
ASIA
USA
Total: 2,864,400

Greenland

CANADA

UNITED STATES OF AMERICA

Mexico City

W. GERMANY

3700
59,900
490,100
Total: 2,168,800
54,000 623,900
PORTUGAL TURKEY
FRANCE 367,000 YUGOSLAVIA
SPAIN 89,300 16,600
MOROCCO 1600 138,400
ALGERIA ITALY 324,300 GREECE

USSR

MONGOLIA

CHINA

N. KOREA
S. KOREA
JAPAN

TAIWAN
Hong Kong

Delhi
Karachi
INDIA
Calcutta
Bombay

Manila
PHILIPPINES

TURKEY
Ankara

ALGERIA LIBYA EGYPT
SAUDI ARABIA
MAURITANIA
MALI NIGER CHAD SUDAN YEMEN
SENEGAL
ETHIOPIA
SOMALIA
Addis Ababa
SRI LANKA
MALDIVES

SAUDI ARABIA
24,600
33,200
40,000 49,800
500
EGYPT 155,100
Total: 1,020,000
93,500 PAKISTAN
55,600 29,700
29,700 INDIA
8300 10,000 OMAN
325,000 65,000
N. YEMEN

MALAYSIA
SINGAPORE
Borneo
INDONESIA
Java
E. Timor
Timor
PAPUA NEW GUINEA

BRAZIL
PERU
Lima
BOLIVIA
PARAGUAY
São Paulo
ARGENTINA
URUGUAY

Caracas
VENEZUELA
GUYANA
SURINAM
COLOMBIA
Bogotá
ECUADOR

ARGENTINA
BOLIVIA PARAGUAY
178,000–650,000 BRAZIL
470,000–700,000
77,000–200,000
URUGUAY
71,000–400,000
CHILE
200,000–700,000
Total: 996,000–2,650,000

ANGOLA ZAMBIA
NAMIBIA BOTSWANA
ZIMBABWE MOZAMBIQUE
SOUTH AFRICA
LESOTHO
SWAZILAND
MADAGASCAR
COMOROS
ZAIRE TANZANIA
Kerguelen

AUSTRALIA

PACIFIC ISLANDS **AFRICA** LATIN AMERICA
EUROPE ASIA
Australia
Total: 449,900

AFRICA ASIA LATIN AMERICA
PACIFIC ISLANDS
EUROPE
New Zealand
Total: 54,800
NEW ZEALAND

Pie charts indicate the total number of immigrants accepted by the USA, Canada, Australia and New Zealand and their proportions by country of origin, 1981–85

Labour flow

- Major net importers
- Minor net importers
- Major net exporters
- Minor net exporters
- Other countries

International migration for work, 1980s

Men and women
→ Major movement
→ Significant movement

Predominantly women
→ Major movement
→ Significant movement

● Cities with informal squatter settlements of over 1,000,000 people, 1980

The total external debt of developing countries multiplied thirteenfold from US$100 billion in 1970 to around $1350 billion in 1990.[16] Borrowing foreign currency is likely to be necessary to finance industrialization, and can in principle lead to a virtuous circle of growth and development, but in practice this high level of debt has become a burden with high economic and social costs.

The graph below shows an annual transfer of almost US$30 billion in long-term loans to developing countries in the late 1970s turning into an annual transfer of over $20 million in the reverse direction in the 1980s. Suddenly, the interest payments on outstanding loans, plus scheduled annual repayments of capital, far exceeded new loans. The cumulative total in net transfers *from* developing countries has been calculated as even higher than appears from the graph, at US$242 billion from 1983 to 1989[17].

The immediate cause of this turnaround was a combination in the early 1980s of increased interest rates with less new lending. In addition, lower commodity prices and higher prices for imports such as fuel and machinery meant that many developing countries had difficulty generating enough foreign exchange from their commodity exports both to pay for imports and to service their debts. Mexico's announcement in August 1982 that it could not meet its repayment commitments is the best known case, and caused the international debt situation to be termed a 'crisis'. Doubt as to the creditworthiness of developing countries led banks to reduce their lending even more.

These changes in the world economy triggered off the debt 'crisis', but several other underlying causes have been suggested. The build-up of debt in the 1970s came largely from the 'recycling' of surpluses held by Middle Eastern oil producers after the oil price rises of 1973–74. At the time there was a decline in international cooperation on monetary issues and no coordinated approach to regulating how these oil surpluses should be invested. Private banks

may also have been too willing to lend large amounts to particular countries while bypassing others.

In addition the loans may not have been invested within the developing countries so as to ensure returns that could meet the required repayments. There are well known cases of loans being used for luxury consumption and extravagant military expenditure, or simply wasted through embezzlement and corruption, e.g. under Marcos in the Philippines or Somoza in Nicaragua. More usually, loans were invested for development but two problems still arose. First, projects such as those in education or infrastructure may have had a high social return but still failed to generate foreign exchange for loan repayment. Loans were often too short-term for such projects, aimed at long-term development, to generate a financial return on the required timescale. Second, 'capital flight', where private citizens of a country export large amounts of their wealth, legally or illegally, to private bank accounts abroad, reduces the amount of capital available for productive investment. This again results in lower returns than required for repayments and in further borrowing.

Much of the total debt is owed by a small number of countries. World Bank figures show that 57% of debt is held by just 20 countries, headed by Brazil, Mexico, Argentina, India and Egypt. However, these are not the worst affected by the debt crisis. The severity of debt or *debt burden* has to be seen as relative to the resources available to a country or the size of its economy. Exports provide the most important resource for earning foreign exchange to enable debt repayments. The map opposite uses two relevant measures. For all low- and middle-income countries it shows: (a) the *debt service ratio*, i.e. annual interest payments plus repayments of capital (*total debt service*) as a percentage of export earnings; and (b) total debt in relation to total GNP. The table (below right) shows debt service in relation to exports and other sources of foreign exchange such as aid and remittances from migrants working overseas, for selected countries.

The UNDP suggests[18] that for any country successful debt servicing depends on several interrelated conditions:

income growth, to generate a surplus that is sufficient both to service debt and to allow for satisfactory increases in domestic consumption and investment;

fair income distribution, to sustain social stability;

an **efficient fiscal system**, to capture sufficient public savings;

a **trade surplus**, to generate sufficient foreign exchange;

high domestic returns on investment, to offer attractive domestic alternatives to international interest rates

Debt is a particular burden to Sub-Saharan Africa. Although the sums involved are smaller than the totals for middle-income Latin America, the total debt of Sub-Saharan Africa (about US$150 billion in 1990) is equivalent to 100% of its GNP (in Latin America this ratio is less than 50%) and 500% of its exports. Great poverty and the

serious structural weakness of African economies make the above conditions hard to meet. Often, lack of a diversified export base due to high concentration on specific commodities (p.18) makes adjustment to changing economic conditions particularly difficult. High population growth rates make the achievement of per capita income growth more arduous. Education and health demands are potentially greater, with high infant mortality and low school enrolment.

Although the factors required for successful debt servicing are not all within the control of developing countries, the approach to debt relief of international agencies such as the World Bank and the International Monetary Fund (IMF) has been to look for solutions on a case-by-case basis and to link rescheduling of debts (i.e. agreeing postponements of interest payments or adding arrears to the capital sum) with the imposition of 'stabilization' or 'structural adjustment' policies. Effectively the IMF or World Bank agrees to make further loans on new terms, thus giving a 'seal of approval'. This leads private banks to agree to rescheduling, on condition that policies are implemented including reduction of state subsidies, privatization, devaluation and trade liberalization. However, the case-by-case approach has not worked for most African countries as it has increased the debt.

Other approaches towards debt relief include writing off bilateral loans or converting loans into grants. The 'Trinidad proposals' passed at a meeting of Commonwealth finance ministers in 1990 envisaged a cancellation of two-thirds of bilateral debt and a rescheduling of the remainder over 25 years. The Brady plan, launched in 1989 to reduce private debt, emphasized debt reduction instead of mere rescheduling, and has been implemented in several countries including Mexico and the Philippines. However, none of these approaches comes near to an overall global solution.

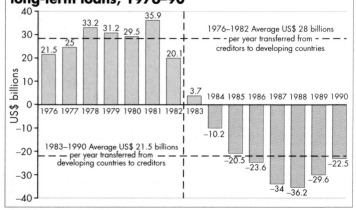

Net transfers to developing countries on long-term loans, 1976–90

1976–1982 Average US$ 28 billions per year transferred from creditors to developing countries

1983–1990 Average US$ 21.5 billions per year transferred from developing countries to creditors

US$ billions

Year	Value
1976	21.5
1977	25
1978	33.2
1979	31.2
1980	29.5
1981	35.9
1982	20.1
1983	3.7
1984	-10.2
1985	-20.5
1986	-23.6
1987	-34
1988	-36.2
1989	-29.6
1990	-22.5

Debt service in relation to sources of foreign exchange for selected countries (all figures as percentages of GNP)[19]

	Debt service 1990	ODA* 1990	Workers' remittances 1989[†]	Exports 1990
Mozambique	3.5	77.4	N/a	24.4
Nigeria	9.3	0.8	<0.05	45.7
Tanzania	6.8	37.5	<0.05	26.3
Egypt	10.8	17.2	13.1	42.1
Jordan	20.4	16.7	10.6	88.7
Turkey	6.7	1.7	4.1	23.6
Bangladesh	3.1	10.5	3.9	12.0
Pakistan	4.8	2.8	4.7	20.9
Philippines	6.4	3.0	0.8	30.2
Thailand	6.8	1.2	N/a	39.8
Jamaica	20.2	9.2	2.4	65.2
Mexico	5.3	0.1	0.2	19.0

* Official development assistance, i.e. aid.
[†] Includes only amounts sent home through official channels by those working abroad.

Debt service ratios and total debt for low-income and middle-income economies, 1990

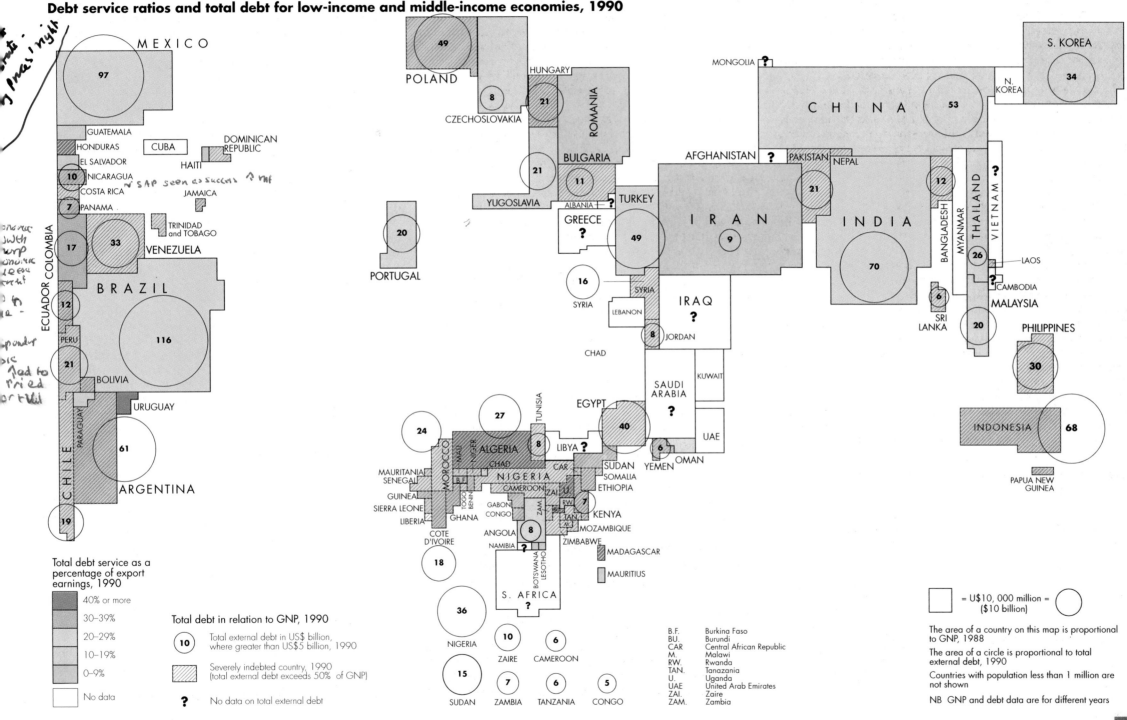

Total debt service as a percentage of export earnings, 1990

- 40% or more
- 30–39%
- 20–29%
- 10–19%
- 0–9%
- No data

Total debt in relation to GNP, 1990

- (10) Total external debt in US$ billion, where greater than US$5 billion, 1990
- Severely indebted country, 1990 (total external debt exceeds 50% of GNP)
- ? No data on total external debt

B.F.	Burkina Faso
BU.	Burundi
CAR	Central African Republic
M.	Malawi
RW.	Rwanda
TAN.	Tanazania
U.	Uganda
UAE	United Arab Emirates
ZAI.	Zaire
ZAM.	Zambia

☐ = U$10, 000 million = ◯
($10 billion)

The area of a country on this map is proportional to GNP, 1988

The area of a circle is proportional to total external debt, 1990

Countries with population less than 1 million are not shown

NB GNP and debt data are for different years

This section ends with four pages summarizing global trends relevant to development as the end of the century approaches.

Population and demographic change

The map opposite shows how many developing countries have populations that are doubling in periods of 35 years or less, while those of many industrialized countries are barely increasing (divide annual growth rate into 70 to get approximate doubling period).

Population growth is not, however, a direct cause of poverty. It is more likely that development reduces population growth. Until around the beginning of the nineteenth century birth and death rates nearly balanced (at quite a high level, indicating large families, high infant mortality and low life expectancy). In countries that underwent an industrial revolution, death rates dropped dramatically, mainly as a result of improved sanitation and public health. Europe's population increased dramatically, and many people emigrated, particularly to North and South America. A generation or so later the birth rate also began to fall in Europe, as continued improvements in living standards, including lower infant mortality, reduced the pressure to have a large family along with the relative benefits.

By 1960, death rates had also been reduced in many developing countries, but birth rates remained high. Fertility rates reduced between 1960 and 1990, but by very different amounts in different

countries (diagram below left). Improvements in women's education and child health care are apparently particularly instrumental in reducing birth rates, and cultural factors also play a part. However, a general reduction in poverty may be required before the birth rates in the remaining high fertility countries show a reduction.

Population growth does not imply *over*-population. Some of the most densely populated areas, such as parts of Europe, are clearly able to maintain large populations at high levels of well-being. Other areas, particularly in South America, Africa and Central Asia, still have low population densities (see map), though this is in places due to inhospitable climate or terrain. An increase in GDP in an industrial country may have more effect on world resources or environmental degradation than an increase in population in poorer countries.

Population factors do constrain development in other ways. Even if fertility rates are reducing, current population growth guarantees future growth as today's babies reach adulthood. Any slowdown must take several generations to work through, in the meantime causing a shift in age structure and a change in the ratio of dependents to working-age population (see diagram above).

The other factor leading to changes in the patterns of populations is movement: international and rural–urban migration. Mass international movements of people are covered on pp.66–67. Some information on rural–urban migration is shown on pp.18–19 and pp.52–53. The proportion of the world's population living in towns and cities is expected to exceed 50% before the end of the century, as a result not only of migration but also of higher rates of reproduction in towns and of villages themselves growing into towns. The map shows the world's major cities and their expected growth.

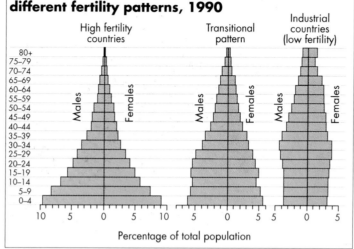

Age distribution of populations in countries with different fertility patterns, 1990

Percentage of total population

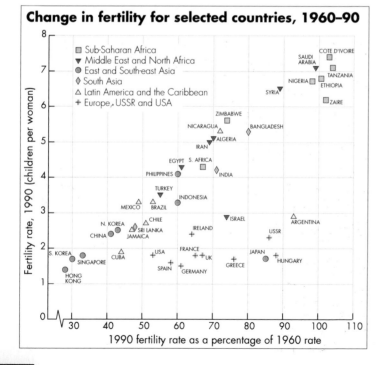

Change in fertility for selected countries, 1960–90

- Sub-Saharan Africa
- Middle East and North Africa
- East and South-east Asia
- South Asia
- Latin America and the Caribbean
- Europe, USSR and USA

Fertility rate, 1990 (children per woman)

1990 fertility rate as a percentage of 1960 rate

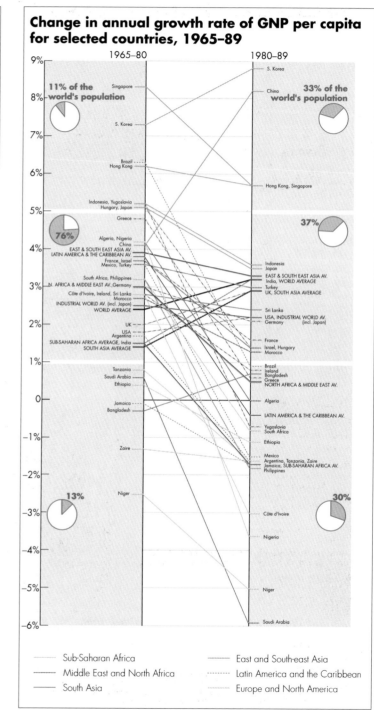

Change in annual growth rate of GNP per capita for selected countries, 1965–89

- Sub-Saharan Africa
- Middle East and North Africa
- South Asia
- East and South-east Asia
- Latin America and the Caribbean
- Europe and North America

Distribution and growth of world population

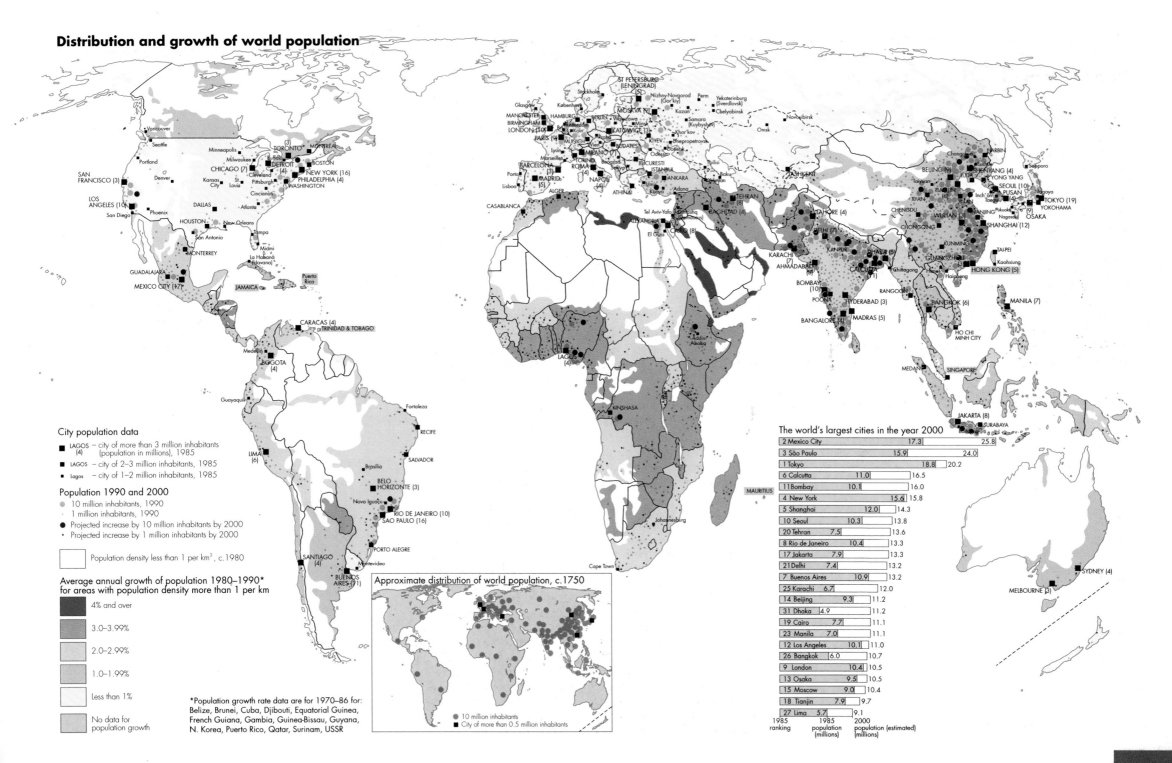

City population data

- ■ LAGOS – city of more than 3 million inhabitants (population in millions), 1985
  (4)
- ■ LAGOS – city of 2–3 million inhabitants, 1985
- ▪ Lagos – city of 1–2 million inhabitants, 1985

Population 1990 and 2000

- ● 10 million inhabitants, 1990
- · 1 million inhabitants, 1990
- ● Projected increase by 10 million inhabitants by 2000
- · Projected increase by 1 million inhabitants by 2000

☐ Population density less than 1 per km², c.1980

Average annual growth of population 1980–1990*
for areas with population density more than 1 per km

- 4% and over
- 3.0–3.99%
- 2.0–2.99%
- 1.0–1.99%
- Less than 1%
- No data for population growth

*Population growth rate data are for 1970–86 for:
Belize, Brunei, Cuba, Djibouti, Equatorial Guinea,
French Guiana, Gambia, Guinea-Bissau, Guyana,
N. Korea, Puerto Rico, Qatar, Surinam, USSR

Approximate distribution of world population, c.1750

- ● 10 million inhabitants
- ■ City of more than 0.5 million inhabitants

The world's largest cities in the year 2000

1985 ranking		1985 population (millions)	2000 population (estimated) (millions)
2	Mexico City	17.3	25.8
3	São Paulo	15.9	24.0
1	Tokyo	18.8	20.2
6	Calcutta	11.0	16.5
11	Bombay	10.1	16.0
4	New York	15.6	15.8
5	Shanghai	12.0	14.3
10	Seoul	10.3	13.8
20	Tehran	7.5	13.6
8	Rio de Janeiro	10.4	13.3
17	Jakarta	7.9	13.3
21	Delhi	7.4	13.2
7	Buenos Aires	10.9	13.2
25	Karachi	6.7	12.0
14	Beijing	9.3	11.2
31	Dhaka	4.9	11.2
19	Cairo	7.7	11.1
23	Manila	7.0	11.1
12	Los Angeles	10.1	11.0
26	Bangkok	6.0	10.7
9	London	10.4	10.5
13	Osaka	9.5	10.5
15	Moscow	9.0	10.4
18	Tianjin	7.9	9.7
27	Lima	5.7	9.1

Trends in economic development

We turn now to trends in economic development. It is not just a question of the old industrialized 'North' retaining its lead by moving first into new areas of technology and gaining new monopoly powers. Broad trends hide big variations within and between countries.

In the North, the trend towards a so-called 'post-industrial society' is affecting different countries in different ways. Some, like the UK, are suffering a relative economic decline along with their older mass-production based manufacturing industries. Others, notably Japan, are consolidating a leading economic position based on a mixture of information technology and new manufacturing techniques. To some extent the standard categorization of economic activity into industry, agriculture and services cannot capture this new distinction. The triangular diagram of changes in the sectoral distribution of the labour force shows simply a strong trend towards 'services', indicating that although manufacturing may remain of central importance, the days of mass industrial employment are gone.

In the 'South', there is also a general trend towards employment in 'services', but one can distinguish on the triangular diagram countries where the trend is also towards industry; these tend to be the only countries where economic development is proceeding at a fast rate.

Differences between the countries and regions of the South are also increasing. Whereas in the 1960s and 1970s most developing economies generally improved, the 1980s have seen much bigger differences. This is illustrated in the graph on p.70 (far right). In the mid-1960s and 1970s over three-quarters of the world's population lived in countries where GNP per capita was growing at between 1% and 5% per year. During the 1980s almost a third were in countries where GNP per capita grew at less than 1% per year or declined. Another third, almost all accounted for by China and the newly industrializing countries of South-east Asia, were in countries which had annual GNP per capita growth rates in the 1980s of over 5%.

The graph below shows changes in real GDP relative to the OECD average and puts this movement into a longer term context. It reinforces the message that Latin America in general is stagnating and Africa is falling ever further behind, while certain countries of East and South Asia are following the earlier example of Japan and beginning to 'cross the gap' that may allow them to approach the economic levels of the industrialized world. The World Bank generalizes this to a positive view of the prospects for Asia as a whole, making certain assumptions.

Change in sectoral distribution of labour force for selected countries, 1960/65 to 1986–89

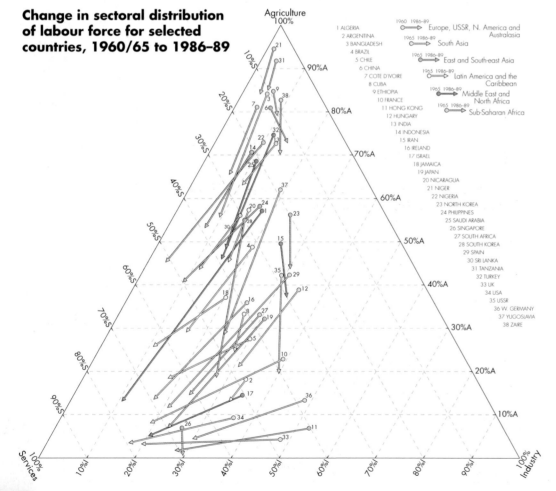

Real GDP per capita as a percentage of OECD average for selected countries, 1913–1987/89 and projections to 2010

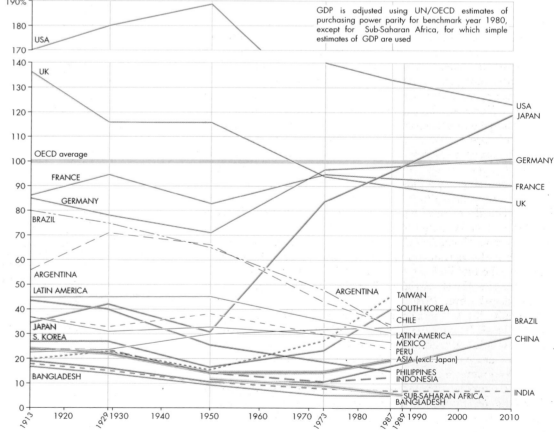

Trends in poverty and human development

According to calculations made by the World Bank, the numbers of absolutely poor in Asia (including China and India) may decline over the next ten years. However, in Africa, even with positive assumptions similar to those made for Asia, there will be a marked increase in the proportion of the population below the World Bank's poverty line. Combined with the greater population growth rate (see map on p.71) this will generate the shift in the global distribution of poverty indicated in the middle two of the set of pie diagrams on the right. The last of the pie diagrams shows that Sub-Saharan Africa's share of total world population is expected to continue to grow until, by the year 2025, it will be almost equal to that of India. It remains to be seen whether Africa will continue to increase its share of the world's poorest people.

The last three diagrams in this section present data from the United Nations Development Programme's (UNDP's) *Human Development Report 1992*. They illustrate how some gaps in human development are widening while others are narrowing, at North–South, regional and country levels.

The three decades to 1990 saw big improvements in aspects of human development such as health and basic education. There was a decrease in disparities in infant mortality, literacy and life expectancy, though many parts of the developing world still have a lot of 'catching-up' to do to equal the standards of the industrialized countries. However, disparities in areas such as technological capability and education, especially at higher level ('human capital formation'), are increasing. The eight small graphs show some relevant changes in these overall disparities between industrialized and developing countries. (Note that the UNDP uses slightly different regional groupings from those used in the rest of this Atlas.)

The histograms illustrate changes in inequalities between regions. The Third World regions shown all have very low shares of the global totals of various economic resources. (The rest is accounted for by Europe, North America, Australasia and Japan, and is not shown on the histograms.) With the exception of East and South-east Asia, and the Middle East and North Africa, and bank lending to Latin America, the shares of the Third World regions declined over the two decades from 1970.

Finally, the tall narrow graph (far right) shows changes at country level. It uses the Human Development Index (HDI) to indicate which countries have advanced more than others in terms of overall human development. (See p.22 for a definition of HDI; the figures for this graph are calculated slightly differently from those on p.22 to take account of data from two years.) It is certainly positive to note that on this measure human development has improved at least slightly in nearly all countries, including some of those with enormous difficulties.

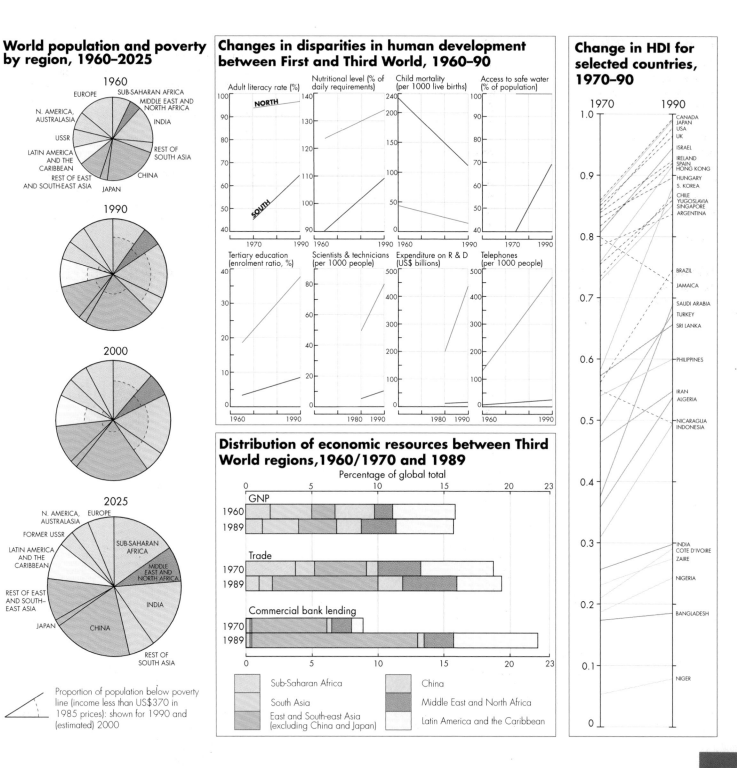

World population and poverty by region, 1960–2025

1960

1990

2000

2025

Proportion of population below poverty line (income less than US$370 in 1985 prices): shown for 1990 and (estimated) 2000

Changes in disparities in human development between First and Third World, 1960–90

Distribution of economic resources between Third World regions, 1960/1970 and 1989

Sub-Saharan Africa
South Asia
East and South-east Asia (excluding China and Japan)
China
Middle East and North Africa
Latin America and the Caribbean

Change in HDI for selected countries, 1970–90

TABLE 1 BASIC DATA AND HUMAN DEVELOPMENT

Countries (with population over 1 million)	Population, 1991 (millions)	Population density, 1991 (per sq.km)	Annual population growth, 1980–91	Date of independence	Pre-independence status	Membership of selected international organizations	Life expectancy 1965	Life expectancy 1991	Infant mortality (per 1000 live births), 1991	Mean years of schooling, 1990	Rate of illiteracy, 1990 Female	Rate of illiteracy, 1990 Total	Real GDP per capita, 1990 (PPP$)	Human Development Index, 1990	
SUB-SAHARAN AFRICA															
ANGOLA	9.5	7.6	2.6d	1976	Portugal	NAM,G77,OAU,SADC	36	46	128	1.5	72	58	840	0.143	ANGOLA
BENIN	4.8	43.1	3.2	1960	France	NAM,G77,OAU,WAf,Fz	42	51	88	0.7	84	77	1043	0.113	BENIN
BOTSWANA	1.3	2.2	3.5	1966	UK	NAM,G77,OAU,SADC,Com	48	68	62	2.4	35	26	3419	0.552	BOTSWANA
BURKINA FASO	9.2	33.8	2.6	1960	France	NAM,G77,OAU,WAf,Fz,Isl	41	48	120	0.1	91	82	618	0.074	BURKINA FASO
BURUNDI	5.7	220.5	2.9	1962	Belgium(Germany)	NAM,G77,OAU,CAf	44	48	108	0.3	60	50	625	0.167	BURUNDI
CAMEROON	11.9	25.5	2.8	1960	France/UK(Germany)	NAM,G77,OAU,CAf,Fz,Isl	46	55	66	1.6	57	46	1646	0.310	CAMEROON
CENTRAL AFRICAN REP.	3.1	5.0	2.7	1960	France	NAM,G77,OAU,CAf,Fz	41	47	106	1.1	75	62	768	0.159	CENTRAL AFRICAN REP.
CHAD	5.7	4.5	2.4	1960	France	NAM,G77,OAU,CAf,Fz,Isl	37	47	125	0.2	82	70	559	0.088	CHAD
CONGO	2.3	6.7	3.4	1960	France	NAM,G77,OAU,CAf,Fz	50	52	83	2.1	56	43	2362	0.372	CONGO
COTE D'IVOIRE	12.4	39.1	3.8	1960	France	NAM,G77,OAU,WAf,Fz	44	52	93	1.9	60	46	1324	0.286	COTE D'IVOIRE
ETHIOPIA	51.4	46.7	3.1	old (Italy 1936–41)	—	NAM,G77,OAU	43	48	125	1.1		34e	369	0.172	ETHIOPIA
GABON	1.2	4.6	3.5	1960	France	NAM,G77,OAU,OPEC,CAf,Fz	43e	54	97	2.6	52	39	4147	0.503	GABON
GHANA	15.5	67.3	3.2	1957	UK	NAM,G77,OAU,WAf,Com	48	47	84	3.5	49	40	1016	0.311	GHANA
GUINEA	5.9	24.1	2.6	1958	France	NAM,G77,OAU,WAf,Isl	35	44	137	0.8	87	76	501	0.045	GUINEA
GUINEA-BISSAU	1.0	35.0	1.9	1975	Portugal	NAM,G77,OAU,WAf	35e	39	143	0.3	76	64	841	0.090	GUINEA-BISSAU
KENYA	24.4	42.8	3.8	1963	UK	NAM,G77,OAU,Com	45	59	68	2.3	42	31	1058	0.369	KENYA
LESOTHO	1.8	59.0	2.8	1966	UK	NAM,G77,OAU,SADC,Com	49	56	82	3.4		22e	1743	0.431	LESOTHO
LIBERIA	2.7	27.6	3.1d	1847	—	NAM,G77,OAU,WAf	43	55	131	2.0	71	61	857	0.222	LIBERIA
MADAGASCAR	12.4	21.3	3.0	1960	France	NAM,G77,OAU,Fz	43	51	113	2.2	27	20	704	0.327	MADAGASCAR
MALAWI	10	106.1	3.3	1964	UK	NAM,G77,OAU,SADC,Com	39	45	144	1.7		53e	640	0.168	MALAWI
MALI	9.5	7.8	2.6	1960	France	NAM,G77,OAU,WAf,Fz,Isl	39	48	162	0.3	76	68	572	0.082	MALI
MAURITANIA	2.1	2.0	2.4	1960	France	NAM,G77,OAU,WAf,Fz,Ar,Isl	41	47	120	0.3	79	66	1057	0.140	MAURITANIA
MAURITIUS	1.1	587.0	1.0	1968	UK	NAM,G77,OAU,Com	61	70	22	4.1		14e	5750	0.794	MAURITIUS
MOZAMBIQUE	14.5	20.1	2.6	1975	Portugal	NAM,G77,OAU,SADC(Isl)	38	47	149	1.6	79	67	1072	0.154	MOZAMBIQUE
NAMIBIA	1.5	1.8	3.1	1990	S.Africa(Germany)	NAM,G77,OAU,SADC,Com	45e	58	73	1.7		60e	1400f	0.289	NAMIBIA
NIGER	8	6.3	3.3	1960	France	NAM,G77,OAU,WAf,Fz,Isl	37	46	127	0.1	83	72	645	0.080	NIGER
NIGERIA	112.1	123.1	3.0	1960	UK	NAM,G77,OAU,OPEC,WAf,Com	42	52	99	1.2	61	49	1215	0.246	NIGERIA
RWANDA	7.3	294.7	3.0	1962	Belgium(Germany)	NAM,G77,OAU,CAf	49	46	112	1.1	63	50	657	0.186	RWANDA
SENEGAL	7.5	39.1	3.0	1960	France	NAM,G77,OAU,WAf,Fz,Isl	41	48	81	0.8	75	62	1248	0.182	SENEGAL
SIERRA LEONE	4.3	59.5	2.4	1961	UK	NAM,G77,OAU,WAf,Com	33	42	146	0.9	89	79	1086	0.065	SIERRA LEONE
SOMALIA	8.9	14.2	3.1d	1960	Italy/UK	NAM,G77,OAU,Ar,Isl	39	48	125	0.2	86	76	836	0.087	SOMALIA
SOUTH AFRICA	38.9	31.8	2.5	1910	UK (Netherlands)	—	47	63	55	3.9		30e	4865	0.673	SOUTH AFRICA
SUDAN	25.9	10.9	2.7	1956	UK	NAM,G77,OAU,Ar,Isl	40	51	102	0.8	88	73	949	0.152	SUDAN
TANZANIA	26.9	30.4	3.0	1961	UK (Germany)	NAM,G77,OAU,SADC,Com	43	51	104	2.0		35e	572	0.270	TANZANIA
TOGO	3.6	67.0	3.4	1960	France(Germany)	NAM,G77,OAU,WAf,Fz	42	54	88	1.6	69	57	734	0.218	TOGO
UGANDA	18.1	90.8	2.5	1962	UK	NAM,G77,OAU,Com,Isl	45	46	105	1.1	65	52	524	0.194	UGANDA
ZAIRE	38.6	17.0	3.2d	1960	Belgium	NAM,G77,OAU,CAf	44	52	96	1.6	39	28	367	0.262	ZAIRE
ZAMBIA	8.4	11.3	3.6	1964	UK	NAM,G77,OAU,SADC,Com	45	49	85	2.7	35	27	744	0.314	ZAMBIA
ZIMBABWE	10.3	26.5	3.4	1980	UK	NAM,G77,OAU,SADC,Com	48	60	61	2.9	40	33	1484	0.398	ZIMBABWE
MIDDLE EAST AND NORTH AFRICA															
ALGERIA	25.6	10.8	3.0	1962	France	NAM,G77,OAU,OPEC,Ar,Isl	50	66	65	2.6	55	43	3011	0.528	ALGERIA
EGYPT	53.6	53.9	2.5	1922	UK (Ottoman)	NAM,G77,OAU,Ar,Isl	49	61	59	2.8	66	52	1988	0.389	EGYPT
IRAN	59.9	36.6	3.6	old	—	NAM,G77,OPEC,Isl	52	65	44	3.9	57	46	3253	0.557	IRAN
IRAQ	18.7	42.7	3.6d	1932	UK (Ottoman)	NAM,G77,OPEC,Ar	52	65	60	4.8	51	40	3508	0.589	IRAQ
ISRAEL	4.9	239.6	2.2	1948	UK (Ottoman)	—	73	76	9b	10.0		5e	10 840	0.938	ISRAEL
JORDAN	4.1	46.6	4.7	1946	UK (Ottoman)	NAM,G77,Ar,Isl	51	69	38	5.0	30	20	2345	0.582	JORDAN
KUWAIT	2.1	117.1	4.4d	1961	UK (Ottoman)	NAM,G77,OPEC,Ar,Isl	63	75	14	5.4	33	27	15 178	0.815	KUWAIT
LEBANON	2.8	272.1		1941	France(Ottoman)	NAM,G77,Ar,Isl	62	66	36	4.4	27	20	2300f	0.565	LEBANON
LIBYA	4.7	2.7	4.1d	1951	Italy	NAM,G77,OAU,OPEC,Ar,Isl	50	63	72	3.4	50	36	7000f	0.658	LIBYA
MOROCCO	25.7	57.6	2.6	1956	France	NAM,G77,Ar,Isl	50	63	72	2.8	62	51	2348	0.433	MOROCCO
OMAN	1.6	7.4	4.3	old (UK 1891–1932)	—	NAM,G77,Ar,Isl	41	69	32	0.9		65e	9972	0.598	OMAN
SAUDI ARABIA	15.4	7.2	4.6	old	—	NAM,G77,OPEC,Ar,Isl	49	69	33	3.7	52	38	10 989	0.688	SAUDI ARABIA
SYRIA	12.8	69.6	3.3	1941	France(Ottoman)	NAM,G77,Ar,Isl	53	67	42	4.2	49	36	4756	0.694	SYRIA
TUNISIA	8.2	53.0	2.4	1956	France	NAM,G77,OAU,Ar,Isl	52	67	45	2.1	44	35	3579	0.600	TUNISIA
TURKEY	57.2	74.3	2.3	old (Ottoman)	—	OECD,NATO,Isl	54	67	60	3.5	29	19	4652	0.717	TURKEY
UAE	1.6	19.5	4.3d	1971	UK (Ottoman)	NAM,G77,OPEC,Ar,Isl	58	72	23	5.1		45e	16 753	0.738	UAE
YEMEN	12.1	22.9	3.8	1919*	Ottoman	NAM,G77,Ar,Isl	38	52	110	0.8	74	62	1562	0.233	YEMEN
SOUTH ASIA															
AFGHANISTAN	17.7	27.1		old (USSR 1979–89)	—	NAM,G77,Isl	35	43	165	0.8	86	71	714	0.066	AFGHANISTAN
BANGLADESH	116.4	894.6	2.2	1971	Pakistan (UK)	NAM,G77,Com,Isl	44	51	111	2.0	78	65	872	0.189	BANGLADESH
BHUTAN	1.6	33.5	2.1	old (UK s-c)	—	NAM,G77	31	48	133	0.2	75	62	800f	0.150	BHUTAN
INDIA	862.7	290.2	2.1	1947	UK	NAM,G77,Com	45	60	90	2.4	66	52	1072	0.309	INDIA
NEPAL	20.1	146.7	2.6	old (UK s-c)	—	NAM,G77	40	53	102	2.1	87	74	920	0.170	NEPAL
PAKISTAN	121.5	157.6	3.1	1947	UK	NAM,G77,Isl	45	59	101	1.9	79	65	1862	0.311	PAKISTAN
SRI LANKA	17.4	269.8	1.4	1948	UK (Netherlands)	NAM,G77,Com	64	71	25	6.9	17	12	2405	0.663	SRI LANKA
EAST AND SOUTH-EAST ASIA															
CAMBODIA	8.6	48.5	2.6d	old (France 1885–1954)	—	NAM,G77	45	50	120	2.0	78	65	1100f	0.186	CAMBODIA
CHINA	1170.7	125.5	1.5	old	—	G77	55	69	29	4.8	38	27	1990	0.566	CHINA
HONG KONG	5.8	5812.1	1.2	UK	—	—	68	78	6	7.0		10e	15 595	0.913	HONG KONG
INDONESIA	187.7	103.6	1.8	1949	Netherlands	NAM,G77,OPEC,As,Isl	44	60	68	3.9	32	23	2181	0.515	INDONESIA
JAPAN	124	329.4	0.5	old (USA 1946–54)	—	OECD,G7	71	79	5b	10.7		1e	17 616	0.983	JAPAN
KOREA, NORTH	22.2	184.3		1948	Japan	NAM,G77		71	25	6.0		5e	2000f	0.640	KOREA, NORTH
KOREA, SOUTH	43.8	443.5	1.1	1948	Japan	G77	58	70	22	8.8	7	4	6733	0.872	KOREA, SOUTH
LAOS	4.3	18.8	2.7	1954	France	NAM,G77	57	50	101	2.9		46e	1100f	0.246	LAOS
MALAYSIA	18.4	56.1	2.6	1957	UK (Netherlands)	NAM,G77,As,Com,Isl	57	71	15	5.3	30	22	6140	0.790	MALAYSIA

Keys to abbreviations and notes on tables are on p.79.   Countries and territories listed are those with population over 1 million in 1991.   Blanks indicate data not available.   — means 'none'.   Figures in italics are for year(s) other than those specified.
*North Yemen independence 1919; South Yemen 1967 (previously UK); Yemen Arab Republic united 1990.

Countries (with population over 1 million)	Population, 1991 (millions)	Population density, 1991 (per sq.km)	Annual population growth, 1980–91	Date of independence	Pre-independence status	Membership of selected international organizations	Life expectancy 1965	Life expectancy 1991	Infant mortality (per 1000 live births), 1991	Mean years of schooling, 1990	Rate of illiteracy, 1990 Female	Rate of illiteracy, 1990 Total	Real GDP per capita, 1990 (PPP$)	Human Development Index, 1990	
EAST AND SOUTH-EAST ASIA (CONT.)															
MYANMAR	42.7	65.0	2.1[d]	old (UK 1886–1948)	—	NAM,G77	48	59	85	2.5	28	19	659	0.390	MYANMAR
MONGOLIA	2.2	1.4	2.8[d]	1921	Russia (China)	G77	44	63	62	7.0		7[e]	2100[f]	0.578	MONGOLIA
PAPUA NEW GUINEA	4.0	8.8	2.3	1975	Australia(Germany/UK)	G77,Com	56	56	56	0.9	62	48	1786	0.318	PAPUA NEW GUINEA
PHILIPPINES	63.8	214.0	2.4	1946	USA (Spain)	(NAM),G77,As	66	65	42	7.4	11	10	2303	0.603	PHILIPPINES
SINGAPORE	2.7	4490.2	1.7	1959	UK (Portugal)	G77,As,Com	57	74	7	3.9		12[e]	15 880	0.849	SINGAPORE
TAIWAN	20.4[a]	568.4[a]		1949	China(Japan1895–1945)	—		74[a]							TAIWAN
THAILAND	55.4	108.4	1.9	old (Japan 1942–46)	—	G77,As	56	69	28	3.8	10	7	3986	0.715	THAILAND
VIETNAM	68.1	209.2	2.1[d]	1954	France	NAM,G77	50	67	39	4.6	16	12	1100[f]	0.472	VIETNAM
LATIN AMERICA AND THE CARIBBEAN															
ARGENTINA	32.7	12.0	1.3	1810	Spain	NAM,G77,OAS	66	71	30	8.7	5	5	4295	0.832	ARGENTINA
BOLIVIA	7.3	6.8	2.5	1825	Spain	NAM,G77,And,OAS	45	59	89	4.0	29	23	1572	0.398	BOLIVIA
BRAZIL	151.6	17.9	2.0	1822	Portugal	(NAM),G77,OAS	57	66	59	3.9	20	19	4718	0.730	BRAZIL
CHILE	13.4	17.9	1.7	1818	Spain	G77,OAS	60	72	17	7.5	7	7	5099	0.864	CHILE
COLOMBIA	32.9	31.6	2.0	1819	Spain	(NAM),G77,And,OAS	57	69	38	7.1	14	13	4237	0.770	COLOMBIA
COSTA RICA	3.1	61.0	2.7	1838	UPCA (Spain)	(NAM),G77,CAm,OAS	65	76	15	5.7	7	7	4542	0.852	COSTA RICA
CUBA	10.7	97.5		1902	USA (Spain)	NAM,G77	67	76	14	7.6	7	6	2200[f]	0.711	CUBA
DOMINICAN REP.	7.3	151.3	2.2	1844(USA var)[†]	Haiti (Spain/USA)	G77,(Car),OAS	55	67	59	4.3	18	17	2404	0.586	DOMINICAN REP.
ECUADOR	10.8	39.0	2.6	1830	GCol (Spain)	(NAM),G77,OPEC,And,OAS	56	66	59	5.6	16	14	3074	0.646	ECUADOR
EL SALVADOR	5.3	254.9	1.4	1838	UPCA (Spain)	(NAM),G77,CAm,OAS	55	66	50	4.1	30	27	1950	0.503	EL SALVADOR
GUATEMALA	9.5	87.3	2.9	1838	UPCA (Spain)	G77,CAm,OAS	49	64	51	4.1	53	45	2576	0.489	GUATEMALA
HAITI	6.6	240.2	1.9	1804	Spain (France)	G77,(Car),OAS	46	55	89	1.7	53	47	933	0.275	HAITI
HONDURAS	5.3	47.4	3.3	1838	UPCA (Spain)	(NAM),G77,CAm,OAS	50	65	62	3.9	29	27	1470	0.472	HONDURAS
JAMAICA	2.4	225.6	1.0	1962	UK	NAM,G77,Com,OAS,Car	65	73	15	5.3	1	2	2979	0.736	JAMAICA
MEXICO	86.3	45.2	2.0	1821	Spain	(NAM),G77,OAS(Car)	60	70	37	4.7	15	13	5918	0.805	MEXICO
NICARAGUA	3.8	32.1	2.7	1838	UPCA (Spain)	NAM,G77,CAm,OAS	51	66	58	4.3		19[e]	1497	0.500	NICARAGUA
PANAMA	2.5	32.5	2.1	1903	GCol (Spain)	NAM,G77,OAS	64	73	22	6.7	12	12	3317	0.738	PANAMA
PARAGUAY	4.4	11.1	3.1	1811	Spain	G77,OAS	65	67	48	4.9	12	10	2790	0.641	PARAGUAY
PERU	22	17.2	2.2	1821	Spain	NAM,G77,And,OAS	51	64	80	6.4	21	15	2622	0.592	PERU
PUERTO RICO	3.6[b]	400[c]	0.9	USA	(Spain to 1898)	(Car)		76	14[b]			12[a]			PUERTO RICO
TRINIDAD & TOBAGO	1.3	243.9	1.3	1962	UK	NAM,G77,Com,OAS, Car	65	71	20	8.0		4[e]	6604	0.877	TRINIDAD & TOBAGO
URUGUAY	3.1	17.8	0.6	1828	Brazil (Spain)	NAM,G77,OAS	69	73	21	7.8	4	4	5916	0.881	URUGUAY
VENEZUELA	19.8	22.4	2.6	1830	GCol (Spain)	NAM,G77,OPEC,And,OAS(Car)	63	70	34	6.3	10	12	6169	0.824	VENEZUELA
W.EUROPE, N.AMERICA AND AUSTRALASIA															
AUSTRALIA	17.3	2.3	1.5	1901	UK	OECD,Com	71	77	8[b]	11.5		1[e]	16 051	0.972	AUSTRALIA
AUSTRIA	7.7	93.6	0.2	old (WW2)	—	OECD,EFTA	70	76	8[b]	11.1		1[e]	16 504	0.952	AUSTRIA
BELGIUM	10	328.1	0.1	1830 (WW2)	Netherlands (France)	OECD,EU,NATO	71	76	8[b]	10.7		1[e]	16 381	0.952	BELGIUM
CANADA	27	2.9	1.2	1867	UK	OECD,NATO,G7,Com	72	77	7[b]	12.1		1[e]	19 232	0.982	CANADA
DENMARK	5.1	121.5	0.1	old (WW2)	—	OECD,EU,NATO	73	75	8[b]	10.4		1[e]	16 781	0.955	DENMARK
FINLAND	5.0	16.4	0.4	1917	Russia	OECD,EFTA	70	76	6[b]	10.6		1[e]	16 446	0.954	FINLAND
FRANCE	57	103.3	0.5	old (WW2)	—	OECD,EU,(NATO),G7	72	77	7[b]	11.6		1[e]	17 405	0.971	FRANCE
GERMANY	79.9	228.6	0.1	1871(partition 1949–90)	Union	OECD,EU,NATO,G7	70	76	7[b]	11.1		1[e]	18 213	0.957	GERMANY
GREECE	10.2	77.6	0.5	1830 (WW2)	Ottoman	OECD,EU,NATO	71	77	10[b]	6.9	11	7	7366	0.902	GREECE
IRELAND	3.5	50.7	0.2	1922	UK	OECD,EU	71	75	8[b]	8.7		1[e]	10 589	0.925	IRELAND
ITALY	57.7	196.3	0.2	1860 (WW2)	Union	OECD,EU,NATO,G7,(OAS)	71	77	8[b]	7.3		3[e]	15 890	0.924	ITALY
NETHERLANDS	15	443.7	0.6	old (WW2)	—	OECD,EU,NATO	74	77	7[b]	10.6		1[e]	15 695	0.970	NETHERLANDS
NEW ZEALAND	3.4	12.8	0.7	1907	UK	OECD,Com	71	76	9[b]	10.4		1[e]	13 481	0.947	NEW ZEALAND
NORWAY	4.3	13.9	0.4	old (Norway–Sweden union 1815–1905)		OECD,NATO,EFTA	74	77	8[b]	11.6		1[e]	16 028	0.979	NORWAY
PORTUGAL	9.9	107.3	0.1	old (France1808–12)	—	OECD,EU,NATO	66	74	11[b]	6.0	19	15	8770	0.853	PORTUGAL
SPAIN	39	78.1	0.4	old (France1809–13)	—	OECD,EU,NATO	71	77	8[b]	6.8	7	5	11 723	0.923	SPAIN
SWEDEN	8.6	20.9	0.3	old (Norway–Sweden union 1815–1905)	—	OECD,EFTA	74	78	6[b]	11.1		1[e]	17 014	0.977	SWEDEN
SWITZERLAND	6.8	170.1	0.6	old	—	OECD,EFTA	72	78	7[b]	11.1		1[e]	20 874	0.978	SWITZERLAND
UK	57.6	238.2	0.2	old	—	OECD,EU,NATO,G7,Com	71	75	7[b]	11.5		1[e]	15 804	0.964	UK
USA	252.5	27.5	0.9	1776	UK	OECD,NATO,G7,OAS	71	76	9[b]	12.3		1[e]	21 449	0.976	USA
E. EUROPE AND CENTRAL ASIA															
ALBANIA	3.3	1.2	2.0[d]	1912 (WW2)	Ottoman	—	66	73		6.0		15[e]	3000[f]	0.699	ALBANIA
ARMENIA	3.4	114.5	0.9	1991	USSR	CIS	70(USSR)[§]	72	22[b]	5.0		7[e]	4741	0.831	ARMENIA
AZERBAIJAN	7.2	83.7	1.4	1991	USSR	—	70(USSR)[§]	71	33[b]	5.0		7[e]	3977	0.770	AZERBAIJAN
BULGARIA	9	81.2	0.1	1908	Ottoman	—	70	72	17[b]	7.0		7[e]	4700[f]	0.854	BULGARIA
BYELORUSSIA	10.3	49.5	0.6	1991	USSR	CIS	70(USSR)[§]	71	15[b]	7.0		5[e]	5727	0.861	BYELORUSSIA
CZECHOSLOVAKIA	15.7	125.2	0.3	1918 (WW2)	Austria	—	69	72	11[b]	9.0		3[e]	7300[f]	0.892	CZECHOSLOVAKIA
ESTONIA	1.6	35.1	0.6	1991	USSR	—	70(USSR)[§]	70	14[b]	9.0		4[e]	6438	0.872	ESTONIA
GEORGIA	5.5	78.5	0.7	1991	USSR	—	70(USSR)[§]	73	16[b]	5.0		7[e]	4572	0.829	GEORGIA
HUNGARY	10.5	114.1	-0.2	1918 (WW2)	Austria–Hungary	—	70	70	16[b]	9.6		3[e]	6116	0.887	HUNGARY
KAZAKHSTAN	16.9	6.2	1.2	1991	USSR	CIS	70(USSR)[§]	69	32[b]	5.0		7[e]	4716	0.802	KAZAKHSTAN
KIRGHIZSTAN	4.5	22.5	1.9	1991	USSR	CIS	70(USSR)[§]	69	40[b]	5.0		7[e]	3114	0.689	KIRGHIZSTAN
LATVIA	2.7	41.6	0.3	1991	USSR	—	70(USSR)[§]	69	16[b]	9.0		4[e]	6457	0.868	LATVIA
LITHUANIA	3.7	57.4	0.8	1991	USSR	—	70(USSR)[§]	71	14[b]	9.0		4[e]	4913	0.881	LITHUANIA
MOLDAVIA	4.4	118.8	0.9	1991	USSR	CIS	70(USSR)[§]	69	23[b]	6.0		5[e]	3896	0.758	MOLDAVIA
POLAND	38.3	125.8	0.7	old (Russia 1815–1918)(WW2)	—	—	69	71	15[b]	8.0		4[e]	4237	0.831	POLAND
ROMANIA	23.3	101.0	0.4	1878 (WW2)	Ottoman	—	68	70	27[b]	7.0		5[e]	2800[f]	0.709	ROMANIA
RUSSIAN FED.	148.7	8.7	0.6	1991	USSR	CIS	70(USSR)[§]	69	20[b]	9.0		6[e]	7968	0.862	RUSSIAN FED.
TADZHIKISTAN	5.5	38.3	3.0	1991	USSR	CIS	70(USSR)[§]	69	50[b]	5.0		7[e]	2558	0.657	TADZHIKISTAN
TURKMENISTAN	3.8	7.7	2.5	1991	USSR	CIS	70(USSR)[§]	69	56[b]	5.0		7[e]	4230	0.746	TURKMENISTAN
UKRAINE	52.1	86.2	0.4	1991	USSR	CIS	70(USSR)[§]	70	18[b]	6.0		5[e]	5433	0.844	UKRAINE
UZBEKISTAN	21	46.9	2.4	1991	USSR	CIS	70(USSR)[§]	69	44[b]	5.0		7[e]	3115	0.695	UZBEKISTAN
YUGOSLAVIA[‡]	23.9[b]	93.3[c]	0.6	1918[‡]	Ottoman/Austria–Hungary	NAM,G77	66	73	21[b]		12	7			YUGOSLAVIA

Sources: Columns 1, 2, 9, 10, 13, 14, *Human Development Report* (HDR) 1993; Columns 3, 8, 11, 12, *World Development Report* (WDR) 1993; Column 7, WDR 1987; except: [a]*Third World Guide* 1993/94 [b]WDR 1993 [c]estimated from World Bank population data. [d]WDR 1992 [e]HDR 1993 [f]UNDP estimates. [†]USA occupied 1916–24, 1965–66 and other short periods. [‡]Break-up of federation in 1991 followed by civil war; several new republics likely to be confirmed. [§]Figure refers to whole of USSR.

TABLE 2 ECONOMIC DATA

Countries (with population over 1 million)	GNP per capita, 1991	Annual growth in GNP per capita, 1980–91	World Bank country groups, 1993	Debt service ratio, 1991	Women as % of labour force, 1990	Agriculture 1965	Agriculture 1991	Industry 1965	Industry 1991	Manufacturing 1965	Manufacturing 1991	Labour Agriculture 1965	Labour Agriculture 1989–91	Labour Industry 1965	Labour Industry 1989–91	
SUB-SAHARAN AFRICA																
ANGOLA	LM	6.1a	Sev,LM,Fu		39		13b		44b		4b	79	73	8	10	ANGOLA
BENIN	380	–0.9	Mod,L,Se	6.2	24	59	37	8	14		9	83	70	5	7	BENIN
BOTSWANA	2530	5.6	Les,UM,PP	3.4	35	34	5	19	54	12	4	88	43	4	5	BOTSWANA
BURKINA FASO	290	1.2	Les,L,Se	9.1	49	37	44	24	20	11	12	90	87	3	4	BURKINA FASO
BURUNDI	210	1.3	Sev,L,PP	31.5		71c	55	10c	16	7c	12	94	92	2	2	BURUNDI
CAMEROON	850	–1.0	Mod,LM,Di	18.7	30	33	27	20	22	10	12	87	73	4	5	CAMEROON
CENTRAL AFRICAN REP.	390	–1.4	Mod,L,Di	11.4	46	46	41	16	16	4		88	83	3	3	CENTRAL AFRICAN REP.
CHAD	210	3.8	Les,L,PP	4.5	17	42	43	15	18	12	16	92	83	3	5	CHAD
CONGO	1120	–0.2	Sev,LM,Fu	21.3	39	19	12	19	37		8	66	62	11	12	CONGO
COTE D'IVOIRE	690	–4.6	Sev,LM,PP	43.4	34	47	38	19	22	11	21	80	65	5	8	COTE D'IVOIRE
ETHIOPIA	120	–1.6	Sev,L,PP	18.6	42	58	47	14	13	7	9	86	80	5	8	ETHIOPIA
GABON	3780	–4.2	Sev,UM,PP	6.5	38	26	9	34	45	7	6		75		11	GABON
GHANA	400	–0.3	Sev,L,PP	26.9	40	44	53	19	17	10	10	61	59	15	11	GHANA
GUINEA	460		Mod,L,PP	17.9	30		29		35		5	87	78	6	1	GUINEA
GUINEA–BISSAU	180	1.1	Sev,L,PP		42	47c	46	21c	12	21c	8		82		4	GUINEA–BISSAU
KENYA	340	0.3	Sev,L,Di	32.7	40	35	27	18	22	11	12	86	81	5	7	KENYA
LESOTHO	580	–0.5	Les,L,Se	4.6	44	65	14	5	38	1	13	91	23	3	33	LESOTHO
LIBERIA	L		Sev,L,PP		31	27		40		3		79	75	10	9	LIBERIA
MADAGASCAR	210	–2.5	Sev,L,PP	32.0	40	25	33	14	14		12	85	81	4	6	MADAGASCAR
MALAWI	230	0.1	Mod,L,PP	25.0	42	50	35	13	20		13	92	82	3	3	MALAWI
MALI	280	–0.1	Sev,L,Di	4.6	16	65	44	9	12	5	11	91	85	1	2	MALI
MAURITANIA	510	–1.8	Sev,L,PP	16.8	22	32	22	36	31	4		89	69	3	9	MAURITANIA
MAURITIUS	2410	6.1	Les,LM,Di	8.8	35	16	11	23	33	14	23	37	19	25	31	MAURITIUS
MOZAMBIQUE	80	–1.1	Sev,L,Di	10.6	48		64		15			87	85	6	7	MOZAMBIQUE
NAMIBIA	1460	–1.2	Les,LM,PP		24		10		28		4		43		22	NAMIBIA
NIGER	300	–4.1	Sev,L,PP	50.4	47	68	38	3	19	2	8	95	85	1	3	NIGER
NIGERIA	340	–2.3	Sev,L,Fu	25.2	20	55	37	12	38	5	7b	72	43	10	13	NIGERIA
RWANDA	270	–2.4	Mod,L,PP	17.6	48	75	38	7	22	2	20	95	90	2	4	RWANDA
SENEGAL	720	0.1	Mod,LM,Di	19.9	26	25	20	18	19	14	13	83	81	6	6	SENEGAL
SIERRA LEONE	210	–1.6	Sev,L,Di		33	34	43	28	14	6	3	78	70	11	14	SIERRA LEONE
SOMALIA	120a	–1.8a	Sev,L,PP		39	71	65b	6	9b	3	5b	81	76	6	8	SOMALIA
SOUTH AFRICA	2560	0.7	Les,UM,Di		33	10	5	41	44	24	25	32	14	30	24	SOUTH AFRICA
SUDAN	400a		Sev,L,Se		29	54		9			4	81	62	5	10	SUDAN
TANZANIA	100	–0.8	Sev,L,PP	24.6	48	46	61	14	5	8	4	91	85	3	5	TANZANIA
TOGO	410	–1.3	Mod,L,PP	7.3	37	45	33	21	23	10	10	78	65	9	6	TOGO
UGANDA	170	–0.8a	Sev,L,PP	70.0	41	52	51	13	12	8	4	91	86	3	4	UGANDA
ZAIRE	L	–1.5a	Sev,L,PP		36	20	30b	32	33b		13b	82	71	9	13	ZAIRE
ZAMBIA	420a	–2.9a	Sev,L,PP	50.3	29	14	16	54	47	6	36	79	38	8	8	ZAMBIA
ZIMBABWE	650	–0.2	Les,L,PP	27.2	35	18	20	35	32	20	26	79	64	8	6	ZIMBABWE
MIDDLE EAST AND NORTH AFRICA																
ALGERIA	1980	–0.7	Sev,LM,Fu	73.7	4	11c	14	41c	50	15c	10	57	14	17	11	ALGERIA
EGYPT	610	1.9	Sev,L,Se	16.7	11	29	18	27	30	12	9	55	34	15	22	EGYPT
IRAN	2170	–1.3	Les,LM,Fu	3.9	18	26	21	36	21		9	49	25	26	28	IRAN
IRAQ	UM		Sev,UM,Fu		6	18		46		8		50	13	20	8	IRAQ
ISRAEL	11 950	1.7	H,Ma		41								3		24	ISRAEL
JORDAN	1050	–1.7	Sev,LM,Se	20.9	10		7		26		13	37	10	26	26	JORDAN
KUWAIT	H	–2.2a	H,Di		14	0	1b	70	56b	3	9b	2		34		KUWAIT
LEBANON	LM		Les,LM,Ma		27	12		21				29	14	24	27	LEBANON
LIBYA	UM	–9.2a	Les,UM,Fu		9	5		63		3		41	18	21	29	LIBYA
MOROCCO	1030	1.6	Sev,LM,Di	27.8	20	23	19	28	31	16	18	61	46	15	25	MOROCCO
OMAN	6120	4.4	Les,UM,Fu		8	61	4	23	52	0	4	62	49	15	22	OMAN
SAUDI ARABIA	7820	–3.4	Les,UM,Fu		7	8	7	60	52	9	7	68	48	11	14	SAUDI ARABIA
SYRIA	1160	–1.4	Sev,LM,Di		15	29	30	22	23			52	22	20	36	SYRIA
TUNISIA	1500	1.1	Mod,LM,Di	22.7	13	22	18	24	32	9	17	50	22	21	16	TUNISIA
TURKEY	1780	2.9	Mod,LM,Di	30.5	33	34	18	25	34	16	24	75	46	11	22	TURKEY
UAE	20 140	–6.3	H,Fu		6		2b		55b		9b	21	5	32	38	UAE
YEMEN	520		Mod,L,Se	7.3	13		22		26		9	73	63	8	11	YEMEN
SOUTH ASIA																
AFGHANISTAN	L		Sev,L,PP		8							69	61	11	14	AFGHANISTAN
BANGLADESH	220	1.9	Mod,L,Di	19.9	7	53	36	11	16	5	9	84	56	5	10	BANGLADESH
BHUTAN	180	7.4a	Les,L,Se	7.2	32		43		27		10	94	92	2	3	BHUTAN
INDIA	330	3.2	Mod,L,Di	30.7	26	44	31	22	27	16	18	73	62	12	11	INDIA
NEPAL	180	2.1	Mod,L,Se	13.6	34	65	59	11	14	3	5	94	93	2	1	NEPAL
PAKISTAN	400	3.2	Mod,L,Di	21.1	11	40	26	20	26	14	17	60	44	18	25	PAKISTAN
SRI LANKA	500	2.5	Mod,L,Di	13.9	37	28	27	21	25	17	14	56	49	14	12	SRI LANKA
EAST AND SOUTH-EAST ASIA																
CAMBODIA	200		Sev,L,Se		39							80	74	4	7	CAMBODIA
CHINA	370	7.8	Les,L,Ma	12.1	43	38	27	35	42	28	38	81	73	8	14	CHINA
HONG KONG	13 430	5.6	H,Ma		36	2	0	40	25	24	17	6	1	53	35	HONG KONG
INDONESIA	610	3.9	Mod,L,Di	32.7	40	51	19	13	41	8	21	70	54	9	8	INDONESIA
JAPAN	26 930	3.6	OE,H,Ma		41	10	3	44	42	34	25	10	7		34	JAPAN
KOREA, NORTH	LM		Les,LM,Ma		46							57	43	23	30	KOREA, NORTH
KOREA, SOUTH	6330	8.7	Les,UM,Ma	7.1	34	38	8	25	45	18	28	55	16	15	34	KOREA, SOUTH
LAOS	220	0.7a	Sev,L,Di	7.6	45							80	76	5	7	LAOS
MALAYSIA	2520	2.9	Les,LM,Di	8.3	31	28		25		9		58	31	13	27	MALAYSIA

Keys to abbreviations and notes on tables are on p.79.   Countries and territories listed are those with population over 1 million in 1991.   Blanks indicate data not available.   Figures in italics are for year(s) other than those specified.

Countries (with population over 1 million)	GNP per capita, 1991	Annual growth in GNP per capita, 1980–91	World Bank country groups, 1993	Debt service ratio, 1991	Women as % of labour force, 1990	Agriculture 1965	Agriculture 1991	Industry 1965	Industry 1991	Manufacturing 1965	Manufacturing 1991	Agriculture 1965	Agriculture 1989–91	Industry 1965	Industry 1989–91	
EAST AND SOUTH–EAST ASIA (CONT.)																
MYANMAR	L		Sev,L,PP		37							63	64	14	9	MYANMAR
MONGOLIA	LM		Sev,LM,PP		45		17[b]		34[b]			54	40	20	21	MONGOLIA
PAPUA NEW GUINEA	830	−0.6	Mod,LM,PP	29.6	39	42	26	18	35	5[c]	10	87	76	6	10	PAPUA NEW GUINEA
PHILIPPINES	730	−1.2	Mod,LM,Di	23.2	37	26	21	27	34	20	26	58	41	16	19	PHILIPPINES
SINGAPORE	14 210	5.3	H,Ma		39	3	0	24	38	15	29	6	<0.5	27	40	SINGAPORE
TAIWAN	H		H,Ma													TAIWAN
THAILAND	1570	5.9	Les,LM,Di	13.1	47	32	12	23	39	14	27	82	70	5	11	THAILAND
VIETNAM	L		Sev,L,PP		47							79	67	6	12	VIET NAM
LATIN AMERICA AND THE CARIBBEAN																
ARGENTINA	2790	−1.5	Sev,UM,PP	48.4	21	17	15	42	40	33		18	13	34	34	ARGENTINA
BOLIVIA	650	−2.0	Sev,LM,PP	34.0	24	23	24[b]	31	32[b]	15	13[b]	54	47	20	19	BOLIVIA
BRAZIL	2940	0.5	Sev,UM,Di	30.0	35	19	10	33	39	26	22	49	28	20	25	BRAZIL
CHILE	2160	1.6	Mod,LM,PP	33.9	31	9		40		24		27	18	29	30	CHILE
COLOMBIA	1260	1.2	Mod,LM,Di	35.2	41	27	17	27	35	19	20	45	1	21	31	COLOMBIA
COSTA RICA	1850	0.7	Mod,LM,PP	18.4	29	24	18	23	25		19	47	24	19	30	COSTA RICA
CUBA	LM		Sev,LM,PP		32							33	24	25	29	CUBA
DOMINICAN REP.	940	−0.2	Mod,LM,Se	11.6	15	23	18	22	25	16	13	59	46	14	15	DOMINICAN REP.
ECUADOR	1000	−0.6	Sev,LM,Di	32.2	30	27	15	22	38	18	21	55	30	19	24	ECUADOR
EL SALVADOR	1080	−0.3	Les,LM,Se	17.2	45	29	10	22	24	18	19	58	10	16	35	EL SALVADOR
GUATEMALA	930	−1.8	Mod,LM,PP	15.3	26		26		20			64	48	15	23	GUATEMALA
HAITI	370	−2.4	Mod,L,Se	6.6	40							77	50	7	6	HAITI
HONDURAS	580	−0.5	Sev,L,PP	30.6	18	40	22	19	27	12	16	68	36	12	17	HONDURAS
JAMAICA	1380	0.0	Sev,LM,Se	29.4	31	10	5	37	40	17	17	37	25	20	12	JAMAICA
MEXICO	3030	−0.5	Sev,UM,Di	30.9	31	14	9	27	30	20	22	49	22	22	31	MEXICO
NICARAGUA	460	−4.4	Sev,L,PP	109.3	34	25	30	24	23	18	19	56	46	16	16	NICARAGUA
PANAMA	2130	−1.8	Sev,LM,Se	3.9	27	18	10	19	11	12	7[b]	46	12	16	21	PANAMA
PARAGUAY	1270	−0.8	Les,LM,PP	11.9	41	37	22	19	24	16	18	54	48	20	21	PARAGUAY
PERU	1070	2.4	Sev,LM,PP	27.7	33	18	7[b]	30	37[b]	17	27[b]	49	35	19	12	PERU
PUERTO RICO	6320	0.9	UM			3[c]	1	34[c]	41	24[c]	39					PUERTO RICO
TRINIDAD & TOBAGO	3670	−5.2	Les,UM,Fu	16.2	27	8	3	48	39	26[c]	9	20	10	35	41	TRINIDAD & TOBAGO
URUGUAY	2840	−0.4	Mod,UM,Di	38.2	31	18	10	35	32		26	20	15	29	18	URUGUAY
VENEZUELA	2730	−1.3	Mod,UM,Fu	18.7	22	6	5	40	47	17[c]	17	30	12	24	32	VENEZUELA
W.EUROPE, N.AMERICA AND AUSTRALASIA																
AUSTRALIA	17 050	1.6	OE,H,Di		41	9	3	39	31	26	15		15		23	AUSTRALIA
AUSTRIA	20 140	2.1	OE,H,Di		41	9	3	46	36	33	25		8		35	AUSTRIA
BELGIUM	18 950	2.0	OE,H,Ma		41		2		30		22		3		20	BELGIUM
CANADA	20 440	2.0	OE,H,Ma		44	6		40		26			5		25	CANADA
DENMARK	23 700	2.2	OE,H,Di		46	9	5	36	28	23	19		4		27	DENMARK
FINLAND	23 980	2.5	OE,H,Ma		47	16	6	37	34	23	24					FINLAND
FRANCE	20 380	1.8	OE,H,Di		43		3		29		21		7		20	FRANCE
GERMANY	23 650	2.2	OE,H,Ma		40	4	2	53	39	40	23		4		30	GERMANY
GREECE	6340	1.1	Mod,UM,Se		36	24	17	26	27	16	14		22		28	GREECE
IRELAND	11 120	3.3	OE,H,Ma		31	17[c]	11	37[c]	9	24[c]	3		13		23	IRELAND
ITALY	18 520	2.2	OE,H,Ma		37	8[c]	3	41[c]	33	27[c]	21		9		20	ITALY
NETHERLANDS	18 780	1.6	OE,H,Di		39	6[c]	4	37[c]	32	26[c]	20		5		22	NETHERLANDS
NEW ZEALAND	12 350	0.7	OE,H,PP		43	12[c]	9	33[c]	27	24[c]	18		9		24	NEW ZEALAND
NORWAY	24 220	2.3	OE,H,Di		45	6[c]	3	32[c]	36	22[c]	14		5		25	NORWAY
PORTUGAL	5930	3.1	Les,UM,Di	21.1	43								17		32	PORTUGAL
SPAIN	12 450	2.8	OE,H,Di		35								10		35	SPAIN
SWEDEN	25 110	1.7	OE,H,Ma		48		3		34		22		3		28	SWEDEN
SWITZERLAND	33 610	1.6	OE,H,Ma		37								6		30	SWITZERLAND
UK	16 550	2.6	OE,H,Se		43	3		46		34			2		20	UK
USA	22 240	1.7	OE,H,Di		45	3		38		28			3		26	USA
E. EUROPE AND CENTRAL ASIA																
ALBANIA	LM		Sev,LM,PP		41								56		26	ALBANIA
ARMENIA	2150		LM,Ma										11		32	ARMENIA
AZERBAIJAN	1670		LM,Di										15		21	AZERBAIJAN
BULGARIA	1840	1.7	Sev,LM,Ma	22.1	46		13		50				17		38	BULGARIA
BYELORUSSIA	3110		UM,Ma													BYELORUSSIA
CZECHOSLOVAKIA	2470	0.5	Les,LM,Ma	11.6	47		8		56				13		50	CZECHOSLOVAKIA
ESTONIA	3830		UM,Ma										9		33	ESTONIA
GEORGIA	1640		LM,Ma										14		30	GEORGIA
HUNGARY	2720	0.7	Mod,UM,Ma	32.5	46	18[c]	10	45[c]	34		29		6		51	HUNGARY
KAZAKHSTAN	2470		LM,Di										20		22	KAZAKHSTAN
KIRGHIZSTAN	1550		LM,Ma										16		24	KIRGHIZSTAN
LATVIA	3410		UM,Ma				20		48		41		9		33	LATVIA
LITHUANIA	2710		UM,Ma				20		45				10		33	LITHUANIA
MOLDAVIA	2170		LM,Ma										21		26	MOLDAVIA
POLAND	1790	0.6	Sev,LM,Ma	5.4	45		7		50				24		41	POLAND
ROMANIA	1390	0.0	Les,LM,Ma	2.0	46		19		49				31		43	ROMANIA
RUSSIAN FED.	3220		UM,Ma				13		48							RUSSIAN FED.
TADZHIKISTAN	1050		LM,Di										14		19	TADZHIKISTAN
TURKMENISTAN	1700		LM,Fu													TURKMENISTAN
UKRAINE	2340		LM,Ma													UKRAINE
UZBEKISTAN	1350		LM,Ma										17		20	UZBEKISTAN
YUGOSLAVIA	3060[b]	2.9[b]	Les,UM,Di	20.4		23	12	42	48							YUGOSLAVIA

Sources: Columns 1, 2, 3, 4, 7, 9, 11, *World Development Report (WDR)* 1993; Columns 5, 12–15, *Human Development Report (HDR)* 1993; Columns 6, 8, 10, WDR 1992; except ᵃHDR 1993 ᵇWDR 1992 ᶜWDR 1993.

TABLE 3 SELECTED INTERNATIONAL ORGANIZATIONS*

NAME	MEMBERSHIP	BACKGROUND	AIMS/BASIS OF ACTIVITIES
ORGANIZATION FOR ECONOMIC COOPERATION AND DEVELOPMENT (OECD)	24 members, mostly Western European countries, including Greece, plus Australia, Canada, Iceland, Japan, New Zealand, Turkey, USA. (The EC Commission also takes part.)	Founded 1961, HQ Paris; replaced Organization for European Economic Co-operation, which was established in 1948 mainly to deal with Marshall Plan aid from the United States after World War II.	Promotes economic and social welfare by assisting member governments' policy formation; encourages world trade; coordinates aid to developing countries. Over 100 committees, e.g. Development Assistance Committee (DAC), High Level Group on Commodities.
EUROPEAN COMMUNITY/UNION(EC, EU)	12 members: Belgium, Denmark, France, Germany, Greece, Ireland, Italy, Luxembourg, Netherlands, Portugal, Spain, UK. Austria, Sweden, Finland, Norway negotiating membership.	Established under Treaty of Rome, 1957. Since 1967, some common institutions with the two other European Communities (EURATOM and the European Coal and Steel Community).	Unified market with common external customs tariff. Promotes harmonious economic activities, closer relations between member states. Political union is regarded as the ultimate aim.
NORTH ATLANTIC TREATY ORGANIZATION (NATO)	16 members, comprising 13 Western European states and Turkey (but not the 5 European neutrals of Austria, Finland, Ireland, Sweden, Switzerland), plus USA and Canada.	Military alliance set up in 1949. Greece, West Germany, Turkey joined later and Spain only in 1982; France has partially withdrawn since 1966.	International collective defence organization linking European states with USA and Canada. NATO has integrated military structure incorporating all members except France.
WESTERN ECONOMIC SUMMIT GROUP OF 7 'G7'	7 leading industrialized states: Canada, France, Germany, Italy, Japan, UK, USA.	Set up in 1975 as emergency response to OPEC oil price increases, 1973–74	Discusses common economic problems.
EUROPEAN FREE TRADE ASSOCIATION (EFTA)	6 members: Austria, Finland, Iceland, Norway, Sweden, Switzerland.	Founded 1960. Originally UK, Denmark and Portugal were also members but these countries have now joined the EC.	Aim of gradual reduction of customs and trade barriers between members was achieved by 1966. Free trade agreement with EC signed 1972; trade barriers removed 1984. EEA (European Economic Area) agreement signed 1992, encompassing all EC and EFTA countries.
COMMONWEALTH OF INDEPENDENT STATES (CIS)	Members are 10 of the 15 former republics of the USSR: Armenia, Byelorussia, Kazakhstan, Kirghizstan, Moldavia, Russia, Tadzhikistan, Turkmenistan, Ukraine, Uzbekistan. (Georgia and the Baltic States did not join; Azerbaijan was a founder but membership lapsed late in 1992.)	Created 25 December 1991.	An alliance of full independent states; policy set through coordinating bodies such as the Council of Heads of State and the Council of Heads of Government. Capital of the Commonwealth is Minsk, Byelorussia.
NON-ALIGNED MOVEMENT	104 full members (1989):102 governments, 2 liberation movements; membership defined by invitation to and attendance at summit conferences. Also several observers and guests.	Grew out of associations between Tito, Nasser, Nehru, particularly June 1956 meeting at Brioni, Yugoslavia. Summits every few years since 1961; 9th and 10th summits 1989 and 1992 in Belgrade and Jakarta, respectively.	Association of countries outside superpower blocs. Anti-imperialist orientation. Has Programme for Economic and Technical Cooperation. More institutionalized since 1973, with Coordinating Bureau. Since 1992 new concerns include environment, promotion of North–South dialogue, democratization of UN.
GROUP OF 77	Membership over 120, overlapping considerably with Non-Aligned Movement.	Originated as 'Caucus of 75' preparing for UNCTAD 1, Geneva 1964. Issued joint declaration of 77 developing countries. More members now but name is unchanged.	Principal comprehensive Third World voice on economic matters. Sub-group on international monetary affairs. Sub-group of 24 (8 each from Africa, Asia, South/Central America) conceived 1971.
ORGANIZATION OF AFRICAN UNITY (OAU)	All states on the continent of Africa except South Africa and Morocco, including the Arab states in North Africa.	Founded in 1963 at Addis Ababa; incorporated both the previous rival 'Casablanca' and 'Monrovia' groupings of African states.	Promotes unity among African states; opposes colonialism and neo-colonialism; mediates disputes between members on basis of territorial integrity; coordinates efforts to improve living standards.
ORGANIZATION OF THE PETROLEUM EXPORTING COUNTRIES (OPEC)	13 members: Algeria, Ecuador, Gabon, Indonesia, Iran, Iraq, Kuwait, Libya, Nigeria, Qatar, Saudi Arabia, United Arab Emirates, Venezuela.	Established 1960; increased importance in 1970s, especially after 1973–74 oil price increases. OPEC members produced 55.5% of world petroleum in 1973 but this figure has reduced considerably from that peak.	Coordinates crude petroleum export price levels, and safeguards members generally. Fund for aid to developing countries.
ASSOCIATION OF SOUTH EAST ASIAN NATIONS (ASEAN)	Brunei, Indonesia, Malaysia, Philippines, Singapore, Thailand.	Founded 1967; area of significant US influence.	Regional economic progress and stability.
CENTRAL AMERICAN COMMON MARKET (CACM)	Costa Rica, El Salvador, Guatemala, Honduras, Nicaragua.	Established 1960 under aegis of Organization of Central American States.	Aims to establish free-trade area and customs union. Serious disputes between members, especially Honduras and El Salvador.
ECONOMIC COMMUNITY OF WEST AFRICAN STATES (ECOWAS)	16 member states	Established by Treaty of Lagos 1975.	Promotes trade, cooperation and self-reliance in the region.
ANDEAN GROUP	Bolivia, Colombia, Ecuador, Peru, Venezuela (Chile left in 1977).	Cartagena Agreement 1969.	Regional cooperation including development finance.
LEAGUE OF ARAB STATES (ARAB LEAGUE)	21 member states, including Palestine (considered independent). Observer status at UN.	Founded 1945.	Strengthens close ties and directs members' policies towards common good of all Arab countries.
ORGANIZATION OF THE ISLAMIC CONFERENCE (OIC)	50 member states plus Palestine Liberation Organization. Iraq is not a member. Observers: Mozambique, Northern Cyprus.	Formally established 1971 after summit meeting of Muslim heads of State at Rabat, Morocco, 1969.	Promotes Islamic solidarity among member states.
SOUTHERN AFRICAN DEVELOPMENT COMMUNITY (SADC)	Angola, Botswana, Lesotho, Malawi, Mozambique, Namibia, Swaziland, Tanzania, Zambia, Zimbabwe.	Grew out of organization of 'front-line states' joined in opposition to apartheid in South Africa. First summit conference Lusaka 1980.	Regional cooperation.
CARIBBEAN COMMUNITY AND COMMON MARKET (CARICOM)	13 members: Antigua, Bahamas, Barbados, Belize, Dominica, Grenada, Guyana, Jamaica, Montserrat, St Kitts, St Lucia, St Vincent, Trinidad and Tobago. Dominican Republic, Haiti and Surinam have observer status.	Established 1973.	Cooperation in economics, health, education, culture, science and technology, and tax administration, as well as foreign policy coordination.
ECONOMIC COMMUNITY OF CENTRAL AFRICAN STATES (ECCAS)	10 members: Burundi, Cameroon, Central African Republic, Chad, Congo, Equatorial Guinea, Gabon, Rwanda, Sao Tome and Principe, Zaire.	Founded 1983.	Seeks to reduce trade restrictions and encourages the establishment of common customs tariffs.
THE COMMONWEALTH	50 independent states, comprising UK and most of its former colonies and other dependencies.	Founded after World War II; membership increased as former colonies became independent; now encompasses one quarter of world's population; secretariat established 1965.	The Harare Declaration of October 1991 outlined new goals, including: promotion of democracy, the rule of law, good government and human rights; equality for women, universal access to education, sustainable development and alleviation of poverty; action against disease and illegal drugs, help for small Commonwealth states and support for UN.
FRENCH COMMUNITY	France and former French colonies in Africa.	Successor to French Union, founded in 1946.	Loose association of states. (The 'Franc Zone' operates as a system of linked currencies.)
ORGANIZATIONS OF AMERICAN STATES (OAS)	35 members: USA and almost all South and Central American states.	Set up in 1948; links the United States, now the dominant external power in South/Central America, though never a colonial power as such, to the other states of the region.	Peace, security, mutual understanding and cooperation among states of western hemisphere. There is a military Inter-American Treaty of Reciprocal Assistance.

*Only selected organizations outside the UN system are shown here. Membership details are for 1992, unless otherwise stated.

The following abbreviations are used in the notes below:

HDR   UNDP (annual) *Human Development Report*, Oxford University Press, Oxford.

TWG   Instituto del Tercer Mundo (annual/biennial) *Third World Guide*, Instituto del Tercer Mundo, Montevideo.

WDR   World Bank (annual) *World Development Report*, Oxford University Press, Oxford.

Introduction (pp.4–9)

1   Brandt, W. *et al* (1980) *North–South: A Programme for Survival*, Independent Commission on International Development Issues (The Brandt Report), Pan Books, London.

2   From a poster published by Christian Aid, London.

3   *TWG* 1991/92, p.150.

Section 1 (pp.10–23)

1   The wars shown on the chart on p.11 are major wars according to Sivard, R.L. (1991) *World Military and Social Expenditures*, World Priorities, Washington DC.

2   Singer, H.W. (1989) *Lessons of Post-War Development Experience: 1945–1988*, Discussion Paper no.260, April, Institute of Development Studies, Brighton.

3   Sutcliffe, R.B. (1971) *Industry and Underdevelopment*, Addison-Wesley, London.

4   North–South Institute (1988) *Telecommunications and Development*, Briefing No. 22, Ottawa.

5   Morris, M.D. (1979) *Measuring the Conditions of the World's Poor: The Physical Quality of Life Index*, Pergamon Press, New York.

6   Nobel Prize winning economist Simon Kuznets' work is best revealed in *Modern Economic Growth: Rate Structure and Spread*, Yale University Press, New Haven, (1966) and *Economic Growth of Nations: Total Output and Production Structure*, Harvard Press, Cambridge, Massachusetts (1971).

7   Data for HDI on p.22 comes from *HDR 1992*. Longevity and educational attainment data are estimates for 1990; adjusted GDP per capita is for 1989.

8   Amnesty International (1990) *Annual Report*, Amnesty International, London.

Section 2 (pp.24–47)

1   Unless otherwise stated, prices on pp.28 and 29 are in British pounds at late nineteenth century prices.

2   Hamilton, E.J. (1929) 'Imports of American gold and silver into Spain, 1503–1660', *Quarterly Journal of Economics*, May, pp.436–437, summarized in Vives, J.V. (1969) *An Economic History of Spain*, Princeton University Press.

3   Frank, A.G. (1978) *World Accumulation, 1492–1789*, Macmillan, London, p.171.

4   Tonnages of metal have been converted to British pounds by weighing contemporary British silver and gold coins held in the British Museum.

5   Messadaglia, cited in Mulhall, M.G. (1899) *A Dictionary of Statistics*, p.307.

6   Quoted in Galbraith, J.K. (1975) *Money*, Penguin, Harmondsworth, p.22.

7   This total, and the statistics on which the figures depicting slavery depend, come from the meticulous study by Curtin, P.D. (1969) *The Atlantic Slave Trade*, University of Wisconsin Press, pp.3, 15, 265–269.

8   Barratt Brown, M. (1963) *After Imperialism*, Heinemann, London, p.40. Another study, *The French Slave Trade*, by Stein, R.L. (1979) University of Wisconsin Press, Madison) suggests that profits were variable and often pocketed by colonists rather than traders.

9   Rinchon, D. (1938) *Le Trafic Négrier*, Brussels, cited in Mandel, E. (1971) *Marxist Economic Theory*, Merlin, London, p.443.

10   Wiseman, H.V. *A Short History of the British West Indies*, cited in Mandel (1971), p.443.

11   Colenbrander, *Koloniale Geschiendenis*, cited in Mandel (1971), p.443.

12   Furber, H. (1948) *John Company at Work*, Harvard University Press, Cambridge, Massachusetts; Irfan Habib (1975) 'Colonization of Indian economy', *Social Scientist* (Delhi), March 1975, pp.23–53.

13   Greenberg, M. (1951) *British Trade and the Opening of China, 1800–42*, Cambridge University Press, pp.1–17.

14   Cain, P.J. and Hopkins, A.K. (1980) 'The political economy of British expansion overseas, 1850–1914', *Economic History Review*, vol. 33, no. 4, p.487.

15   Mulhall, M.G. (1899) *A Dictionary of Statistics*, and (1911) *A New Dictionary of Statistics*.

16   Quoted in Thorner, D. (1950) *Investment in Empire*, University of Pennsylvania Press, Philadelphia, p.1.

17   Barratt Brown, M. (1963) *After Imperialism*, Heinemann, London, p.52.

18   Barratt Brown, M. (1974) *The Economics of Imperialism*, Penguin, Harmondsworth.

19   The graph is based on Figures 32–3 in Hobsbawm, E.J. (1969) *Industry and Empire*, Penguin, Harmondsworth. Data on the geographical distribution of British investments is incomplete and the graph is based on interpolation.

20   Bairoch, P. 'The main trends in national economic disparities since the Industrial Revolution', in Bairoch, P. and Levy-Leboyer, M. (Eds) (1981) *Disparities in Economic Development since the Industrial Revolution*, Macmillan, London and Basingstoke.

21   Low, D.A. quoted in Ranger, T.O. (1968) 'Connexions between 'primary resistance' movements and modern mass nationalism', *Journal of African History*, vol. IX, no. 3, p.450.

22   Jeffrey, R. (1982) *Asia – The Winning of Independence*, Macmillan, London.

Section 3 (pp.48–73)

1   Source: UNEP (1990) *Environmental Data Report 1989/90*, Table 7.1, United Nations Environment Programme, New York.

2   *South* magazine, July 1989, p.12.

3–5   UNIDO (1990) *Industry and Development: Global Report 1989/90*, United Nations Industrial Development Organisation, p.18, 28–29, 295.

6   *South* magazine, August 1989, p.19.

7   *WDR* 1991, p.105

8   Lambert, A.J. (1990) 'New EC initiatives seek to alleviate the environmental repercussions of Britain's agricultural policy', *Geographical Magazine*, May 1990, p.32

9   Sen, A. (1981) *Poverty and Famine: An Essay on Entitlement and Deprivation*, Oxford University Press, Oxford.

10   World Health Organization data quoted in *WDR* 1993, pp.32–33.

11   ILO (1989–90) *Yearbook of Labour Statistics*, International Labour Office, Geneva, p.3.

12   Oldeman, L.R., Hakkeling, R.T.A. and Sombroek, W.G. (1990) *World Map of the Status of Human-induced Soil Degradation: An Explanatory Note*, 2nd edn, International Soil Reference and Information Centre, Wageningen, The Netherlands.

13   World Resources Institute figures, 1990, also quoted in *WDR 1992*, p.58.

14   World Commission on Environment and Development (1987) *Our Common Future* (The Brundtland Report), Oxford University Press, Oxford.

15   *HDR* 1992, p.85, Table 5.1 gives 13.9% in 1990. All data in the text on this page is from this source.

16–18   *HDR* 1992, pp.45 and 47. All data in the text on p.68 is from this source.

19   Cols 1 and 4 are calculated from *WDR* 1992, Table 24; Cols 2 and 3 are taken from *HDR* 1992, Tables 18 and 19. N/a = not available.

Tables 1 and 2 (pp.74–78)

Data in these tables is the most up-to-date available at the time of going to press. It may be for a later year than similar data in the maps and figures on pp.4–73.

The main sources for the tables are the *WDR* 1993 and *HDR* 1993. These generally agree, but for some data (e.g. infant mortality rates) they differ considerably in their assumptions for some countries. These tables have generally used the *WDR* for economic data and the *HDR* for population data and social development indicators, except that where the two are in close agreement the data is given for the most recent year available (e.g. *WDR* 1993 gives estimates for life expectancy for 1991 whereas *HDR* 1993 gives data only for 1990).

Despite the 'official' nature of the sources, comparative national data like this can convey spurious accuracy. Often, official statistics are projections based on past data. Life expectancy data, for example, should ideally be based on 10-year censuses and revised to take into account actual births and deaths each year. But seven developing countries have not conducted a census since independence and 22 others not since before 1975. Almost half of all developing countries have no reliable data on life expectancy (*HDR* 1993, p.108).

Table 1: Notes to columns

4, 5   These attempt to summarize complex changes in territory, political control and forms of state, mostly since 1800, and constitute only a rough guide. For Africa, Asia, and Latin America and the Caribbean, more detailed information is provided on pp.32–35 and 43.

Key for Column 4

old   independent since before 1800

(US 1889–96)   short period of occupation, occupying power and dates

(WW2)   temporary occupation during World War 2

UK   not independent, indicating controlling power

s-c   semi-colonial status for some or all of period

Key for Column 5

UPCA   United Provinces Of Central America

GCol   Greater Colombia

Union   date given is for union of several smaller political entities

Entry in ordinary type means state was a colony of or occupied by that power immediately before independence.

Entry in brackets indicates previous colonial status or occupation.

Entry in italics (e.g. *GCol*) means state was previously an integral part of, in that case, Greater Colombia.

6   Membership is given for international organizations listed in Table 3, p.78. Brackets indicate associate member or observer status.

Key

And	Andean Group	Com	British Commonwealth
Ar	Arab League	EU	European Union
As	ASEAN	Fz	Franc Zone
CAf	ECCAS	G77	Group of 77
CAm	CACM	Isl	Organisation of Islamic Conference
Car	CARICOM	WAf	ECOWAS

13   For explanation of the idea of real GDP per capita and purchasing power parity (PPP), see pp.14 and 22.

14   HDI is an idea developed by UNDP, giving equal weight to life expectancy (Col. 8 gives this for 1991), educational attainment (combination of Cols 10 and 12), and utility derived from income (Col. 13). See p.22.

Table 2: Notes to columns

1   Estimates for 1991: H, UM, LM, L – see note on Col. 3 below.

3   *Indebtedness* uses standard World Bank definitions, averaged over three years 1989–91:

Sev   severely indebted

Mod   moderately indebted

Les   less indebted

OE = high-income members of the Organisation for Economic Cooperation and Development (OECD).

Income groups: economies are divided according to 1991 GNP per capita:

L   low-income (US$635 or less)

LM   lower middle-income ($636–2555)

UM   upper middle-income ($2556–7910)

H   high-income ($2556–7910)

Major export category: 50% or more of total exports of goods and services from one category, 1987–89:

Di   diversified (no single major category)

Fu   fuels (mainly oil)

Ma   manufactures

PP   non- fuel primary products

Se   services

4   Debt service ratio is total payments in one year, including interest payments and repayment of principal, as a percentage of exports of goods and services.

5   See pp.60–61 for comments on the extreme difficulty of obtaining consistent definitions and measurement in this area.

6–11   The manufacturing sector is part of the industrial sector, but its share of GDP is also shown separately. The percentage of GDP in services is not shown, but can be calculated simply by deducting the sum of the percentages in agriculture and industry from 100. So, for example, 49% of Benin's GDP was obtained from services in 1991 (i.e. 100 – (37 + 14) = 49).

12–15   Note that, as for GDP in Cols 6–11, the percentage of labour force in services can be calculated as a remainder.

SOURCES

Grateful acknowledgement is made to the following sources for permission to reproduce material in this Atlas:

Introduction

p.7 (bottom left, top right) Mapping © Bartholomew 1977. Extracts taken from the *Bartholomew World Atlas*, 11th Edn. Reproduced with permission.
(bottom right) *Third Atlas of the Environment*, Heinemann Educational, © GLA Kartor AB, Stockholm.

p.8 (right) Adaptation of a map for Saudi Arabian Airlines (1981) Saudi Arabian Airlines.

p.9 (bottom right) *Third World Guide, 1988/89, 1991/92*, published by Instituto del Tercer Mundo.

pp.5–9 Electronic artwork created by RH Illustration and Design from materials compiled and produced by The Open University. Reproduced by permission of Robert Harrington.

Section 1

p.18 (bottom left) United Nations Environment Programme, *Industry and Environment*, April, May, June 1990.

p.19 (bottom left) UN (1985) *Urban and Rural Population Projections 1950–2025: The 1984 Assessment*, in *Habitat News*, vol. 10, no. 2, 1988, United Nations Centre for Human Settlements;
(bottom right) UNDP (1990) *Human Development Report*, Oxford University Press.

p.23 'The map of Freedom', *Freedom Review, Vol. 22, No. 1* (1991) Freedom House Publishers.

Section 2

p.27 (large map) Faruqi, I. and Sopher, D. (Eds) (1974) *Historical Atlas of the Religions of the World*, Macmillan Publishing;
(inset map) *Times Atlas of the World* (1990) Bartholomew.

p.28 (all figures) Curtin, P.D. (1969) *The Atlantic Slave Trade*, The University of Wisconsin Press.

pp.30, 32, 33, 35, 43 Maps based on the detail contained in *The New Cambridge Modern History Atlas* by Darby, H.C. and Fullard, H. (Eds) (1970) © George Philip Ltd.

p.34 Schwartzberg, T. (1978) *A Historical Atlas of South Asia*, © The Regents of The University of Minnesota.

p.38 (bottom left) Rostow, W.W. (1978) *The World Economy*, University of Texas Press.

pp.39 (top), 40 (top) Barraclough, G. (1978) *Times Atlas of World History*, Times Books Ltd.

p.40 (bottom right) Vaizey, I. (1980) *Revolutions of our time: Capitalism*, George Weidenfeld and Nicolson Ltd.

p.46 Reproduced from *Oxford Atlas of Modern World History* (1989) by permission of Oxford University Press.

Section 3

p.49 (table) United Nations (1989–1990) *UN Environment Programme – Environmental Data Report*, United Nations Environment Programme.

p.50 (bottom left) *Industry and Development: Global Report* (1986) United Nations Industrial Development Organisation;
(bottom centre) *Industry and Development Global Report* (1989–1990) United Nations Industrial Development Organisation (1990);
(top right) Gwynne, R.N. (1990) *New Horizons, Third World Industrialisation in an International Framework*, Longman Group UK.

p.52 (bottom left) *The Economist Vital World Statistics* (1990) The Economist Books;
(top centre) adapted from The World Bank (1991) *World Development Report*, Oxford University Press; World Resources Institute (1992) *World Resources 1990–91*, Oxford University Press; and *The Economist Vital World Statistics* (1990) The Economist Books;
(bottom right) Findlay, A.M. and Findlay, A. (1987) *Population and Development in the Third World*, Methuen and Co.

p.56 (top centre) *World Health Statistics Annual 1990*, World Health Organisation (1991).

p.67 (labour flow, case studies) Kidron, M. and Segal, R. (1978, revised 1991) *New State of the World Atlas*, Touchstone Books, reproduced by permission of Simon & Schuster Ltd.

p.68 UNDP (1992) *Human Development Report*, Oxford University Press.

p.70 (top centre) *World Population Monitoring 1991*, United Nations.

Photographs

Cover Angolan handpump, Carlos Guarita/Reportage; Sunset, Still Pictures/ Adrian Arbib.

p.4 Andes Press Agency/Carlos Reyes.

p.10 Mark Edwards/Still Pictures.

p.24 Brenda Price/Format.

p.48 Julio Etchart/Reportage.

In addition to the above, data for maps and figures were obtained primarily from the sources given below. The following abbreviations are used:

CHM   Ashdown, P. (1979) *Caribbean History in Maps*, Longman Caribbean.
HDR   UNDP (annual) *Human Development Report*, Oxford University Press, Oxford.
HHA   Moore, R.J. (Ed.) (1981) *Hamlyn Historical Atlas*, Hamlyn.
NCMH   Darby, H.C. and Fullard, H. (Eds) (1970) *The New Cambridge Modern History*, Vol. XIV *Atlas*, Cambridge University Press.
TAWH   Barraclough, G. (Ed.) (1978) *Times Atlas of World History*, Times Books Ltd.
TWG   Instituto del Tercer Mundo (annual/biennial) *Third World Guide*, Instituto del Tercer Mundo, Montevideo.
WDR   World Bank (annual) *World Development Report*, Oxford University Press, Oxford.

Introduction

p.5 (centre) UNICEF (1991) *The State of the World's Children*, Oxford University Press; *WDR* 1990; World Bank (1991) *World Debt Tables*; (right) *TWG* 1991/92.

p.8 (left and centre) Cole, J.P. (1979) *Geography of World Affairs*, Pelican.

p.9 (top left, top right, bottom left) *WDR* 1990;

Section 1

pp.14, 15 *WDR* 1990.

p.16 (centre) Sutcliffe, R.B. (1971) *Industry and Underdevelopment*, Addison-Wesley.

p.17 (manufacturing data) *UN Yearbook of Industrial Statistics*, 1975, 1976, 1977, in Kidron, M. and Segal, R. (1981) *The State of the World Atlas*, Pan; (industrial areas) *Philips International Atlas* 1981.

p.18 (map) (export concentration index) *TWG* 1991/92; (bottom right) General Agreement on Tariffs and Trade *International Trade 1988–9*.

p.19 (map) United Nations Education Scientific and Cultural Organisation *Statistical Yearbook 1990*.

p.20 (bottom left and right) *WDR* 1990; (bottom centre) *WDR* 1990, UNICEF (1991) *World Fact Book*.

p.21 (top left, top right, bottom left) *WDR* 1990; (bottom right) *WDR* 1988.

p.22 (map) *HDR* 1992; (top right) *HDR* 1992, *WDR* 1990.

Section 2

p.25 (left) (migration data) Woytinsky, W.S. and Woytinsky, E. (1953) *World Population and Production: Trends and Outlooks*, The Twentieth Century Fund; (trade routes) *TAWH*.

p.29 (slave trade numbers) Curtin, P.D. (1969) *The Atlantic Slave Trade*, University of Wisconsin Press.

p.33 *NCMH, HHA, CHM*.

p.34 Schwartzberg, J. (1978) *A Historical Atlas of South Asia*, University of Chicago Press; *NCMH*.

p.35 *NCMH; HHA*.

p.36 (top right) Kocher, S.L. (1981) *Tropical Crops: a Textbook of Economic Botany*, Macmillan International.

p.37 (bottom centre) Deerr, N. (1950) *The History Of Sugar*, Vol. 2, Chapman and Hall.

p.38 (top centre) UNCTAD (1981) *Fibres and Textiles*, United Nations Commission on Trade and Development.

p.39 (bottom) Mulhall, M.G. (1899 and 1911) *The Dictionary of Statistics*.

p.41 (left) (investment data) *HHA*; (railway densities) Mulhall, M.G. (1899 and 1911) *The Dictionary of Statistics*; (bottom right, centre right) Hobsbawm, E. (1969) *Industry and Empire*, Penguin; (top right) *TAWH*.

p.42 (bottom left) calculated from Bairoch, P. (1968) *The Working Population and its Structure*, Gordon and Breach; (right) Bairoch, P. 'The main trends in national economic disparities since the Industrial Revolution', in Bairoch, P. and Levy-Leboyer, M. (Eds) (1981) *Disparities in Economic Development since the Industrial Revolution*, Macmillan.

p.43 *NCMH, HHA*.

p.44 (left) *CHM*; the typology (listed in column 1 of the text) on which the maps on pp.44 and 45 are based was suggested by Dr Robert Holland and is similar to that used in Rotberg, R.I. and Mazrui, A.A. (Eds.) (1970) *Protest and Power in Black Africa*, Oxford University Press.

p.47 (arms data) Stockholm International Peace Research Institute (1981) *SIPRI Yearbook 1981*, Taylor and Frances.

Section 3

p.49 (bottom left, top centre) *WDR* 1990; (top right) *South* magazine, July 1989, pp.12–16.

p.51 (growth rate) *WDR* 1990; (pie charts and bar chart) UNIDO (1990) *Industry and Development, Global Report* 1989/90, United Nations Industrial Development Organisation.

p.53 (large map) World Resources Institute (1991) *World Resources 1990/91*, Basic Books, Table 18.2; (top right, centre right) Food and Agricultural Organisation (1990) *FAO Production Yearbook 1989*; (bottom right) *WDR* 1992.

p.54 Seaman, J. and Holt, J. *Markets and Famines in the Third World*, Disasters, Vol. 4, No. 3, pp.283–297.

p.55 (dietary energy supply) *WDR* 1991.

p.56 (bottom left) *WDR* 1990, 1992; *HDR* 1992 (adjusted); (bottom right) *WDR* 1990.

p.57 (life expectancy) UNICEF (1991) *The State of The World's Children*, Oxford University Press; (health expenditure) *HDR* 1991.

pp.58, 59 UNICEF (1991) *The State of The World's Children*, Oxford University Press.

p.60 (bottom left) *WDR* 1992; (bottom right) *HDR* 1992.

p.61 (bottom left) *WDR* 1992; (top right) *HDR* 1992; (bottom right) (1990 data) *HDR* 1992, (1985 data) *TWG* 1991/92.

p.62 (bottom left) World Resources Institute (1991) *World Resources 1990/91*, Basic Books; (top centre) Lean, G., Hinrichsen, D. and Markham, A. (Eds) (1990) *Atlas of the Environment*, Arrow Books/WWF; (bottom right) Greenpeace.

p.63 Lean, G., Hinrichsen, D. and Markham, A. (Eds) (1990) *Atlas of the Environment*, Arrow Books/WWF.

p.64 (bottom left, centre right, bottom right) Stockholm International Peace Research Institute (1991) *SIPRI Yearbook 1991*, Oxford University Press; (top centre) *SIPRI Yearbook 1991*; Sivard, R.L. (1991) *World Military and Social Expenditures*, World Priorities.

p.65 (military controlled governments) Sivard, R.L. (1991) *World Military and Social Expenditures*, World Priorities; (major armed conflicts, battle-related deaths) Stockholm International Peace Research Institute (1991) *SIPRI Yearbook 1991*, Oxford University Press, (UN peacekeeping forces) UN Dept of Public Information, April 1992.

p.66 *UNHCR World Map 1990*; (Palestinian refugee population) UN (1992) *World Population Monitoring 1991*, United Nations; (refugee movements in Sub-Saharan Africa) *World Population Monitoring 1990*.

p.67 (pie diagrams) UN (1990) *World Population Monitoring 1989*, United Nations; (international migration) Seagar, J. and Olson, A. (1986) *Women in the World: An International Atlas*, Pan; (cities) Lean, G., Hinrichsen, D. and Markham, A. (Eds) (1990) *Atlas of the Environment*, Arrow Books/WWF.

p.68 *HDR* 1992, World Bank (1991) *World Debt Tables* 1990/91.

p.69 *WDR* 1990.

p.70 (bottom left and right) *HDR* 1992.

p.71 (population growth, population) *WDR* 1992, *TWG* 1991/92; (cities) Lean, G., Hinrichsen, D. and Markham, A. (Eds) (1990) *Atlas of the Environment*, Arrow Books/WWF.

p.72 (bottom left) *HDR* 1992; Crow, B. et al. (1983) *Third World Atlas*, 1st Edn, Open University Press; (bottom right) OECD (1989) *The World Economy in the 20th century*, Organisation for Economic Cooperation and Development.

p.73 *WDR* 1992, *HDR* 1992.

Among the many other sources consulted, the following were particularly useful:
Encyclopaedia of World History (Ed. W.L. Langer) 5th Edn, Harrap.
Keesing's Contemporary Archives.
New Cambridge Modern History (14 vols), 1970, Cambridge University Press.
Times Atlas of the World, comprehensive edition, 1980, Times Books.
Kiernan, V.G. (1982) *European Empires from Conquest to Collapse 1815–1960*, Fontana.
Kinder, H and Hilgerman, W. (1978) *The Penguin Atlas of World History* (2 vols), Penguin.
McEvedy, C. (1980) *Atlas of African History*, Penguin.